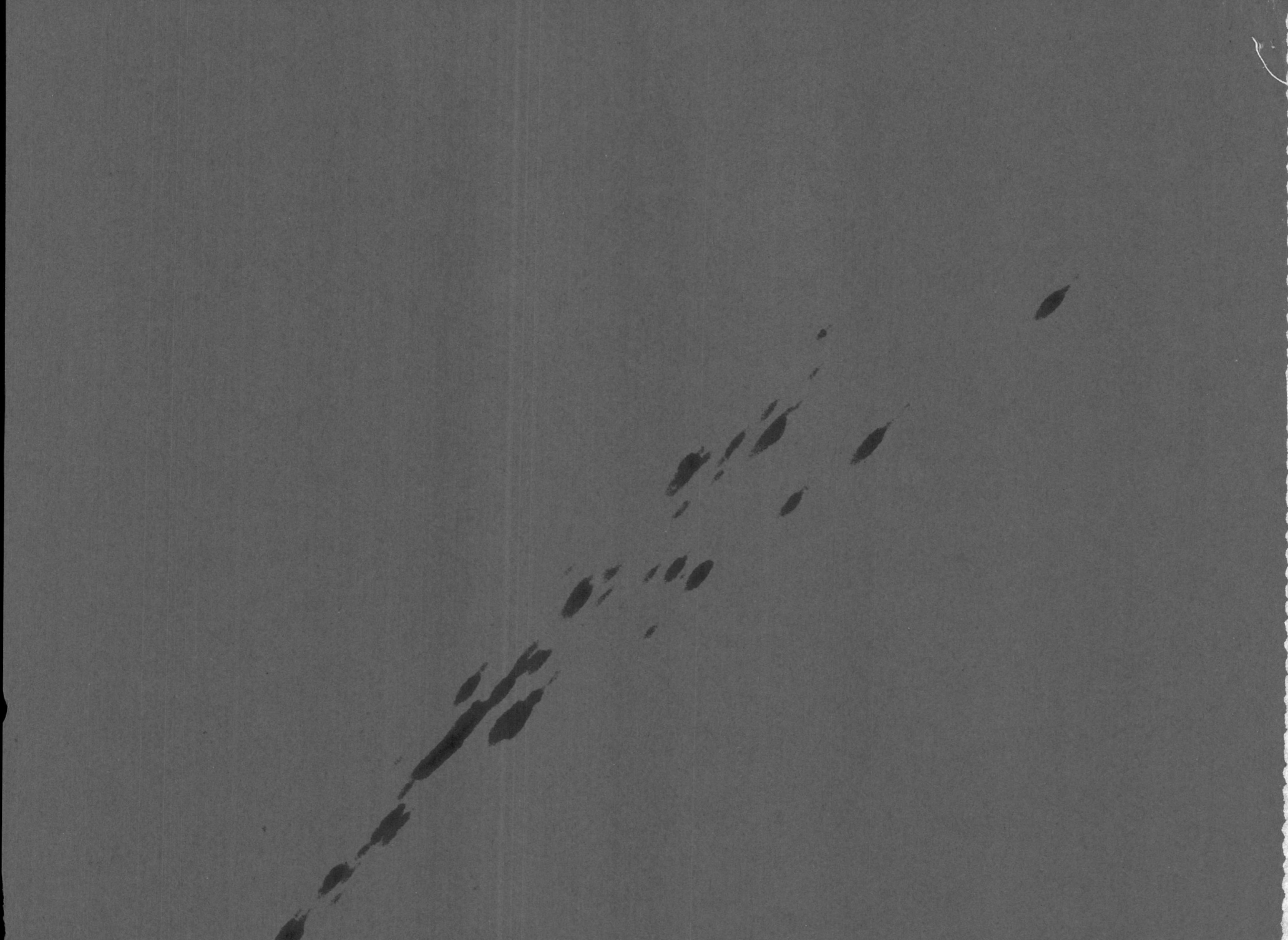

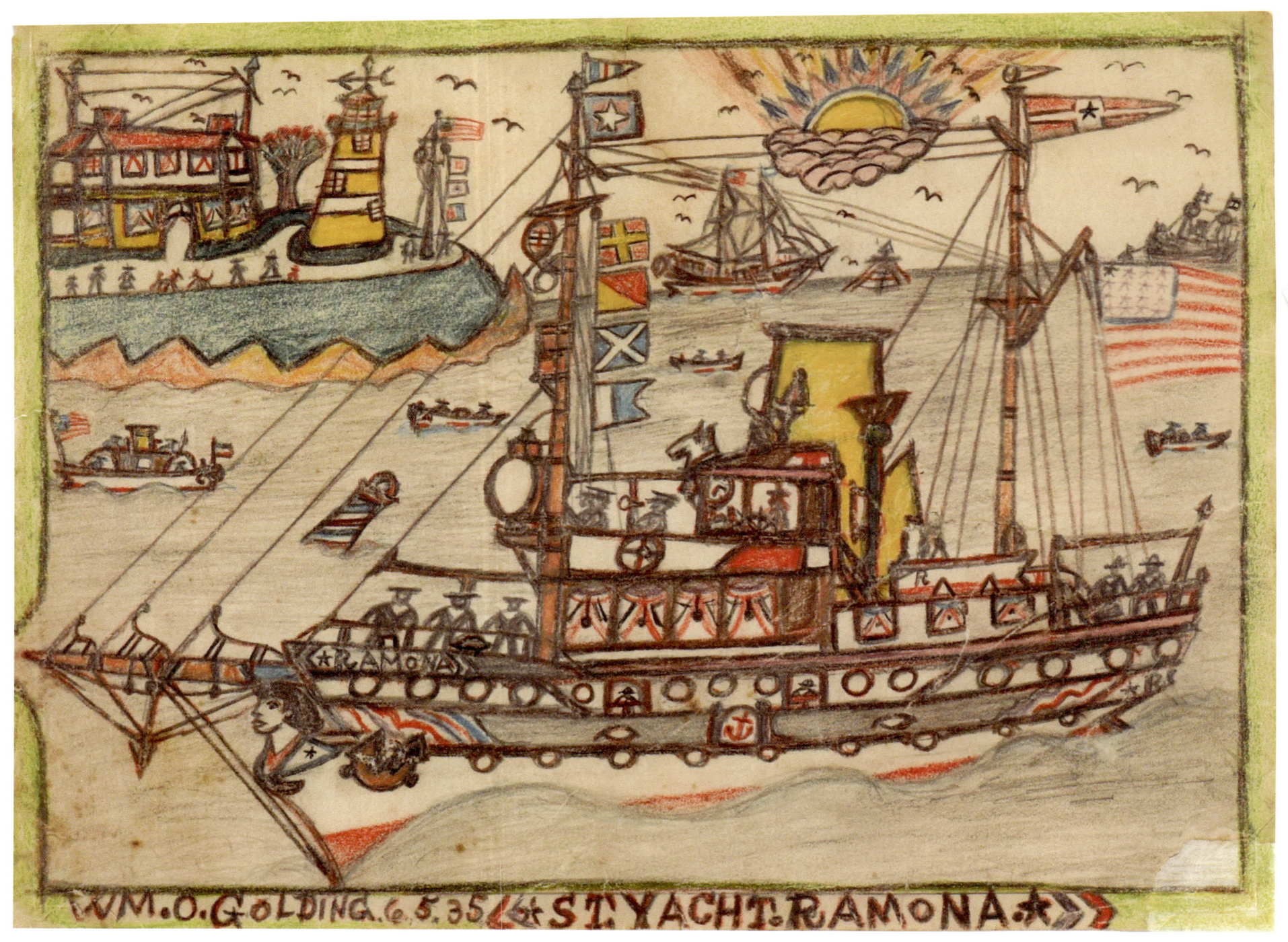

WM. O. GOLDING. 6. 5. 35. ☆ ST. YACHT. RAMONA. ☆

THE ART OF
WILLIAM O. GOLDING

HARD KNOCKS, HARDSHIPS,
AND LOTS OF EXPERIENCE

HARRY DELORME

with contributions by

AHMAURI WILLIAMS-ALFORD

JACKIE CLEVELAND COX-CRITE

TELFAIR BOOKS

2022

DIRECTOR'S FOREWORD

So the captain calls me and I went on board and they took me down in the cabin and made much of me but when I wanted to go back ashore I found that I could not for the very reason that I was out at sea about 45 or 50 miles offshore. When I come up on deck I saw a man standing by a big wheel. I ask him what light is that and he told me that it is Savannah light, Tybee light. And that is the way how I left home on the ship Wandering Jew. I never saw home again until May 25th 1904.

Letter from William O. Golding to Margret Stiles
Savannah, GA
July 10th, 1932
US Marine Hospital, Savannah

In 2020, Telfair Museums acquired seventeen drawings by William O. Golding, an African American mariner born in Liberty County, Georgia, who in the 1880s, at a very young age, had been kidnapped on the Savannah waterfront, and spent the next five decades of his life at sea. In the 1930s, convalescing from chronic bronchitis in the Marine Hospital on Savannah's Oglethorpe Square, Golding created a remarkable group of more than 130 illustrations chronicling his life on the high seas aboard a dizzying range of vessels paying call at major ports around the world from Nova Scotia to Hong Kong. Golding's work takes us on an imaginative journey from the busy post-bellum docks of Savannah to the most distant entrepots of the world, and presents a kind of visual autobiography, developed in retrospection, of a truly global life.

Telfair Museums' exhibition and accompanying publication also reflect the multi-decade journey of Telfair's Director of Education and Senior Curator Harry H. DeLorme, Jr. DeLorme first spotted several of Golding's works in a private collection in the mid-1990s, and has spent the last twenty-five years on a journey pursuing the elusive archival record of Golding's life and artistic output. Golding's drawings featured in the landmark 1976 exhibition *Missing Pieces: Georgia Folk Art, 1770–1976*, which debuted at the Atlanta History Center before traveling to the Telfair Museum of Art and then to the Columbus Museum in Columbus, Georgia. In 2000, DeLorme organized Telfair's exhibition *Hard Knocks, Hardship, and a Lot of Experience: The Art of William O. Golding*, which featured some forty-two works of the roughly sixty pieces then known. Since then, DeLorme and other colleagues have identified more than 130 illustrations by Golding.

With the acquisition of two additional pieces in 2021, Telfair Museums' collection now represents one of the two largest repositories of Golding's work, the other being the Morris Museum of Art in

Augusta, Georgia. Golding's work is also represented in the collections of the Smithsonian American Art Museum (SAAM), the Williams College Museum of Art, the Philadelphia Museum of Art, and the Georgia Museum of Art. In early 2021, Telfair received an NEA grant supporting the exhibition and the accompanying catalogue. In pursuing his research for the exhibition and catalogue, DeLorme has worked closely with the Morris Museum of Art and with Golding's great-grandniece, Jackie Cleveland Cox-Crite. We are very grateful for the contribution of essays by Kevin Grogan, Director and Curator of the Morris Museum of Art, and Jackie Cleveland Cox-Crite. Special thanks also go to Ahmauri Williams-Alford, Assistant Curator of Historical Interpretation and Programs at the Telfair, who assisted DeLorme with research for the exhibition and catalogue and contributed an essay. We would also like to thank Janice Shay of Pinafore Press for her work on this catalogue, photographer David Kaminsky, and all of the lenders to the exhibition.

William O. Golding wrote to his friend and supporter, Savannah socialite Margaret Stiles: "In all that time since I left home I have been all over the world from North, South East and West and plenty of ports in the Seven (7) Seas from England to China, Japan, India, Australia, Africa, West Indies, Central America, South America, around Cape Horn 23 times, Cape of Good Hope 25 or 30 times. Am old now. 59 years old." From the vantage point of his bed in the US Marine Hospital, Golding was able to recreate and document a life spent at sea. And although his true home was on the waters of the world, in some sense, Telfair Museums' exhibition and catalogue represent a homecoming for this native son.

Benjamin T. Simons
Executive Director and CEO
Telfair Museums

FOREWORD

Savannah enjoys a reputation as a community that has, over the years, nurtured remarkable artists, including a group of richly imaginative and accomplished self-taught artists. Among those self-taught artists, William O. Golding stands out as the creator of a body of work that did not depend on Savannah and its environs for subject matter. Instead, at a time when the vast majority of Americans lived and died within fifty miles of their place of birth, Golding drew on his experience of the wider world gained during his years as a merchant seaman. He led a life that was rich with incident and unique experiences, captured in drawings that he created late in his life.

In the St. Crispin's Day speech in Act IV of *Henry V*, Shakespeare's King Henry declares, "Old men forget." Not William Golding. He captured a life that was filled with adventure in a series of highly detailed, colorful, and informative drawings that showed in minute detail the ships on which he served and the places he visited over the half century he spent at sea. As Shakespeare wrote, he remembered "with advantages, what feats he did."

Although the details of Golding's life at sea are not described in their full particulars beyond those he chose to share through his drawings, this much is known: he did not seek it. As Harry DeLorme notes in his illuminating essay here, Golding, then six or eight years of age, and a young friend were walking down River Street—even in the daytime, a place noted for public drunkenness, open gambling, and prostitution (in other words, a place where two little boys had no business being)—when Golding was invited aboard a ship. Before

he knew it, the ship was well out to sea, and his new life had begun. He had been kidnapped in the early 1880s and did not see his home again until he was well into adulthood in 1904. He left again, returning to service on a number of different ships, and did not return to live in Savannah until more than another twenty years had passed.

Even on his final return to Savannah, his health compromised by the sailor's life he had led, the sea—and what he described as the glorious experience of seeing the world—never really left him. He sailed "in his sleep," he said. In 1932, while a patient at the US Marine Hospital in Savannah, he began to capture those dreams, as well as the stories shared and traded with fellow mariners, in the drawings that are the subject of the present exhibition.

Long thought to have been a modest archive, it turns out to have been a body of work now thought to include over 100 drawings that capture the sights he saw. Golding was less a documentarian than he was (to use a self-descriptive phrase coined by the Swiss artist Paul Klee) a "painter of remembered dreams," but his drawings are meticulous in their detail and richly illuminating in surprising ways, providing useful, interesting information about the port cities he visited, the ships he served on, and the captains of those ships. He was nicknamed "Deep Sea" by his cronies at the hospital, though "Sharp Lookout" would have seemed more apt. He was a keen observer of the world around him and an ardent recorder of the things he saw.

One can only presume that life aboard the variety of ships on which he served was not an unalloyed treat. The work was hard and the wages low. Perhaps it is generosity of spirit that led him to record that life as if it were a succession of halcyon, sun-dappled days. Golding's experiences did not, apparently, mirror those recorded by Richard Henry Dana in *Two Years Before the Mast*. There is none of the descendent gloom of Melville or Conrad. But neither is his work frivolous or cartoon-like. It is disciplined, colored by affection, and touched by genius. Golding had the gift of synesthesia, an ability to render his own experience so evocatively as to make it palpable. He makes a life at sea—a life one can only presume was filled with unceasing toil and fraught with danger—seem irresistible.

His was a life well lived and well remembered. His drawings condense that life of adventure so successfully that one is left with a sense of the man who created them: as a sunny optimist who embraced life and welcomed experience which he eagerly shared with others. Rafael Sabatini's entertaining romantic adventure *Scaramouche* begins with the famous line, "He was born with a gift of laughter and a sense that the world was mad." That, it has often seemed to me, captures the essence of William Golding and his art. His drawings certainly attest to that sense of life.

William Golding had a great champion in Margaret Stiles, the recreation director at the US Marine Hospital where Golding was resident for long periods of time during the 1930s. She, an artist in her own right who was also a member of the board at the Telfair Academy and a member of the Savannah Art Club, provided him with the materials to make his art, and she made it her mission to see that it was seen and purchased.

Now, nearly eighty years after his death, Golding has found another champion in the person of Harry DeLorme, Director of Education and Senior Curator for Telfair Museums. He has made it his mission to secure Golding's reputation for all time. The result of his effort is the present exhibition and the publication that accompanies it, as complete and well-documented an effort as one could ask for. The Morris Museum of Art owns thirty of Golding's drawings, and we regard Harry DeLorme and what he's done on behalf of this important artist with something approaching awe. Though we can't take credit for the hard work invested in this exhibition, we are very pleased to share it as an exhibitor.

Kevin Grogan
Director and Curator
Morris Museum of Art

LENDERS TO THE EXHIBITION

Telfair Museums, Savannah, Georgia

The Morris Museum of Art, Augusta, Georgia

Georgia Museum of Art, Athens, Georgia

American Folk Art Museum, New York, New York

Ashantilly Center, Inc., Darien, Georgia

Fleisher Ollman Gallery, Philadelphia, Pennsylvania

The Miller Collection

Mr. and Mrs. E. Brian Culver

Mr. and Mrs. Edwin H. Culver

Private Collections

FUNDING FOR THE EXHIBITION

Exhibition and catalogue support is provided by:

The National Endowment for the Arts

The City of Savannah

The Georgia Council for the Arts

Inge Brasseler

Additional support provided in memory of Arnold and Lorlee Tenenbaum

through the Labelle and Meyer Tenenbaum Education Endowment

TABLE OF CONTENTS

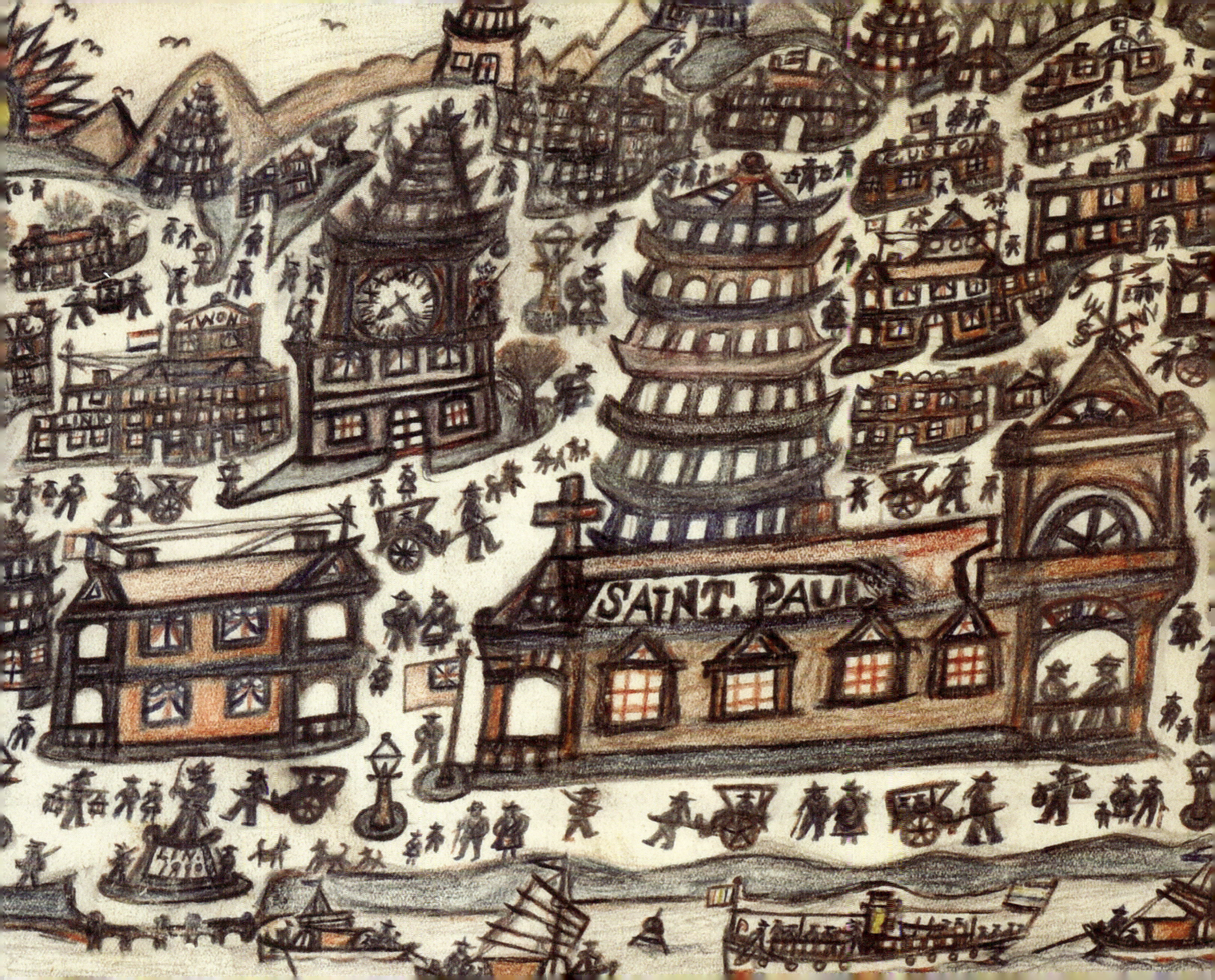

WILLIAM O. GOLDING

AMERICAN MARINER AND ARTIST

In the first of his two surviving letters, the artist and mariner known as William O. Golding presented his life story, one that seems both a fantastic sea yarn and a poignant summary of a half-century of maritime experience (fig. 1). Full of vivid detail, anecdote, specific dates, and even dialogue, this beautifully told story is utterly believable. The artist was clearly a practiced storyteller who had lived a hard life, seen the world, and returned to tell the tale. Accepted as factual for many years, this story may be more akin to yarns spun by an older sailor—a mixture of memory, legend, and a bit of embellishment. His drawings likewise combine fact and invention, sometimes juxtaposing different time periods and locations. While loosely following maritime painting types, such as portraits of ships and views of foreign and domestic ports, Golding's drawings come from more personal territory and transcend mere documentation. Autobiography, private symbolism, and sailor's lore color his works, which contain worlds of information embedded in signal flags, waterfronts, and expressive miniature figures on ship and shore. His experience was rooted in the South and in his identity as an African American living through the Jim Crow era, but with the added perspective of a sailor and world traveler who was a firsthand witness to the rise of American sea power, Western colonialism, and war overseas. Expressive and idiosyncratic, his existing drawings stand out in the history of American art and are long overdue for closer examination.

Facts about the man and the experiences that inspired him are still scant. His very name is elusive. Census records, veterans' documents, and his death certificate all record his surname as "Golding," the name he signed on many of his drawings. In private life, however, he seems to have gone by the surname "Golden," as indicated in family memory, in accounts by individuals who knew

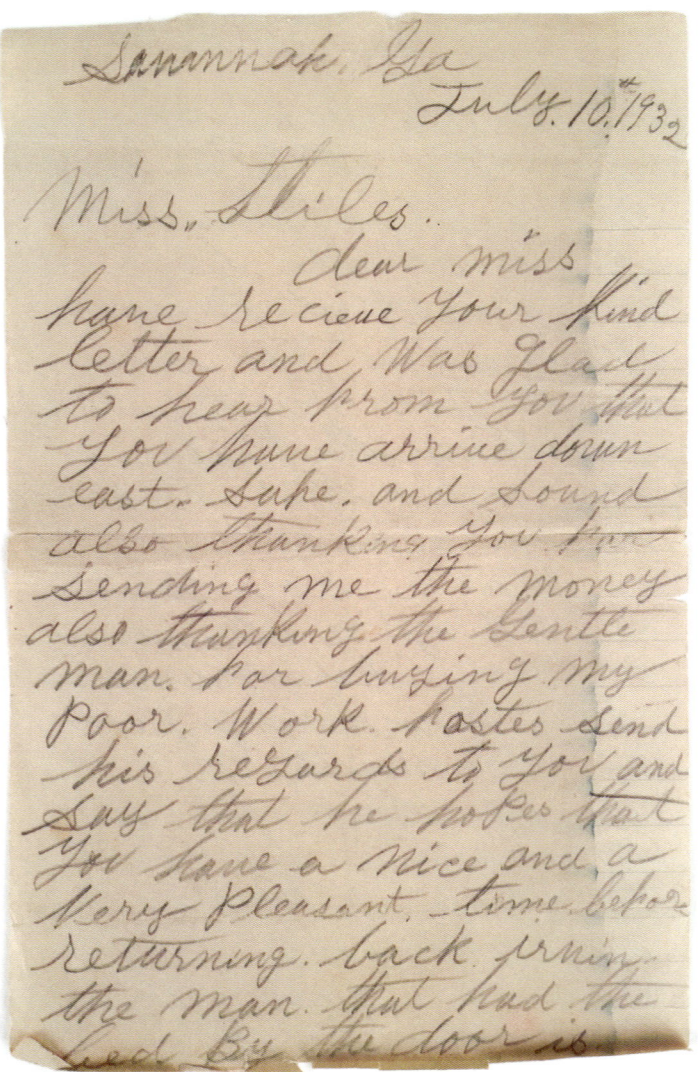

Fig. 1. *William O. Golden letter to Margaret Stiles, July 10, 1932. Courtesy Fleisher/Ollman Gallery, Philadelphia, Pennsylvania.*

(2)

dead, he died Sunday morning. at. 6. 30. may he Rest. in Peace. the Rest of the boys is all. Right at Present. Miss. Stiles You said that You Wanted me to draw the Picture of the Ship that took me from Savannah When i Was a boy am Sending a drawing of. her. her name is the. Wandering Jew. of. Yarmouth. N.S. 3. masted. Ship. tons 1800. Comamanded. by. capt. William. O. Potter. Bro of. capt John. Potter Who. own and Sail the Ship. Minister. of marine

Note: In the letter at right, punctuation and capitalization were added to the transcription for clarity.

Savannah, Ga
July 10th, 1932

Miss Stiles,

Dear Miss, have receive your kind letter and was glad to hear from you that you have arrive down east, safe and sound. Also thanking you for sending me the money also thanking the gentleman for buying my poor work. Foster send his regards to you and say that he hopes you have a nice and a very pleasant time before returning back. Irving the man that had the bed by the door is dead. He died Sunday morning at 6:30 may he rest in peace. The rest of the boys is all right at present. Miss Stiles you said you wanted me to draw the picture of the ship that took me from Savannah when I was a boy. Am sending a drawing of her. Her name is the Wandering Jew of Yarmouth, N.S. 3-masted ship, tons 1800. Commanded by Captain William O. Potter, bro. of Capt John Potter who own and sail the ship Minister of Marine. On the 15 of July 1882 I went with my cousin down to the bluff better known now as the Coast line wharves passing astern of the Wandering Jew. The Captain and his wife was walkin the quarterdeck this morning when I went down there I heard the Captain ask his wife Now Polly you always say that you wanted a boy, now there is two (2) of them now, pick your choice wich one (1) of them you will take. She says I will take that little fat boy with the pretty nice white teeth meaning me. So the captain calls me and I went on board and they took me down in the cabin and made much of me but Iwhen I wanted to go back ashore I found that I could not for the very reason that I was out at sea about 45 or 50 miles offshore. When I come up on deck I saw a man standing by a big wheel. I ask him what light s that and he told me that it is Savannah light, Tybee light. And that is the way how I left home on the ship Wandering Jew. I never saw home again until May 25th 1904. I come back home to Savannah. In all that time since I left home I have been all over the world from North, South, East, and West and plenty of ports in the Seven (7) Seas from England to China, Japan, India, Australia, Africa, West Indies, Central America, South America, around Cape Horn 23 times, Cape of Good Hope 25 or 30 times. Am old now. 59 years old. Can't get along like I used to do on the ship so I have to give up going to sea. Now only go to sea in my sleep and get among other old shellbacks and swap yarns of old times is all I can do now. Well 49 years is long enough to be going to sea. All that time I never accumulate any fortune but hard knocks, hardships and a lots of experience. Was in all kinds of ships from a whaler to a man o' war. So I have had my time knocking around the world. Am sending the drawings that you said to send.

The Wandering Jew and the Minister of Marine is two (2) sister ships built by the same company. The Marine was lost in 1890 with all hands off the horn. The Wandering Jew was burnt by fire off Fiji Island in 1899. So ends a good captain and a good ship. May they rest in peace. Hoping that these few lines will find you well and enjoying the best of health. So I will bid you a pleasant afternoon and a safe return. I remain a friend and servant.

William O. Golding
U.S. Marine Hospital, Savannah

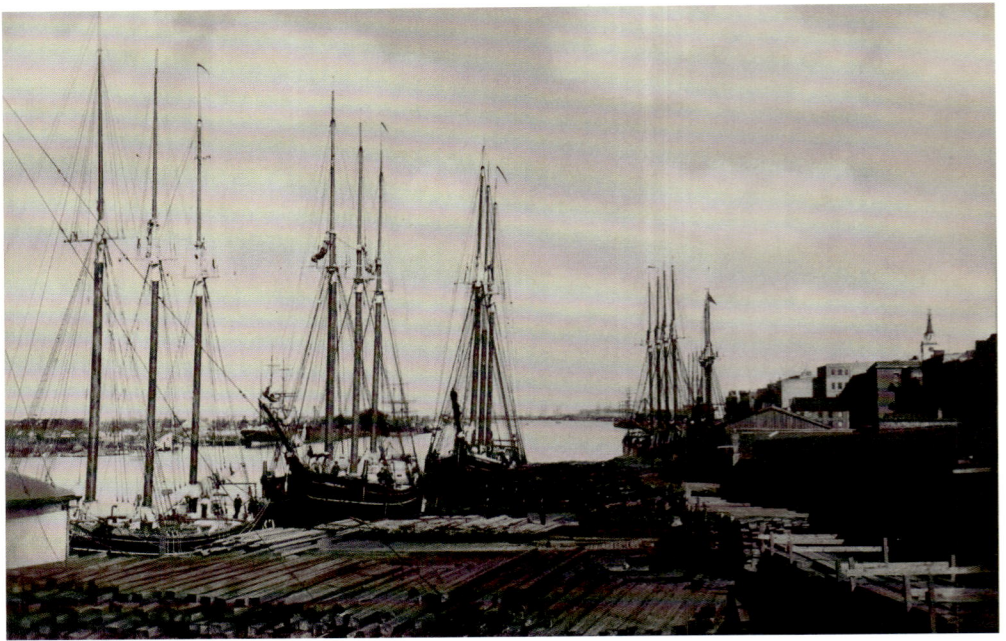

Fig. 2. *Savannah River Docks and Wharves, Lumber, prior to 1905. MS 1360 Cordray-Foltz Photography Studio collection. Courtesy the Georgia Historical Society, 1360-29-15-01.*

him, and in a drawing in which he names a steamship after himself (see detail, page 61). [1] For the purposes of this essay, the name "Golden" will be used to refer to the man, and "Golding" will be used in the context of his drawings and their life beyond the artist. Despite a lack of personal accounts of Golden beyond his two surviving letters, a few details about his life have emerged in recent times that provide clues to his upbringing and experiences.

EARLY LIFE

William O. Golden's life intersected with historical events from his earliest days. Records indicate that he was born on January 15, 1874, in Liberty County, Georgia, about thirty miles southwest of Savannah. He first appears on record in the 1880 US Census for Liberty County as the six-year-old adopted son of William Anthony Golding (Golden), age sixty, and Harriet Golding, fifty-nine. [2] Young William O. Golden may have been orphaned along with a sister; the more likely scenario is that his birth parents were rela-

tions or neighbors who simply did not have the means to raise him. Many people in the community were formerly enslaved men and women eking out a living as farmers. By contrast, William Anthony Golden was one of the most important men in Liberty County's African American community. A former state legislator, one of the first thirty-three African Americans to serve in Reconstruction-era politics in Georgia, the elder Golden was a distinguished local leader. Born enslaved, William A. Golden rose to leadership almost immediately following the Civil War, playing an important historical role in Liberty County on several fronts—political, religious, and educational. Through the Freedmen's Bureau he was closely involved in the establishment of the Homestead School, where his wife, Harriet, taught in the late 1860s. In 1870, Golden petitioned the American Missionary Association to send a teacher and minister to the community. An expanded school, christened the Dorchester Academy, opened in 1879 when William O. Golden was five years old, and may be where he briefly attended school before he was taken from Savannah. [3]

Some sixty years later, in 1940, the final census in which Golden would appear recorded that he had no school or college, but that he had attended elementary school to second grade. This may indicate that he received education at the school originally founded by his stepparents; his stepmother could have also provided early instruction in reading and writing. Golden may have later had access to instruction after his enlistment in the US Navy in 1892, and he likely encountered opportunities to read and write during his long years at sea. Writing, in the form of descriptive titles, later became a hallmark of his visual art. Beyond basic literacy, William may have taken more with him from his early experience growing up with a famous father figure, whose vision and example were likely important touchstones for his young stepson. A 1975 article in the *Savannah Morning News* quotes an employee of the Marine Hospital who knew William O. Golden, and states that he was a "deeply religious man, proud of his race." [4] That pride in his identity as an African American man, as well as religious faith and the foundations of an education, were important gifts from his stepparents—gifts that he carried with him from Liberty County into an unimaginably wider world than the one he experienced as a child.

LEAVING HOME

The circumstances of young William's childhood kidnapping and departure from Savannah aboard a ship are known almost entirely from his own account, written some fifty years after the events. His written recollections may, intentionally or not, be mixed with other early memories of his life at sea. Names of captains and ships may have been changed or substituted for others; and some facts could have been exaggerated or even invented. To begin with, he gave the year of his kidnapping from Savannah as 1882, but, as we shall see, evidence suggests that it may have been as early as 1880.

William O. Golden vividly described the story of his abduction while exploring the Savannah wharves with a male cousin sometime between 1880 and 1882. He was likely in Savannah with his family or stepfather, who was said to have worked for a time as a custodian at the US Custom House on Bay Street near the riverfront. [5] Savannah's waterfront had been the hub of the city's commerce and shipping activity since its founding, and in 1880, the city's maritime business was rebounding in the wake of the Civil War, with ongoing improvements taking place in the harbor. Between 1880 and 1882, vessels in Savannah's port were largely loading the region's staples of cotton, lumber, and, increasingly, naval stores bound for destinations in the US and abroad (Fig. 2).

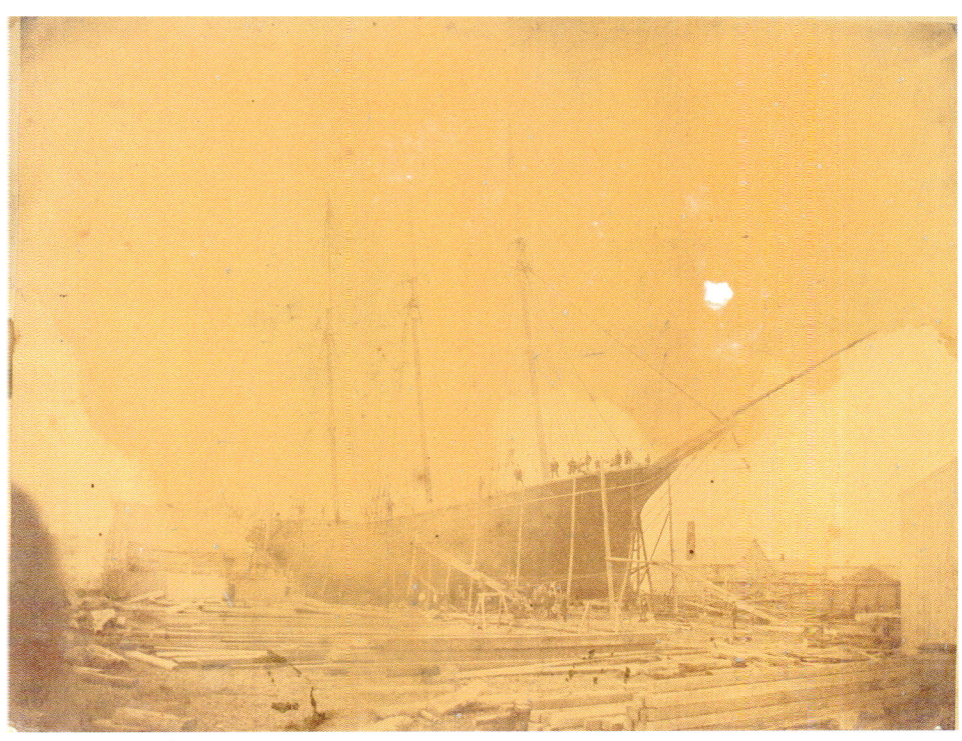

Fig. 3. *Barkentine Wandering Jew Under Construction, c. 1880. Courtesy the Oysterponds Historical Society, Orient, NY.*

In his 1932 letter, Golden recounted in detail how at Savannah's wharves he was lured aboard a vessel named the "Wandering Jew of Yarmouth, Nova Scotia" by a captain and captain's wife in need of a cabin boy. Golden gives the captain's name as William O. Potter, who refers to his wife as "Polly." Golden provides a description of *Wandering Jew* as a "3-masted ship, tons 1800," which would have made it a large sailing vessel for the time. He further states that the vessel had a sister ship, the *Minister of Marine*, made by the same company and sailed by captain Potter's brother John. Golden describes how both vessels met their end: the *Wandering Jew* "burned by fire off Fiji Island in 1899" and the *Minister of Marine* "lost with all hands off the Horn [Cape Horn] " [6]

Records of the time call Golden's story into question, however. Perhaps due to the young age at which he left Savannah, Golden may

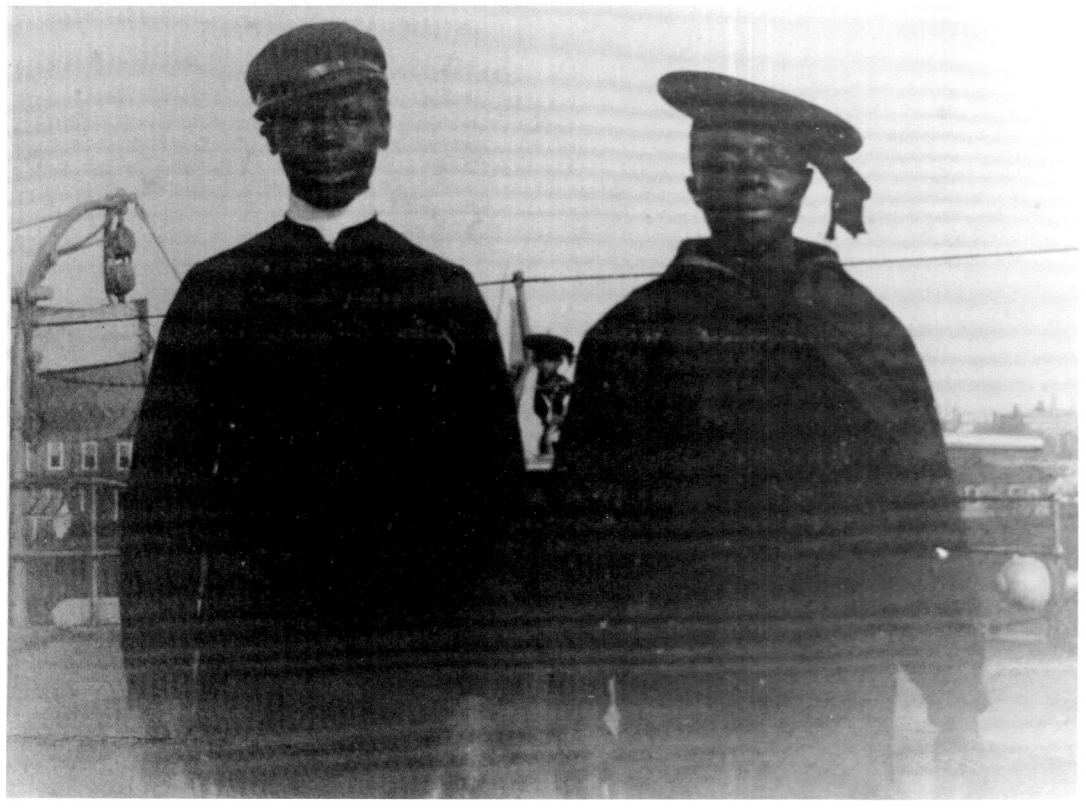

Fig. 4. USS Newark (Cruiser #1), Two African American members of the cruiser's crew, 1898. Man on left is wearing a steward's uniform. Copied from the scrapbook of William D. Edwards, by courtesy of Robert W. Edwards, 1974.
NH 80782. Courtesy the Naval History & Heritage Command.

Island, the *Wandering Jew* was a brand-new, three-masted bark of 670 tons when it first visited Savannah (Fig. 3). Considerably smaller than the ship Golden describes, this vessel was mostly engaged in coastal trade and was in Savannah to load lumber. [8] The bark's master was Frank Norton, a captain from Orient, a Long Island community that was home to numerous mariners and ship masters. (Orient was even home over time to captains named Potter, though none of them were master of the ship *Wandering Jew*, or are a good fit with Golden's story.) Coastal trade vessels like the *Wandering Jew* also ventured to ports in Atlantic Canada and may have provided a means by which Golden reached Nova Scotia and Newfoundland, which figure in some of his drawings. Given the presence of a few British Canadian ships in Savannah during the period between 1880 and 1882, another possibility is that he left on a Canadian ship and changed the name in his story.

If Golden did leave Savannah between six and eight years of age, he would have been quite young to work aboard a ship, even as a cabin boy, though children were present on ships in the nineteenth century. The US and Royal navies actively recruited boys in their early teens. A Canadian crew database from the period shows a number of children of ages eleven and younger serving on vessels. [9] Whaling-ship crew lists also include some ten- and eleven-year-olds. The practice of obtaining crew for a ship against their will or by means of trickery or force—historically called "shanghaiing"—was still taking place in the late nineteenth century. "Crimps" in some ports secured and signed crew for ships by any means necessary while retaining a large portion of a sailor's pay. Less frequently does one hear of captains engaging in the practice directly and specifically in the abduction of children. Some captains were known to have adopted younger children who were orphans, or with the consent of their parents, although this would not seem to apply to Golden.

conflate one ship or captain with another, and even misremember the year he departed the city. The *Savannah Morning News* shipping-news section and a registry of ships in the Savannah harbor for Golden's stated abduction date of July 15, 1882, show neither a ship named the *Wandering Jew* nor any large Canadian vessel in port at the time. Golden's story of Captains William and John Potter could potentially connect to two brothers of those names from King's County, Nova Scotia: William Russell Potter and John Henry Potter, who were both masters of large ships in the 1880s. [7] Their ships, however, do not appear to have traveled to Savannah.

A ship by the name of *Wandering Jew* was in Savannah's port, however, on the exact day of the month Golding recounts, July 15, but a full two years earlier, in 1880. Built in Greenport, Long

NAVAL SERVICE

As Golden matured into young manhood, the harsh experience of seagoing labor may have led him to seek more stable employment at sea, resulting in his enlistment in the US Navy. A veteran's master index card and a pension application card show that "William O. Golding" of Savannah enlisted in the US Navy in 1892 and was discharged in 1902. [10]

The US Census of 1930 provides further evidence of Golden's military activity during a turning point for America on the global stage. Appearing on the census at the US Marine Hospital in Savannah, Golden's service is recorded as "Sp. Phil.," meaning the Spanish-American War, and specifically the Philippine War that followed the initial conflict and US victory over Spain in the battle of Manila Bay in 1898. [11] A small subset of Golden's drawings speak to these wars, in which he depicted at least one key warship that participated in the conflict with the Spanish in Cuba, two drawings of a tug from the Savannah area that ran guns to Cuban rebels, and two drawings of the Philippines, including a view of Cavite with US warships in the harbor. Other drawings depict United States, British, and French warships at key locations and military installations abroad. In images of Saigon, the Rock of Gibraltar, and St. Helena, Golden depicts groups of turn-of-the-century US warships. Golden also made drawings of historically famous ships that were in use as military and merchant training vessels during his early years in the Navy. These included the famed USS *Constellation*, which made its last major cruise as a training ship to Gibraltar in 1892, and the USS *St. Mary's*, a former sloop of war based at the New York Nautical School. [12]

The 1890s were a period during which Navy recruitment increased in the build-up to the Spanish-American War. In 1890, nearly ten percent of US Navy recruits were African American, and a number became naval apprentices (Fig. 4). [13] Although African Americans were recruited for service, they faced ever-more-restricted opportunities in the roles that they were allowed to play, a trend that continued into the era of the First World War and beyond.

In the US Navy of the 1890s, African Americans served in a variety of ranks aboard ships, from seaman and machinist to coal passer, as well as steward and messman. The latter became more prescribed roles for African Americans entering the service as Jim Crow practices became more prevalent in the Navy, and African Americans were increasingly segregated from white crew members aboard ship. A cruel irony is that African Americans performed heroically in both the Navy and the Army during the wars in Cuba and the Philippines. While some African Americans thought ill of American imperialism, others hoped their distinguished military service would bring greater respect and opportunity. But despite the vital role African American troops played in America's rise to global power at the turn of the century, racism prevailed in the services and in American society in the years that followed. Golden's discharge in the spring of 1902 coincided with the US defeat of the Philippine rebels. Although Golden did not reenlist, perhaps due to the pressures and limitations he would have faced in an increasingly discriminatory Navy, his occupation as a mariner would play a supporting role in a later, larger war.

After his discharge from the Navy, Golden apparently went to work on merchant ships and may have spent time serving aboard luxury steam yachts. A biographical statement that accompanied one of his drawings indicates that Golden claimed to have served aboard the *Viking*, the *Nourmahal,* and the *Warrior,* all steam yachts belonging to America's wealthy elite (though the article's writer stated that he tended to exaggerate and may have only seen some of these vessels). [14] The era of the steam yachts waned with the onset of the First World War, and Golden, then serving aboard merchant vessels, experienced the dangers of the Great War firsthand. German U-boats prowled the Atlantic, stoking the

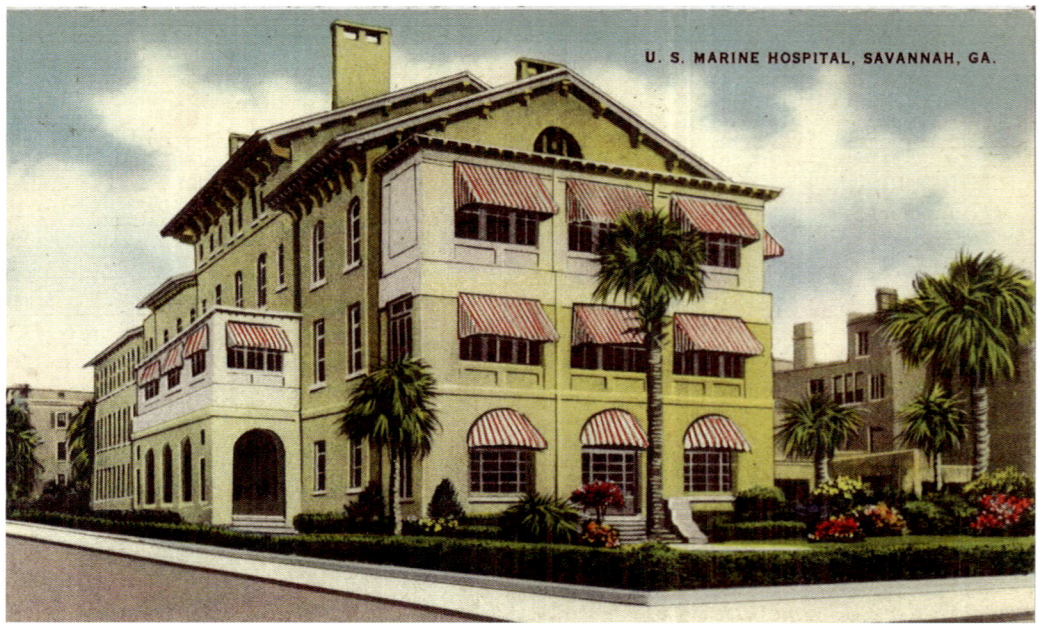

U. S. MARINE HOSPITAL, SAVANNAH, GA.

Fig. 5. U.S. Marine Hospital, Savannah, GA (Postcard), circa 1940s, Pub. by Coastal News Co., Savannah, Ga. A "Colourpicture" publication, Cambridge, Mass. U.S.A.

fears of merchant seamen, ocean-steamship passengers, and US Navy personnel. In June 1917, Golden made perhaps his only appearance in the press when he was named among the survivors of a merchant ship named the *Galena*, which was captured and sunk in the English Channel by a German U-boat. Apparently, this incident did not deter Golden from returning to sea, as he continued to serve on merchant vessels into the 1920s.

THE US MARINE HOSPITAL AND MARGARET STILES

By the mid-1920s Golden's health had affected his ability to go to sea. One source indicates that he may have initially retired in Baltimore before returning to Savannah. A 1975 Savannah newspaper article cited a record stating that by 1925, Golding was an intermittent patient at the US Marine Hospital in Savannah, where he was treated for chronic bronchitis. [15] Years of sleeping in crowded forecastles, exposure to toxins and dust in cargoes, the ravages of

the elements, and, possibly, habits like smoking had taken their toll. Golden likely stayed closer to home during this time, as evidenced by drawings of vessels that would have been familiar sights on the Savannah waterfront in the 1920s. By 1930, he was in residence at the Marine Hospital (Fig. 5).

Savannah's US Marine Hospital offered Golden not only medical treatment but a refuge, a place where his service may have set him apart and provided opportunities for him to talk to men like himself, particularly African American sailors. Marine hospitals were established by the US government in 1798 for the care of merchant seamen, and the Savannah area had several sailors' hospitals over the years. The edifice Golden knew was the largest, constructed in 1907 on York and Whitaker Streets, just a few blocks from the city's waterfront. In addition to providing medical services, marine hospitals had played a role in the quarantine of sailors, immigrants, or war prisoners who might be carrying infectious diseases. [16] In Golden's time at Savannah's hospital, merchant mariners, fishermen, and veterans of early-twentieth-century wars—black and white—could all be found on the patient roster, though wards were almost certainly segregated in Jim Crow Savannah. The 1930 census recorded sixty-seven white patients at the Marine Hospital, and twenty-eight African Americans, with a majority of patients listed by profession as "Merchant Marine." Golden, appearing as "William O. Golding," was listed as "home," meaning not currently employed and one of only a handful of veterans among the patients, along with two other black veterans of World War I and one Black veteran of the Spanish-American War. [17] Golden, who claimed to have served on "all kinds of ships, from a whaler to a man o war," enjoyed swapping seagoing yarns with the other men, who knew him by the nickname "Deep Sea." Around the time of the census, when Golden was residing at the hospital, he began drawing. Some eighteen months later, in late 1931 or early 1932, he met Margaret Stiles, a white educator and artist from a privileged Savannah family who organized recreational programs at the hospital, likely including art activities (Fig. 6).

Born into an old and moneyed Georgia family, Margaret "Margie" Stiles was of a generation of Southern white women of means who sought formal education as visual artists in the north and internationally (often this followed the arts-and-craft-instruction that was part of women's education and finishing-school experience in the nineteenth century). Stiles is known to have studied art in New York City and made trips abroad to visit museums. As a young woman, her travels and art studies were often reported in the society column of the *Savannah Morning News*, one story from 1902 mentioning that she was remaining in New York to complete an art course. [18] Later that year, Stiles is listed as a teacher at a Savannah private school operated by Miss Emelyn Hartridge. Stiles also taught art at Hartridge's boarding school for girls in Plainfield, New Jersey, which was established in 1903. By the 1930s, Margie Stiles was also heavily involved in affairs in her home city, particularly at the Telfair Academy, Savannah's art museum, where she served as a trustee during the 1930s, overlapping with her years in contact with Golden. At the Telfair from 1932 to 1936, she was chair of the Mechlin education program, named for Leila Mechlin, a noted art critic and founder of the American Federation of Arts, who consulted with the Telfair to create educational programs and exhibitions. [19] Stiles administered the program, which took outreach presentations on art history to local schools, including segregated schools for African American youth. Secondhand accounts indicate that Stiles and perhaps others in her circle volunteered to lead activities for patients at the US Marine Hospital in downtown Savannah, which was several blocks from the Telfair Academy.

The extent of Stiles's involvement with Golden is not entirely known, but she played a large role during his creative period, and through her family helped to preserve the majority of his works that survive today. Stiles appears to have served as patron and agent for Golden. Either directly or indirectly she arranged sales of small groups of his drawings to a number of collectors in her circle in Savannah and farther away. Five works were purchased by Anne Lee, an art teacher at Savannah's private Pape School, who was also involved with the Telfair. Lee is said to have bought these after "meeting Golding in a retirement home," meaning the Marine Hospital. [20] Other drawings were purchased by prominent Savannah residents, including Malcolm Bell, later a photographer and banker, and Mary Haskell Minis, friend and sponsor of the Lebanese-born writer and artist Kahlil Gibran. Interest in Golden's work continued to grow through the efforts of Stiles and her family. Stiles traveled between Georgia and the Northeast throughout her life, often visiting her sister in New York and on one trip attending the wedding reception for her niece Margaret Screven and husband A. J. M. Tuck. The latter would play a role in selling four of Golden's drawings to prominent New York businessman and yacht

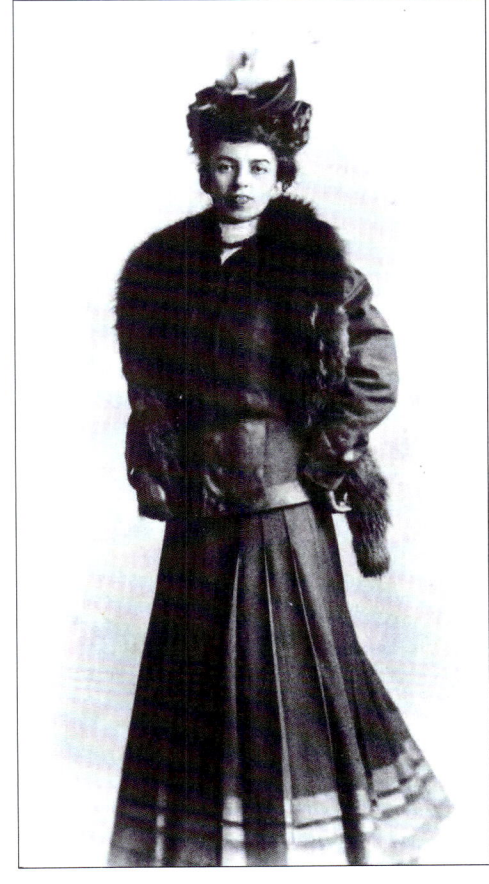

Fig. 6. Margaret C. Stiles, 1906.
Courtesy Hugh Golson.

owner George F. Baker, Jr. A biographical statement about Golden, which accompanied the latter group of drawings sold to Baker in 1933, appears to have been written by either Stiles' niece, Margaret Screven Tuck, or A. J. M. Tuck himself. The statement outlines the beginnings of Golden's work and his relationship with Stiles:

My aunt, Miss Stiles first met him only about 13 months after he had just commenced to draw, and only did sailing ships and the Savannah water front. Miss Stiles suggested his trying to draw some of the places he had seen—also the ships—but everything he does is entirely out of his head. He has never had. . . lessons, or advice, or criticism, nor pictures to copy. [21]

This description points out that Golden was already drawing before he met Stiles and suggests that Stiles heard Golden's colorful stories of places and ships, encouraging him to draw additional subjects. It also mentions that Stiles brought Golden paper and crayons from local dimestores. Perhaps the best document of the relationship may be found in Golden's two surviving letters to Stiles. In them he chats about weather and storms (as one might expect of a seaman), crime in Savannah, and the health of other patients. More importantly, he discusses his life and provides insight into his dealings with her and how he approached his art and subject matter.

His first letter begins thanking Stiles for arranging for a sale of his drawings, referring to his art in a self-deprecating manner: "Thanking you for sending me the money also thanking the gentleman for buying my poor work." The letter goes on to provide a capsule history of his seagoing experience, seemingly in response to a query by Stiles, who perhaps used Golden's backstory to help sell his art. Golden then wistfully discusses his current situation at the Marine Hospital, saying that he "now only goes to sea in my sleep, and get among other old shellbacks and swap yarns of old times is all I can do now." He points out that his time at sea has left him without any personal wealth: "All that time I never accumulate any fortune but hard knocks, hardships and a lots of experience." This statement lays bare the truth of the life he experienced, one that was notoriously unfair to seamen, and dramatically less so to African Americans. It underscores Golden's hope that Stiles will use the sixteen drawings he encloses to generate income on his behalf. [22]

His second letter, written a little over a year later, in August 1933, provides another look at Stiles as a promoter of Golden's work, as well as Golden's growing sense of pride in his development as an artist:

I have took great pain with some of them for some have taken 2 to 3 days making. They are some you can pick out for exhibition purposes. The Constellation and the Constitution those two are a pair you can keep them or sell them as you see fit. There is 2 two drawing of the Isendaga. The reason why is that I draw one and it was a little dark to me so I turn to and draw another. The nurse Miss Shooks say it is fine there is nothing wrong with it so am sending it on to see how you like it. [23]

In this statement Golden mentions the long hours spent on each drawing, even dropping a hint that Stiles may be exhibiting his work. The letter makes clear that Golden was well able to critique his own work, redrawing a piece that didn't satisfy him, though sending both versions to Stiles to get her opinion. He goes on to discuss his image of the Rock of Gibraltar, and his pride is obvious.

I think you will like this picture better than the other picture I made of the Rock. In this one you see the soldiers marching to relieve the guards with a band of music in front with the band master swinging his staff from right to left. I think it is my best. [24]

He closes his second letter soliciting Stiles for other suggestions for future commissions while also citing the physical discomfort caused by his often minutely detailed work:

If you have any special picture something I knows write and let me know. Am tired and my eyes is paining. I will I rest up a little while. Drawing is straining to the eyes. No more orders on hand. Will rest until I hear from you. No more to say. Must close by saying thank you for all you have done for me and wishing you good luck and happiness. [25]

Beyond the comments found in his letters, it is nearly impossible to tell what Golden really thought of Stiles. His letters are thankful and deferential, though one must keep in mind the racially oppressive times and the paternalism and power represented by well-meaning whites like Stiles. She apparently thought a good deal of his work, enlisted family to help make sales for him, and perhaps arranged exhibitions. The money paid for Golden's work was likely meager—A. J. M. Tuck referred to it as "pocket money for his luxuries"—but records of specific payments have not survived. [26] Neither have Stiles's communications to others on behalf of Golden, making it difficult to fully assess her motives. Stiles's own writings to or regarding Golden and his work have not surfaced. This was a time, however, when the so called "primitive" art of painters without academic training was beginning to gain wider notice, and not long before black artists from the South like Bill Traylor and William Edmondson attracted the patronage and paternalistic interest of white, academically trained artists who saw parallels in their work to the reductivist inclinations of modern art. Stiles herself may not have subscribed to any particular brand of modernism; her own art was apparently quite traditional. She was sixty-four or sixty-five when she met Golden, who was six years or more her junior. Single, an educator, and supporter of the arts and civic causes, Stiles herself was independent minded, though not necessarily progressive. In all likelihood, she was taken with Golden's undeniably appealing work and perhaps thought about her assistance to him in a philanthropic or humanitarian context, though one almost certainly still rooted in the Southern white perceptions of racial hierarchy in that time and place.

Golden continued to produce his drawings until the end of 1939, with one notable gap year. A handful of drawings are not dated, but his most productive period appears to have been between 1932 and 1935. The latter year alone yielded twenty-four or more drawings. His output begins to slow in 1936. Only three known drawings date from 1937, and none from 1938. He returns to work the next year after this hiatus with a strong group of some fifteen drawings in 1939. The last dated work, a whaling picture, was made on December 14, 1939. It seems unlikely Golden stopped there. If he did, one explanation may be that Stiles stopped visiting him. A number of drawings from 1939 descended through Stiles, so Golden's production may have ebbed and flowed as he had contact with her or as she made requests for work. Perhaps his health and eyesight deteriorated, though his drawings of 1939 seem assured, and a few are quite complex. If Stiles stopped her visits, he may have had less access to art materials. Finally, Golden may have spent more time away from the Marine Hospital. Interestingly, 1940 is the only year that Golden definitively appears in the Savannah City Directory, in which he is listed as "William O. Golden," living with his wife, Josephine. [27] Nevertheless, Golden was at the Marine Hospital on April 5, 1940, when he was again recorded in the US Census. A much smaller contingent of men, only twenty-two, was listed in residence at the hospital. [28] Sometime during the late 1930s or early 1940s, Golden was also receiving visits from family at the hospital, including a young great-nephew, James W. Cleveland. According to Jackie Cox-Crite, Cleveland's daughter, James saw Golden there several times, remembering playing with the gold buttons on his uniform and seeing the older man drawing (see Cox-Crite's essay in this catalogue). [29] Golden made an impression on the youngster, no doubt telling exciting stories of his experiences at sea. James W. Cleveland, Sr., went on to Merchant Marine service as an adult, as did his two sons, continuing the tradition of seagoing in the family, a personal legacy Golden inspired beyond his work as an artist.

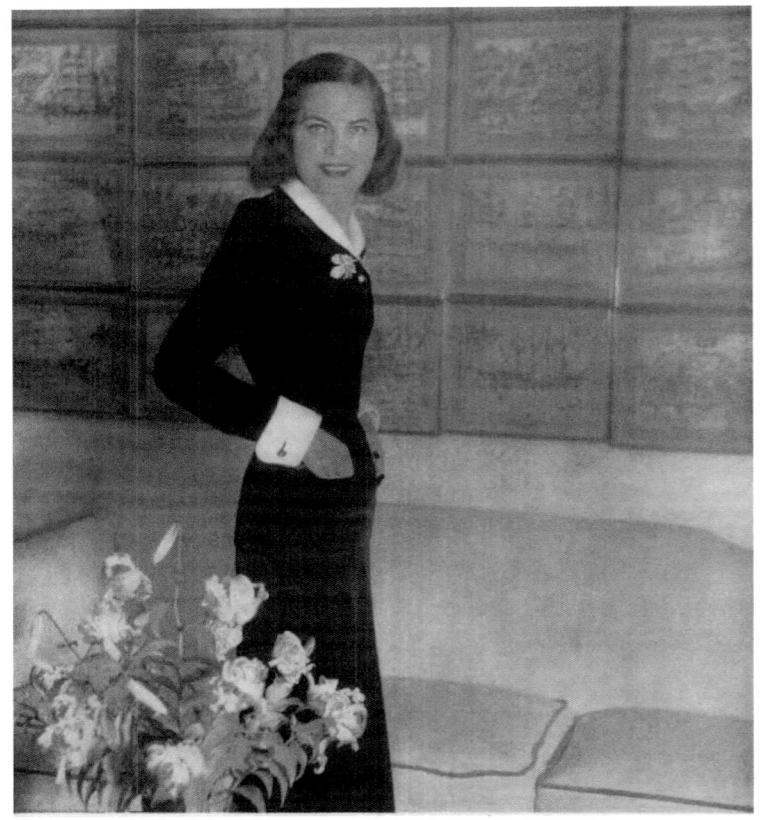

Fig.7. *Margaret Screven Duke with Golding drawings, 1947. Originally appeared in* Town & Country, *November 1947, a publication of Hearst Magazine Media, Inc.*

and culturally important cemetery, holding the remains or markers of formerly enslaved individuals and free people of color from the years prior to the Civil War, and prominent black Savannahians from early influential ministers to twentieth-century civil rights leaders.

SURFACING: THE ART OF WILLIAM O. GOLDING

William O. Golden's art entered the larger world through several pathways. Small groups of works of an unknown total number were sold to early collectors through Margaret Stiles and her connections. At least fourteen drawings can currently be traced to these sales, but anecdotal information suggests a higher number. Stiles herself retained many of Golden's works and a large group were already in the possession of her niece, Margaret Screven Tuck Duke, by the mid-1940s. Remarried in 1940 to American diplomat Angier Biddle Duke, Margaret Duke appeared in a photo shoot for the December 1947 issue of *Town and Country* magazine. The fashionable Duke is shown standing in her New York residence in front of a grid-like backdrop arrangement of Golden's drawings (Fig. 7). This first known appearance of Golden's work in print does not mention the artist, and decades passed before his work appeared in publications again. More than twenty-five works Duke owned were inherited by a Savannah family and exhibited many years later at Telfair Museums before being acquired by the Morris Museum of Art in Augusta in 2006. Golden's drawings are not known to have entered a museum collection in his lifetime, and no records indicate that Stiles offered his work to the Telfair Academy, despite her close involvement. The reasons are almost certainly due to race and to Golden's lack of formal training and reputation. Telfair would not mount its first exhibition of work by African American artists until 1959. Golden's drawings did, however, make their way into a museum collection in 1953, when Mrs. Mills B. Lane of Savannah donated three excellent early drawings to the Williams College Museum of Art.

William O. Golden died on August 25, 1943, at the US Marine Hospital. The cause of death was given as "surgical shock," during surgery for an "epigastric hernia." He is recorded on his death certificate as "William O. Golding," his usual occupation is indicated as "merchant seaman," and his treatment at the Marine Hospital is indicated as being for "bronchial asthma, duration 12 years." Next of kin listed are his wife, Josephine Golding, and sister, Sarah Quarterman. [30]

Several days after his death, Golden was buried in Savannah's historic Laurel Grove South Cemetery. Developed by 1850, Laurel Grove was established with segregated white (North) and black (South) sections. Laurel Grove South is noted today as a historically

Margaret Stiles retained sixty or more Golding drawings until her death in 1954 at the age of eighty-seven. The works in her estate passed to her nephew, Franklin Buchanan (Buck) Screven. This cache of drawings was acquired from him in the 1960s by Kai Olesen, then of Savannah, and his stepson, David Lee Cotton of Miami. Olesen, a former merchant seaman, researched Golden's life and career, while Cotton sought to establish the value of the drawings. [31] The two made contact with local and national media and may have consulted with Herbert W. Hemphill, Jr., a major collector of American folk art. According to Olesen, Cotton sold drawings to an executive of the Jim Beam company for display on his yacht and loaned works to an exhibition in Miami in 1969. By the late 1960s and early 1970s, Golden's drawings began to appear in art publications and commercial galleries, primarily Hirschl and Adler in New York, and the Philadelphia-based Janet Fleisher Gallery, later Fleisher/Ollman Gallery. In 1969 his work appeared in the *Artists and the Sea* exhibition at the Miami Art Center. In Golden's most prominent art-press coverage, three drawings belonging to Cotton were reproduced in a full-color, two-page article in *Art in America*'s January/February 1970 issue under the title "Rediscovery: William O. Golding." [32]

The 1970s marked a period of transformation in the way that the art world and museums were exhibiting what was called "folk art." Always an inadequate term, "folk art" had been applied in America to the products of artists without academic training working prior to the twentieth century. Encompassing traditional art forms passed down in communities as well as the art of individual untrained makers, many works under the "folk" umbrella were initially celebrated as Americana, evoking a nostalgia for the country's scrappy beginnings. By the 1920s and 30s, folk art appeared in exhibitions connected to colonial American history, albeit a version that often played to white fantasies about America's past. Margaret Stiles was likely aware of these trends, as the colonial craze had manifested

at the Telfair Academy in the form of "colonial kitchen" displays of vernacular objects. During the 1930s and '40s, the work of non-academically trained artists began to receive consideration within the context of modern art. Pieces by African American artists, including William Edmondson and Bill Traylor, were promoted by white artists, critics, and galleries.

Flashing forward to the 1970s, the book and exhibition *Twentieth-Century American Folk Art and Artists*, organized by Herbert Hemphill, brought together traditional and popular art forms with the work of contemporary, so-called self-taught artists in an exhibition at the American Folk Art Museum in New York. Among the pieces included were memory paintings of rural subjects, sculptural shop signs, kachina dolls, and a William O. Golding drawing, presented with other marine paintings by untrained artists. [33] Hemphill's involvement with Golden's work extended to an advisory role in a Georgia exhibition and catalogue that coincided with the US Bicentennial. *Missing Pieces: Georgia Folk Art, 1776–1976*, organized by Anna Wadsworth, included the gamut of work produced by artists throughout the state's history, from eighteenth-century portraits to quilts, basketry, paintings, and documentation of sculptural environments by Howard Finster and others. Three Golding drawings appeared in the catalogue and exhibition, shown at the Telfair Academy, the Atlanta Historical Society, and the Columbus Museum. [34] Hemphill also apparently acquired and sold works by Golding, and donated a Golding drawing of the USS *Tybee* to the Smithsonian American Art Museum. Twelve photographs of Golding works reside in Hemphill's files at the Archives of American Art. Two of those works can be traced back to Kai Olesen, who acquired works from Margaret Stiles's nephew and wrote a biographical article on Golden for the *Savannah Morning News* in 1975. Olesen's article and related comments that he circulated to other publications were based on research of Golden's records at the former Marine Hospital and an interview with Isaac Aiken, an employee at the hospital who remembered Golden. A longtime seaman himself, Olesen is informative and at times insightful regarding details found in Golden's drawings, as in this description of his port views:

> A drawing by Golden is actually more than a picture. Rather it is a happening replete with seaman's lore, as he saw it with his innocent sailor's eye: The teeming roadstead, the lighthouse, seaman's symbol of security and salvation, the signal station from whose mast a flag hoist would eventually decide a ship's future destination; the ubiquitous seagulls, the emblems of authority in the form of custom houses and fortresses high above the waterfront, where the Sailor's Home beckons with promise of peace and quietude and where attractive and easily accessible worldly pleasures are offered in the American Bar. [35]

Four years later, a Golding drawing of the USS *Texas* would appear in Robert Bishop's book *Folk Painters of America*.

Despite their occasional inclusion in publications and exhibitions, Golding drawings made their way into relatively few museums. The Georgia Museum of Art in Athens acquired two drawings in 1977, the same year as the *Missing Pieces* exhibition. Several Golding drawings were acquired by Robert P. Coggins and illustrated in a catalogue of his Southern art holdings, which in 1989 became a core collection at the Morris Museum of Art. Three drawings from Georgia private collections were included in the Telfair Museums' 1996 exhibition and catalogue *Looking Back: Art in Savannah, 1900–1960*, followed by the first survey exhibition of the artist's work at the Telfair in 2000, after the Golding collection formerly belonging to Margaret Screven Duke surfaced in Savannah. Works owned by David Lee Cotton and his partner Bill Ellington, likely the largest remaining group of drawings connected to Margaret Stiles, were sold by heirs in 2012. Most were purchased by a Savannah collector and acquired by Telfair Museums in 2020. Telfair's collection now provides an important repository for the study of Golden's work in the city he left as a child, and where, as an adult, he recorded his experiences in pencil and crayon on paper.

GOLDEN'S ART PRODUCTION

Over a period of eight to ten years, beginning around 1930 and ending in late 1939, William O. Golden produced a small but compelling body of work. Once thought to include only sixty drawings—a number derived from works bequeathed to Margaret Stiles's nephew—Golden's known production now numbers more than 130. His subject matter may be loosely divided into ship portraits, views of harbors, and navigational landmarks. Although reminiscent of earlier marine paintings and prints, and of memory paintings by artists with no formal art training, Golden's drawings are distinctive and idiosyncratic, brimming with visual invention, symbols, and conventions that he used repeatedly. Golden reiterated subjects and compositions, and while some of his work appears repetitive, stylistic elements evolve throughout the years of his creative output. Even subjects that Golden drew three or four times are often quite different, depicting the same vessel in different settings or with different details.

Golden's work, though bearing his own unique stamp, suggests some familiarity with marine painting and folk-art forms practiced by seamen. His drawings echo two staple types of marine painting: the ship portrait and the harbor view. Images of ships date back thousands of years in human culture, emerging as a distinct genre in the art of Western sea powers, particularly seventeenth- and eighteenth-century Dutch and later British paintings. Marine painting and ship portraits were taken up by other European, American, and Chinese painters, some who trained in England or came into contact with British marine artists. [36] It is possible that Golden encountered work by American marine artists, perhaps a contemporary like the prolific Antonio Jacobsen, in captains' quarters or shipping offices, or encountered the work of "pierhead" painters in ports. Like Jacobsen, James Bard, and numerous other self-taught painters of ship portraits, Golden favors a broadside view of his subjects. Golden may also have seen print portraits of vessels, produced in large numbers by Currier and Ives and other publishers depicting vessels in profile with the ship's name and pertinent information below the image.

Harbor scenes, Golden's other predominant subject, are found throughout the history of marine art. Perhaps the most intriguing examples in Golden's output are his views of Chinese treaty ports, some of which recall the work of eighteenth- and nineteenth-century Chinese painters that depict harbors with waterfront "hongs" or Western-owned factories. [36] As in those images, Golden frequently depicts multiple flags, typically American, British, and French, flying from buildings near Chinese harbors.

Golden's work, made with readily available materials and without academic training in art, could have also been influenced by the myriad art forms produced by sailors. In a long career spent on vessels of various types, Golden could have been familiar with these traditional arts, from the pictorial scrimshaw of whaling ships, to sailors' tattoos, to stitched wool-work ship portraits by mariners utilizing the sewing skills developed in their trade. Golden's whaling drawings bear some resemblance to the drawings and whale "stamps" made in the logbooks of whale ships, recording whale sightings or catches. [37] Whether or not he practiced any of these arts, Golden did represent traditional maritime woodcarving in his drawings of expressive figureheads on sailing ships, and the carved birds or eagles that sit atop the pilothouses of his steam vessels. Sailor's folklore is also visible in Golden's drawings, from the shark's tail fin nailed to the bowsprit of a sailing vessel to Golden's interpretation of Cape Horn's mythical post office. [38]

Although it is difficult to confirm specific influences from marine art in Golden's drawings, some of the conventions he used suggest his familiarity with representations of ships, particularly his incorpo-

Golden's work, though bearing his own unique stamp, suggests some familiarity with marine painting and folk-art forms practiced by seamen. His drawings echo two staple types of marine painting: the ship portrait and the harbor view.

ration of ship and place names as visual elements. With the exception of small studies, and perhaps his earliest works, Golden always identified his subjects at the lower border of the composition. In early drawings from 1932, Golden included ship and place names in a drawn, plaque-like inset in the bottom center of the image. At the corners of this plaque he went so far as to include tiny, drawn screw heads, imitating name plates on framed images of ships. In some cases, the title is flanked by stars and bordered with chevrons. By 1933, these drawn nameplates often extended to occupy the entire lower border of the picture, and soon after transformed into a drawn frame around the entire image. This border is usually filled in with color, typically brown, orange, or green. In early works, Golden included his initials or abbreviated name, date, and place near the title. "Savannah, GA" or "SAV. GA" and often "U.S.M.H." (for United States Marine Hospital) appear in smaller print outside of the title "plate." Golden later incorporated this information into the lower border, occasionally adding more description, such as a vessel's home port, names of captains or owners, or locations where the vessel is depicted. Golden often interrupted his drawn frames at the top or sides to accommodate a bowsprit, mast head, pennant, or building that did not fit within the border.

During approximately nine years of art production, Golden's approach to drawing remained remarkably consistent, with small stylistic and compositional variations and evolutions. His drawings from 1932, simpler and slightly less colorful at the start, quickly evolve into complex compositions like his drawing of Chefoo, China, of that year. From the spring of 1932 through 1934, his images are rich in detail and color. His drawings from the mid-1930s are more assured, streamlined, and occasionally less complex in composition. After a hiatus in parts of 1937 and all of 1938, Golden resumed work in a productive, perhaps final year of art-making in 1939, with a somewhat colder, less colorful palette, incorporating new subjects as well as fresh takes on images he had rendered previously.

In terms of general characteristics, Golden's drawings were all composed in pencil and crayon on white paper, materials easily found at downtown Savannah dimestores. Golden's works are all line drawings, with local color accenting specific details. On ships, bright color is most often used for flags and pennants, with tans and browns applied to wooden masts, bowsprits, and cabins. Figureheads and decorative bow ornaments are treated in more detailed color. The traditional red color of the hull below waterline is often glimpsed through waves. Steam vessels sport yellow funnels. Golden's limited use of color may be due to either judicious use of available supplies or aesthetic preference. Typically, the sky is left the color of the paper, but the sea is always shaded in gray with pencil. In several works from 1933 and 1934, large clouds animate the skies, reflecting pinks and orange from a setting or rising sun. Golden always renders a ship drawing water, reflecting its weight, with undulating waves at the waterline overlapping the vessel's hull to indicate movement. Background and foreground are often peppered with shorthand "m" shapes representing birds. In some drawings from the mid 1930s, Golden renders seabirds larger in scale, floating on the ocean's surface, or the fins of a pod of dolphins arcing through the waves.

Golden's ship portraits typically depict the named vessel surrounded by smaller watercraft. In these images, small launches, sailboats, tugboats, and rowboats abound. Larger vessels are depicted smaller in scale in the background or near the horizon in a more accurate depiction of spatial depth, but they sometimes appear wildly smaller in scale in front of the featured ship. Examples include Golden's 1934 drawing of the steam yacht *Nourmahal* (Pl. 25), in which a five-masted schooner and two other large vessels appear in miniature in the foreground. Golden's ship portraits often depict the featured vessel entering or leaving a harbor, with attention paid to signaling between the ship and the light stations or military bases on land. Golden's imagination is visible in the figureheads of men, women, or birds that grace his sailing ships and other vessels, often not matching the actual carvings on the historical ships he depicted.

Human figures, another integral component of Golden's scenes, are always small in scale, as if seen from a distance from an approaching vessel, and are largely rendered in silhouette. Golden packs a surprising amount of detail and expressive quality into his tiny figures, communicating their activities with exceptional economy. He draws sailors going about their business, standing atop yardarms or aligned on deck as a vessel cruises into harbor. In his whaling pictures, lookouts are posted in crow's nests, while in whaleboats harpooners stand by or are poised to strike, while oarsmen guide them toward their prey. In other scenes, officers bark orders from speaking trumpets aboard ship or from onshore fortifications. Port scenes bustle with animated, antlike human figures—women are shown in dress of the early twentieth century, men walk with canes, soldiers carry rifles. Dogs are shown roaming the roads, while people are depicted riding in cars, trucks, or—in Chinese port scenes—rickshaws. Golden's ports abound with largely the same sorts of buildings or establishments wherever in the world they are set. All are the types of places a sailor would frequent or take note of, among them sailors' rests, hotels, hospitals, "Anglo-American" bars, custom houses, ships' chandleries, and churches.

Space is compressed and flattened in Golden's harbor views, owing to the artist's lack of formal training. What might have been a limitation often yields exciting and animated compositions in Golden's hands, the lack of perspective resulting in tilted-up views of harbors or ports that allow the viewer to see more of the terrain in works like *Saigon, China* (Pl. 49). In other works, buildings spread out across a city appear on the same plane, as in his views of Chinese cities and drawings of his home port of Savannah.

Perhaps the most noteworthy signature element recurring in Golden's work is the sun, which he draws in the form of a compass rose (Fig. 8). Developed as early as the 1300s and used on nautical maps, charts, and ships' compasses, the compass rose typically lays out thirty-two navigational points radiating out from the center. [39] Golden includes this striking feature, transformed into a sun, in all but a handful of his drawings. This emblem appears in many variations throughout his work and is nearly always present, even when Golden has to include it in miniature or crop it at a border. His compass-rose sun usually appears to burst forth from behind a floating bed of clouds, emanating rays of yellow, orange, or pink, perhaps signaling a new day at sea. In a few drawings, the sun appears rising or setting behind the horizon at sea, behind mountains in foreign port scenes, or icebergs in his Arctic whaling pictures, appearing at its largest in the latter. Interestingly, the compass-rose sun is absent from several of his images of the Savannah waterfront. In seamen's lore, a compass-rose tattoo is said to guide the wearer home. Perhaps, for Golden, the sun was a personal symbol, one guiding constant in his nomadic existence, the compass rose a reminder of his way home and of the cardinal directions he had traveled so many times.

Harry DeLorme, *Director of Education and Senoir Curator, Telfair Museums*

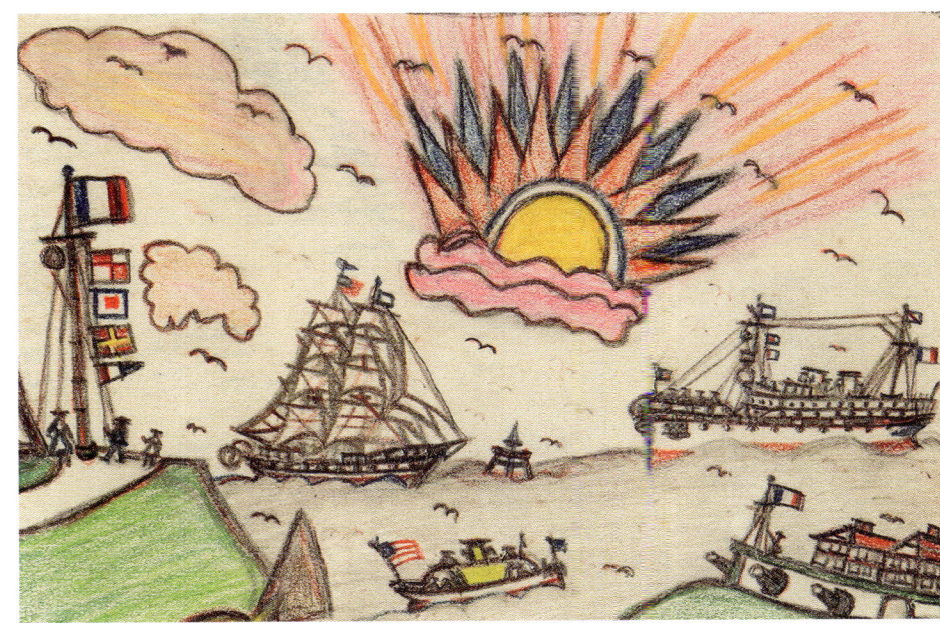

Fig. 8. *Compass rose sun, from William O. Golding, Saigon, China, 1934, Telfair Museums (detail, Pl. 49)*

EARLY LIFE: GOLDEN AND THE DORCHESTER ACADEMY

Little is known about William O. Golden's parentage and early childhood. In the 1880 US Federal Census for Liberty County, Georgia, he is listed as the adopted son of William Anthony Golden and Harriet Rebeca Bacon. This is the first time he shows up in the US Federal Census and he does not appear again until the 1930 census. This is largely attributed to his capture and years he spent at sea.

It is not known how William O. came to be under the care of the Goldens, or what his biological parents' surname was. It is likely that William O.'s biological parents did not have the means to care for him. They would have sought out someone powerful, or least someone with considerable influence in the black community, like William A. Golden, to look after their son. Listed on the 1880 census is also an adopted sister, Nancy Mallard, who seems to disappear from the record after 1900. [1] William O.'s death certificate lists a sister, Sarah Quarterman, who could have been a blood relation.

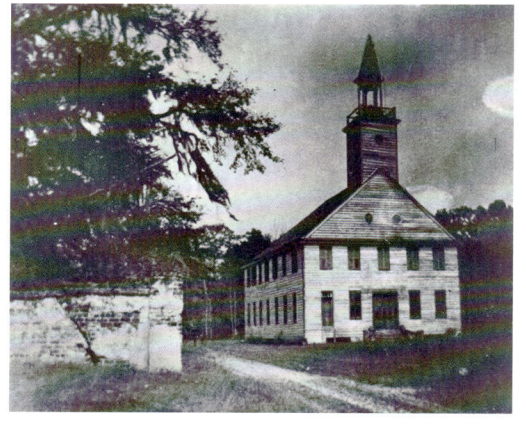

Fig. 1. *Photograph of Midway Church, Midway, Liberty County, Georgia, ca. 1875. Courtesy of the Georgia Archives, Vanishing Georgia Collection, lib023.*

William Anthony Golden was born about 1805 in Liberty County. He was enslaved by John Boyd Mallard, a prominent enslaver in Liberty County, as noted in a Southern Claims Commissions record. [2] Although he was enslaved by Mallard, Golden did not live on the plantation in the 1860s but instead in Walthourville with Harriet, who had been emancipated by Charlton C. Hines in 1861. It is not

known where he resided before his marriage to Harriet. Golden played an important role in his community, serving as a legislator, congregational minister, and an advocate for education.

Following the Civil War and Emancipation, Golden and thirty-three other African Americans were elected to the Georgia legislature in 1868 to serve in Reconstruction-era politics. These men were among some of the first African American state legislators in the United States. However, less than two months later, on September 3, 1868, Golden and these men were expelled from the house by the white majority. Subsequently, these men, "The Original 33" as they came to be called, petitioned the federal government to intervene, and in 1870 The Original 33 were reinstated for a term after the Georgia Supreme Court ruled that Black people did have a right to hold office in Georgia. [3] Golden also served from 1873 to 1874 but refused to serve afterwards, choosing to dedicate his time to improving the educational system for African Americans in Liberty County.

Along with being a state legislator, Golden was a man of faith. The grandson of Larson Sharper Jones, the first Black preacher of Liberty County, Golden joined the Midway Congregational Church in 1839 (Fig. 1). Golden played an active role in Black membership at the church and served as selectman. William A. obviously had a significant religious influence on William O., who was noted as being a deeply religious man.

Although William A. Golden was poorly educated, he was an ardent activist for education for his race. In 1868, with the support of the Freedmen's Bureau and the American Missionary Association (now the United Church of Christ), Golden offered up some of his own land and established the Homestead School, a one-room school building, at Golding's Grove in Liberty County. In 1870, Golden petitioned the AMA to send a teacher, "preferably southern-born and colored... a young man with good moral character and a preacher if possible." [4] The AMA responded by sending Eliza Ann Ward, a white teacher and staunch abolitionist from Monson, Massachusetts.

Ward's first appointment by the AMA was at Beach Institute in Savannah, Georgia, in 1867, and she spent the next couple of years teaching on a few plantations in Hilton Head, South Carolina, before arriving at Homestead School in 1870. Ward notes that despite "always hanging back r ever ready to do their work at the proper time," the students had a strong desire to learn and made rapid progress. [5] Unfortunately, much to the community's dismay, Ward only remained at the school for two academic school years before having to leave due to ill health. Even after her departure, she remained in regular contact with the school and continued to send clothing and school supplies to them.

Upon Ward's departure, the school ceased to operate for two years. African Americans in Liberty County continued to plea for educational assistance. The community was poor and couldn't offer much money for another teacher. Funds often came from parents bartering chickens, eggs, greens, and rice to pay for school supplies and operating costs. Finally in the spring of 1874, the AMA announced that they were sending Reverend Floyd Snelson of Andersonville, Georgia, to teach and preach in Liberty County.

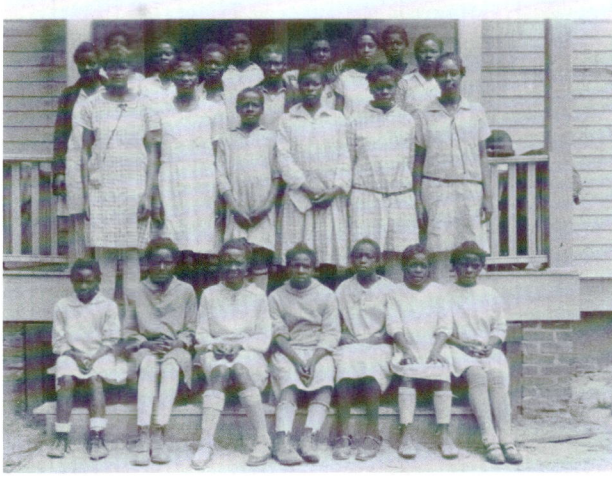

Fig. 2. Photograph of young women on the porch of a wooden building. American Missionary Association Photographs: 1887-1952, Dorchester Photographs: students, staff, grounds; 1898-1927. Amistad Research Center, New Orleans, LA.

Snelson, like Golden, was formerly enslaved. However, unlike his contemporary, Snelson received a formal education at Atlanta University, present-day Clark Atlanta University. With Snelson and Golden's presence and persistence, the school quickly evolved. It continued to grow with funding from the AMA, constructing more buildings for the growing number of enrollments.

By 1879, the school expanded and was renamed Dorchester Academy in honor of its Puritan heritage. It is unclear if William O. ever officially attended classes there. He might have been too young if he was shanghaied from the Savannah waterfront at age six instead of eight. According to the 1940 census, his highest grade completed was grade two. If he did not attend Dorchester Academy, it is possible his adoptive mother taught him basic literacy, as she served as a teacher for a time at Homestead School in the 1860s.

Dorchester Academy went on to become a major success. By 1917, it had eight frame buildings and a student population of three hundred. (Fig. 2) It continued operating as a school until 1940, and the site became a National Historic Landmark in 2006.

Ahmauri Williams-Alford, *Assistant Curator of Historical Interpretation and Programs, Telfair Museums*

SEARCHING FOR WILLIAM O. GOLDEN

Mid-May, 1975, my dad, James W. Cleveland, Sr., sent me a copy of *Ebony* magazine featuring an article about my great-granduncle, William O. Golden. I quickly flipped through the colorful drawings and was immediately impressed and very curious about the tiny crewmen on board the vessels. Also, what were those aquatic creatures leaping in the water? I didn't have time to read the article, but I filed the magazine safely with my packing boxes, as I was too busy preparing for my upcoming college graduation to be held at 10 a.m., my first wedding in the campus chapel at 3 p.m., and a huge community reception at the Black Philanthropies Hall in Mattapan, Massachusetts, at 6 p.m.—all on the same day.

Many years later, after relocating with my husband to Georgia, I had a moment to finally unpack boxes and settle into the Atlanta area. My search for William O. Golden began in earnest. Evening and weekend research became my mission at various Atlanta libraries. I gathered information on collectors, museums, exhibitions, Miss Margaret Stiles, and the Savannah Marine Hospital where Uncle Golden spent a good amount of time being treated for chronic bronchitis.

On trips from Atlanta to Savannah, I would talk with my grandmother, Lillie Mae Cooper, about Uncle Golden. She shared that whenever he was in Savannah, he spent time with her and my dad, who was a toddler. My dad would later share with me that he remembered sitting on Uncle Golden's lap and playing with the shiny buttons on his uniform.

Years later (after Uncle Golden's art received notice), Grandmother Cooper said it was very annoying when the press and others would badger her for days with calls, interruptions without any invitation, and unplanned visits, to ask if she had any of Uncle Golden's drawings, and if she would she go and search for them. She would always reply, "I had thrown those old scraps of paper out years ago!"

Uncle Golden's stories about traveling the world obviously impressed my dad, and he began his sailing career at the age of sixteen. After two years of active duty in the Korean conflict, he returned to Savannah as a reservist, and enrolled at Savannah State College. After he graduated, he then sailed again as a Merchant Marine, raising his family from a distance. He became a lifelong learner, eventually completing a master's degree program. I must mention that I never heard any other family member speak of William O. Golden, except for my grandmother and dad.

While living in Atlanta I decided to take my research on Uncle Golden to the next level, persistently writing to and calling individuals whose names were mentioned in exhibition catalogues I found in libraries. I finally reached a stockbroker in Savannah who was sharing Uncle Golden's artwork with museums and collectors in a tri-state area. When I returned to live and work in Boston, we had several long-distance calls.

As my job positions in corporate finance began to grow with more responsibilities, I had less time for Golden research. So I decided to make a four-city round trip, to stay grounded and not lose all the goodwill that was growing from strangers I had reached out to for information. The first trip was scheduled to Miami to see Mr. Cotton, who told me he had two Golden artworks on his living room walls and that I was welcome to see them anytime. The second was scheduled to Savannah to visit the stockbroker, who told me he had twenty or twenty-two Golden items displayed in the entrance hallway of his condo, and that I was welcome to see them. Third, I scheduled a visit to Atlanta to continue library research before returning to Boston. After confirming that everyone was fine with my tentative arrival schedules, I booked my round-trip ticket and confirmed my ETA with everyone.

MIAMI

While on the phone, standing at the Miami airport, I was informed by a male voice that Mr. Cotton had died earlier in the week. I was speechless and confused because I had spoken with him a week earlier. Once I managed to compose myself, I expressed my sympathies for his loss and hung up. I stood there crying like a baby because this visit was going to be my very first viewing of original William O. Golden art, other than in newspapers, magazines, and exhibition catalogues.

Still crying, I called my favorite Uncle Kenneth, and tried to explain why I was upset. He told me to relax: he would come to the Miami airport to pick me up, and I could stay overnight with him and Aunt Diane. Since I knew it would take hours for him to reach me, I decided that I would catch a cab downtown and visit the Miami Art Museum. [1] I arrived one hour before closing time and the place was empty, except for one nice security guard, on the last day for viewing the Queen of England's first-ever showing of her drawing collection. I was stunned, with my nose almost touching the delicate, small drawings—six inches or smaller—by Michelangelo, Leonardo da Vinci, Rembrandt, and other great artists from history. I talked about the drawings with Uncle Kenneth on the way from the Miami Art Museum to West Palm Beach, then repeated my stories to Aunt Diane. This visit was a learning experience I will always remember. The small drawings showed how much information you can convey from a slight tilt of the head or shoulder, the arch of an eyebrow, or the positioning of the fingers. These small markers can speak volumes of emotions: sadness and joy, heartbreak and exaltation, pleasure and

disgust. If you look at an image a dozen times, you should go back to look a dozen more. There is always something new to discover, if you look carefully.

SAVANNAH

The next day I made it to Savannah, my hometown. I located the stockbroker's office in a tall building near one of the grand historic squares downtown. Sitting in his office, he shared wonderful stories about his aunt's collection that he inherited when he went to help close out her New York apartment after her death. I listened very closely, with no interruptions or questions. Finally, I asked how soon I might see the William O. Golden artworks, and we made plans to meet at his condo the following afternoon.

The next day I went by; there was no answer at the door. I called, no answer. I called into the evening hours; still no answer. I had to catch my flight early the next morning to Atlanta. Needless to say, I was very disappointed... again. No sighting yet of an original William O. Golden drawing. Later, when I was back in Boston, he shared that he got tied up at Tybee Island with friends and was in no condition to drive back to Savannah. I quietly forgave him and was glad he was safe.

ATLANTA

I rented a car in Atlanta and drove down to the Morris Museum of Art in Augusta, where a William O. Golden piece was on display in their current exhibition. I stared, mesmerized, at the small drawing, and couldn't have been happier to just gaze and smile at the beauty of it. I left, quietly and completely satisfied. I was gratified to discover the small Golden drawing after the earlier disappointments. How else would I have known to appreciate the subtle nuances, to look closely for landmarks, and to feel the joy and happiness in every new William O. Golden sunburst? The Atlanta trip was completed via this detour visit.

FAMILY

As young children we watched my dad lovingly care for our Auntie Bill, Willie Mae Shulman, who was in Charity Nursing Home (where I was born in 1953 when it was Charity Hospital). Dad would lift her from her bed into our car and drive her home to spend a full day with us, away from the nursing home. She was delighted to spend time with us, even though she was unable to speak or walk

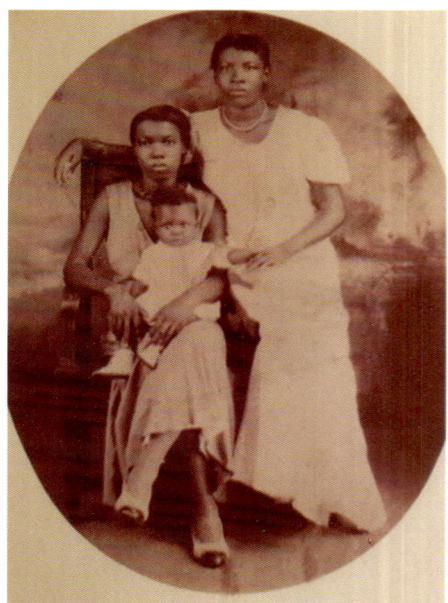

Fig. 1. *James W. Cleveland, Sr., 9 months old, with his mother, Lillie Mae Cleveland Cooper, and her sister Willie Mae Cleveland Shulman (right), circa 1934. Courtesy Jackie Cleveland Cox-Crite.*

after a serious stroke that affected her entire left side. She and Dad had their own language—Dad with very simple questions, she with simple grunts and laughter. My mom, Katherine Marie Cleveland, would take us to visit with Auntie Bill after every Sunday Mass.

Auntie Bill and Grandmother Cooper grew up together as sisters in Midway, Georgia, in Liberty County, the place where William O. Golden spent his earliest years. I loved staring at the beautiful black and white photograph of them dressed so elegantly, with fancy shoes and jewelry—they were so young then (Fig. 1). That photo remained in the living room for decades.

Frequently Mom would drive to Midway, with or without Grandmother, to visit the family there. Her visits always included boxes of dry goods, toiletries, and whatever she thought they could use. And we would be gifted with whatever fresh produce was in season. Because we were very young, I really don't remember the adults' names. I believe Aunt Soda (Sarah Missouri Quarterman) was also raised with all the children—Lillie Mae (Cleveland) Cooper, Willie Mae (Cleveland) Shulman, and Uncle Dave Mack—in Midway. [2]

As a child I often went on road trips to Jacksonville, Florida, to visit Aunt Soda and Uncle Walter, Sr., and the other adult cousins: Tomassina, Walter, Jr., and Ella. We usually hung out with Aunt Doris (Doris Quarterman Bell), Uncle "Joe" Louis Quarterman, Sr., and their children who were closer to our exact ages. I am now discovering that some of the older children raised with Grandmother were adopted and that each was accepted as a sister or brother. William O. Golden was a member of this fine family.

I am very proud to know that William O. Golden's spirit has been in such close proximity to me my entire life, through the same places near downtown Savannah where I have lived (Hall Bottom—a small, black community off East Broad and Hall Streets) and attended school. I also spent time on the Savannah waterfront, shopping, vacationing, and producing art shows at the Savannah Hyatt Regen-

The search for William O. Golden by his descendants will go on— today and into the future— because across nine states and forty-four households, there are more than 125 loved ones who are his family.

cy and the Hilton Head Island Hyatt Regency (where I first met the stockbroker, who attended my private exhibitions of work by Boston artists). I've always felt empowered by my education, knowing that my family expected me to do my best academically, in sports, in employment, and as an advocate for art and artists.

William O. Golden documented his worldwide travels at sea through drawings and memories. Like Golden, my dad traveled the world many times over, around Cape Horn; through the Suez Canal; exiting the Straits of Gibraltar; back and forth to Free China; and on tours of Japan, with his cameras documenting people, places, and things. I am the proud new archivist, ready to sort thirty-three years of boxes of Dad's photographs, albums, and cherished memories.

Dad encouraged me to apply for the National Maritime Scholarship. I did and was awarded a full four-year scholarship to attend any college of my choice.

My younger brothers, James Jr. and Jerome Douglas, were encouraged by my father to become merchant seamen— James Jr. as a college graduate and Jerome as a high-school graduate. Dad leveraged all of his influence as a Chief Steward and helped them secure gainful employment. James Jr. had some trouble adjusting to the assumed class and privilege attached to the white officers and white seamen in general, and the subservient roles that most blacks and people of color were expected to adhere to. He didn't remain a merchant seaman for very long, even though identical attitudes were expressed stateside. Jerome, however, thrived in his role as a merchant seaman. He had friends worldwide, looked at every opportunity as a learning experience, collected antiques, and loved his time at sea.

The search for William O. Golden by his descendants will go on— today and into the future—because across nine states and forty-four households, there are more than 125 loved ones who are his family. We are William O. Golden, and he is breathing deeply and calmly inside each of us.

Jackie Cleveland Cox-Crite

Author's note: I wish to express sincere appreciation to my sister, Joan Cleveland Emerson, for her dedication and loving support of our Dad throughout his decline and death and the distribution of his estate.

In Memory of James W. Cleveland, Sr. (1932–2020)

PLATES

GOLDEN'S AGE OF SAIL

William O. Golden said that he left Savannah aboard a sailing vessel, and named sailing ships later became the most prevalent subject in his art. They are portrayed either solo or in larger scale in some forty drawings and appear in miniature in many of his port views. Among Golden's earliest works are a drawing of the ship that he claimed took him from Savannah; also his first pictures of whalers. By 1933 Golden was drawing famous sailing ships that figured in US or world history. Although they are not as common in his work of the mid-1930s, Golden resumed drawing sailing vessels in his last year of artmaking, 1939. Though particularly fond of fully rigged three-masted ships, Golden also portrayed barks, barkentines, schooners, and yachts. Numerous smaller sailing-vessel types appear in a secondary role in his port views, from simple catboats to Chinese junks.

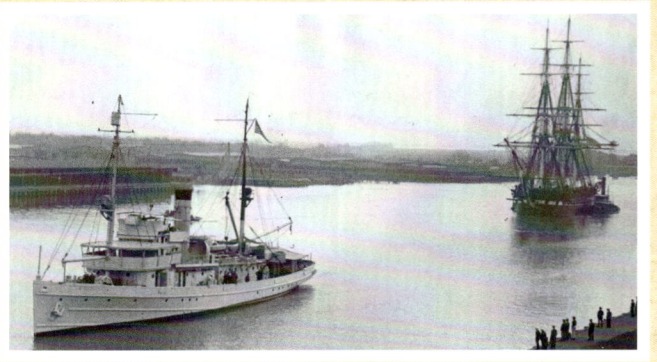

Fig. 1. *USS Constitution on a nationwide port tour arriving in Savannah, 1931,* The Atlanta Journal-Constitution, 21222645963022.

Key among Golden's portraits of historic sailing vessels were his drawings of the USS *Constitution* and the USS *Constellation*, both mentioned in his 1933 letter to Margaret Stiles. Perhaps due to its popularity and visibility during Golden's artmaking years, the *Constitution* was the subject of four drawings made between 1932 and 1939. One of the most beloved and iconic ships in American history and the oldest sailing warship still afloat, the *Constitution,* known as "Old Ironsides," was completed in 1797 and defeated British warships in the War of 1812. Golden may have had the opportunity to lay eyes on the vessel when the *Constitution* visited Savannah from December 7 to 11, 1931, during a post-restoration tour of the Eastern Seaboard. [1]

If he didn't see the vessel itself, Golden could have seen images of the *Constitution,* which appeared in paintings, prints, and publications throughout its storied history. In the mid-1920s a popular print and the silent film *Old Ironsides* helped popularize efforts to restore the ship. Photographs of the *Constitution* were run in newspapers, including the *Atlanta Constitution,* at the time of its visit to Georgia (Fig. 1).

On two occasions Golden drew another iconic US warship of the age of sail, the USS *Constellation* (Pl. 7), now a museum ship based in Baltimore's harbor. In his earlier drawing of the *Constellation,* Golden patriotically included the Great Seal of the United States. To another drawing of the USS *Ranger* (Pl. 5), Golden proudly added the descriptive phrase "First ship to fly American flag." The *Ranger* appeared in a popular print in 1898 based on an Edward Moran painting picturing the *Ranger* in a French harbor, noting the occasion as the "first recognition of the American flag by a foreign government." [2] Whether Golden saw this image is unknown, but his drawing depicts the *Ranger* entering a French port and flying the French ensign as a courtesy from its foremast.

Golden's sailing-vessel subjects seem to have as much to do with a vessel's historic interest as with patriotism, and included such notable British vessels as the HMS *Victory* (Pl. 9) and the HMS *Bounty.* Other famous ships Golden drew included the *Thomas W. Lawson* (Pl. 14), a seven-masted vessel said to be the largest schooner ever built. On two occasions, Golden also drew the Confederate States cruiser *Alabama* (Pls. 11, 12), a commerce raider of the Civil War. The vessel ran on steam rather than sail power, but Golden shows the *Alabama* with its auxiliary sails billowing.

In other cases, Golden portrayed merchant sailing vessels that he could have conceivably seen, including the Barkentine Josephine of Baltimore (Pl. 16). Built in Belfast, Maine, the four-masted barkentine engaged in coffee trade with Brazil. The vessel's name has added resonance, given that Golden's wife was named Josephine, leaving one to wonder if the woman depicted as the figurehead was intended as a portrait.

Whalers are a distinctive subset of Golden's sailing-ship drawings. The artist claimed to have served aboard one and created some eight images that speak to this experience. He drew four named whaling vessels: the *Emma'ina, Petre', Neptune,* and *Saluda*. The *Saluda* seems to have special significance, appearing in four drawings and a study, though a whaler by that name remains elusive in the records. Golden's whaling pictures follow a similar composition, as if this particular scene was burned into his memory. The main whaler is always shown entering from the right, while in most cases another whaler approaches from the left. Whales, usually white, gray, or brown, are flanked by the ships, while smaller whaleboats and their crews engage in the hunt. In the boats, whalemen are seen either with harpoons held vertically or poised to strike a target within a pod of whales. A steamship always appears near the horizon, while the left center background is dominated by undulating ice mountains, over which Golden's compass rose-shaped sun emerges.

Golden appeared familiar with whaling, as evidenced in details of the ships themselves and the activities of the crew. His whalers are almost always three-masted square-rigged ships. A shark's tail fin is shown attached to the tip of the featured whaler's bowsprit, a tradition said to bring good luck. Sailors positioned atop the masts keep watch for whales. In smaller whaleboats, Golden accurately records a crew of six or seven. A harpooner is always shown at the bow, either standing at the ready or preparing to strike. Four to five oarsmen are depicted propelling the craft, while at the stern, the boatheader controls the steering oar. Golden simultaneously shows a whaling vessel at full sail, with whaleboats both in use and stowed on ship, combining different moments in time in one image. He also compresses distance as whaleboat crews were often far separated from their ships.

In most of his whaling scenes, Golden gives the Arctic Ocean as the location, with one specifically identified as "North Cape," perhaps a reference to Norway's North Cape. The larger-than-typical compass rose-shaped sun that Golden uses here may be a representation of the midnight sun of arctic summer. Another distinct feature of the whaling pictures is the presence of a two-masted steamship on the horizon. Steam vessels were used in whaling, so perhaps Golden intended to illustrate the presence of both sail and steam in the industry. Whether Golden served on one whaler or more, his memory of this brutal hunt in a harsh and beautiful environment created an indelible image to which he returned frequently.

Aside from portraits of warships, merchant ships, and whalers, sailing vessels also fulfill a secondary role in many of Golden's drawings, coexisting with steam vessels as they would have during this period of transition in maritime travel. In some works, a sailing ship incongruously leads a fleet of steam warships, perhaps depicting different time periods at once, but the sailing ship may also be one of Golden's personal symbols. Like sailors' tattoos of full-rigged ships, which signified the wearer's journey around Cape Horn, Golden's frequent inclusion of this type may be a similar emblem of his experience. Although a good bit of Golden's service was likely aboard steam vessels, his lovingly rendered sailing ships and their detailed rigging figured proudly in his memory. —H.D.

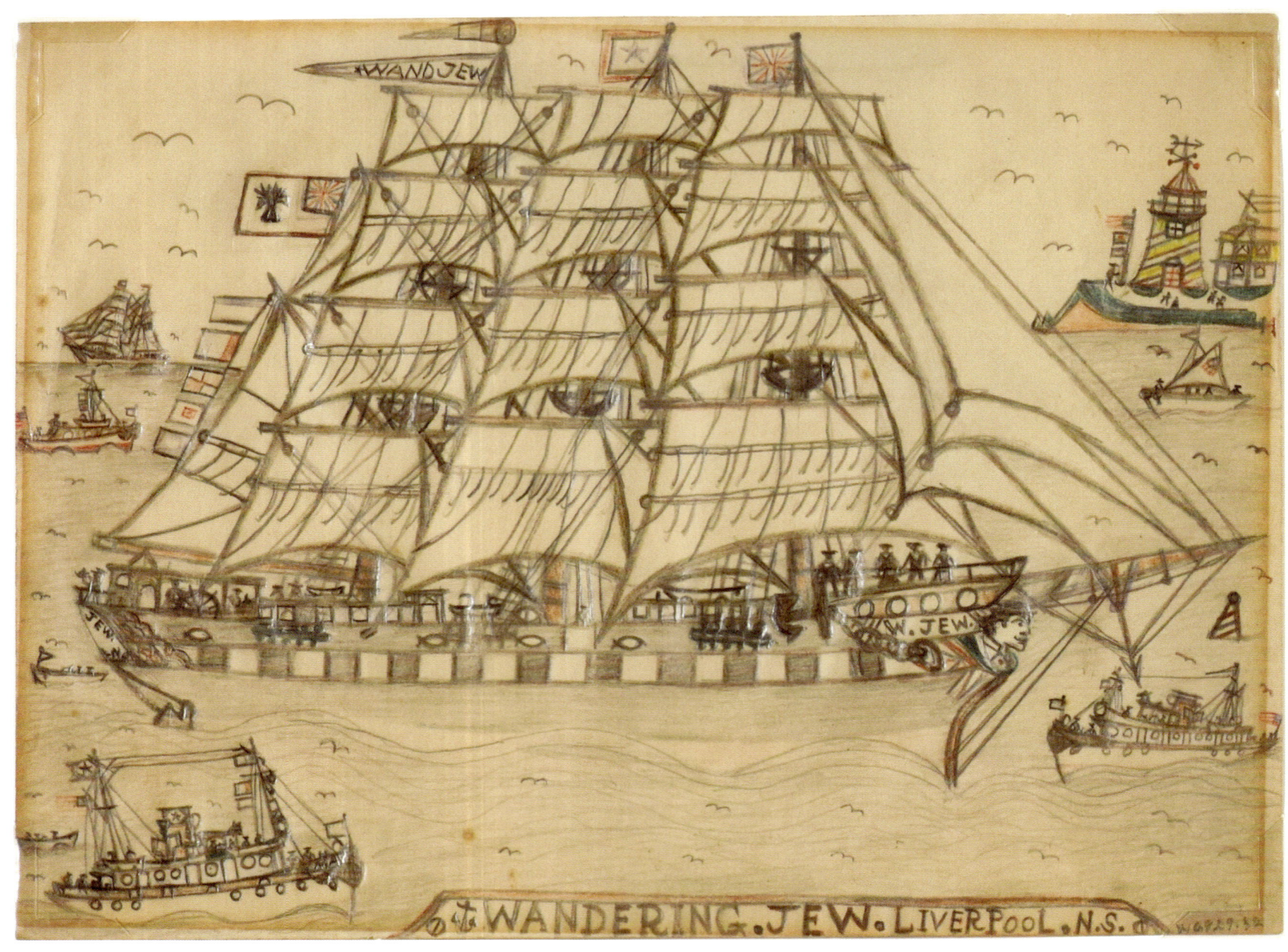

PLATE 1. *Wandering Jew, Liverpool, N.S.,* 1932

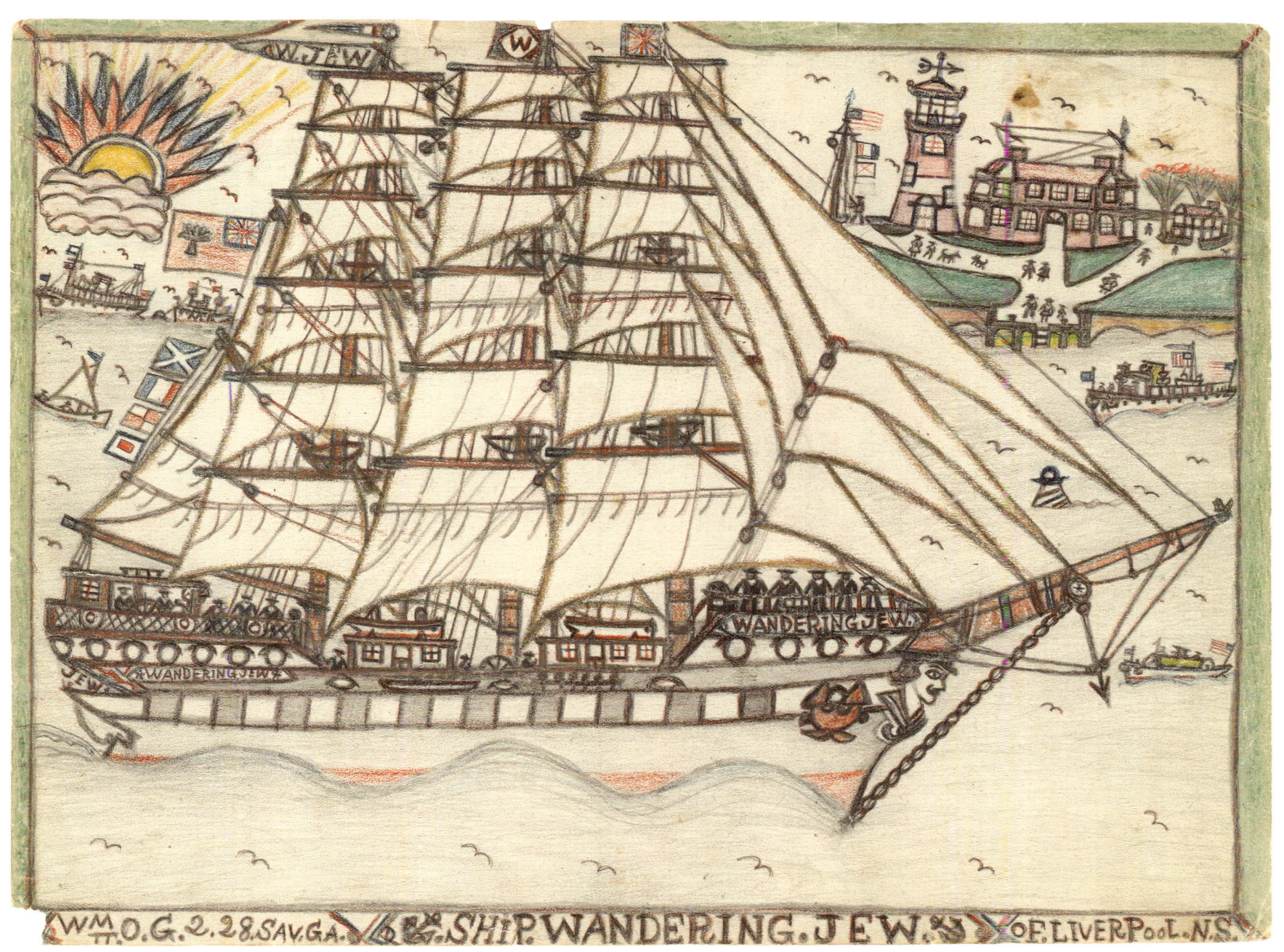

PLATE 2. *Ship Wandering Jew of Liverpool, N.S.,* n.d.

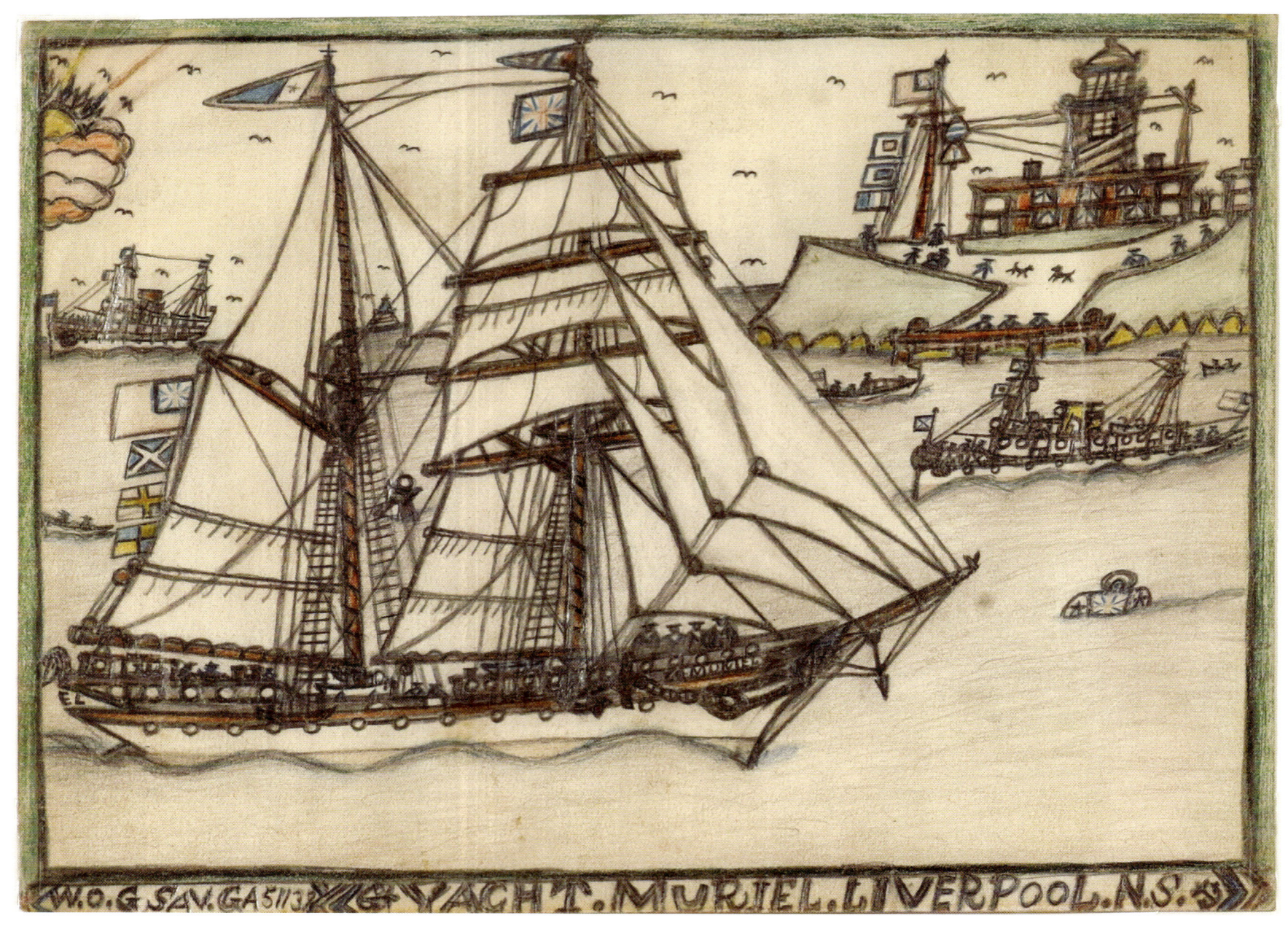

PLATE 3. *Yacht Muriel, Liverpool, N.S., 1939*

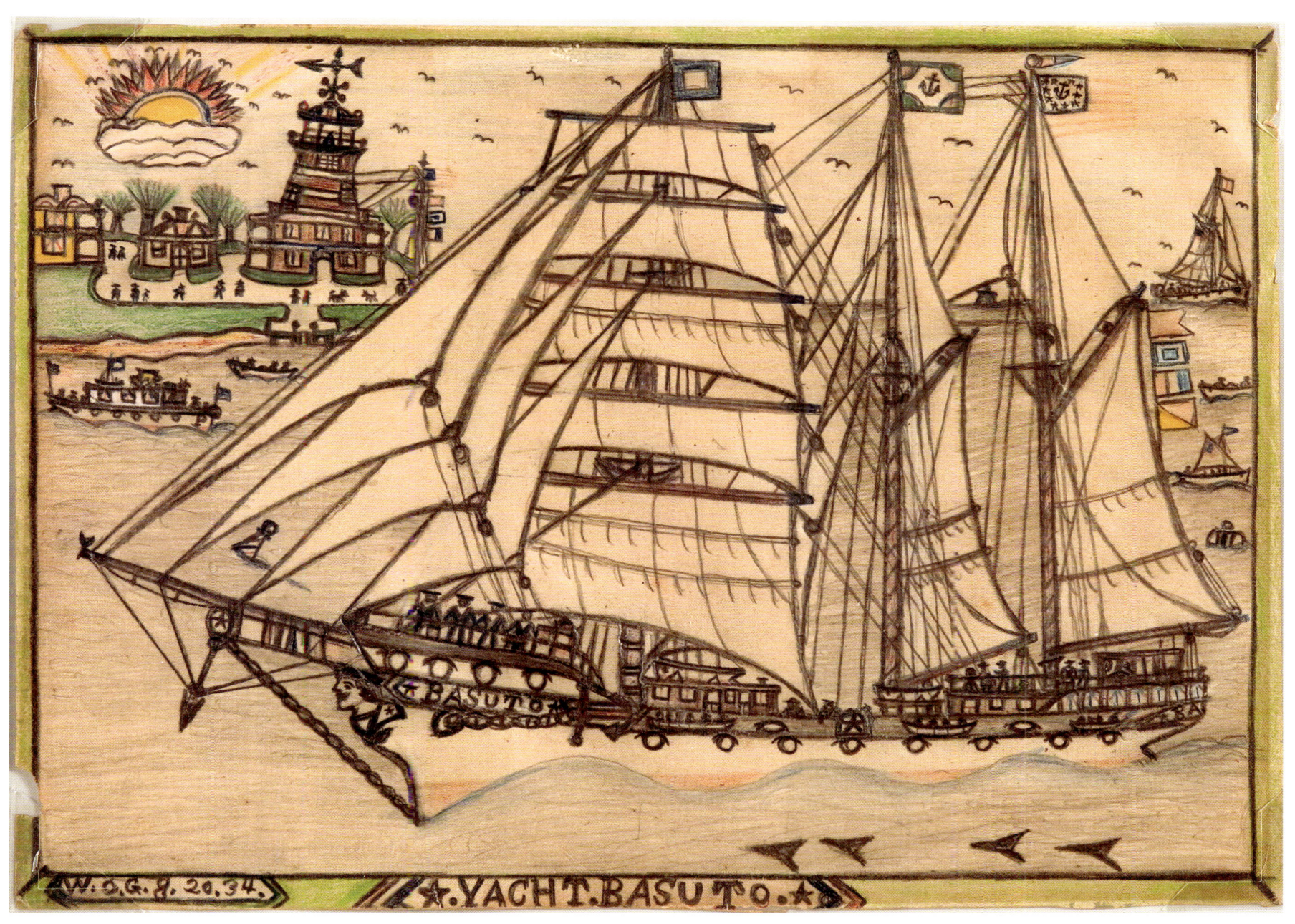

PLATE 4. *Yacht Basuto*, 1934

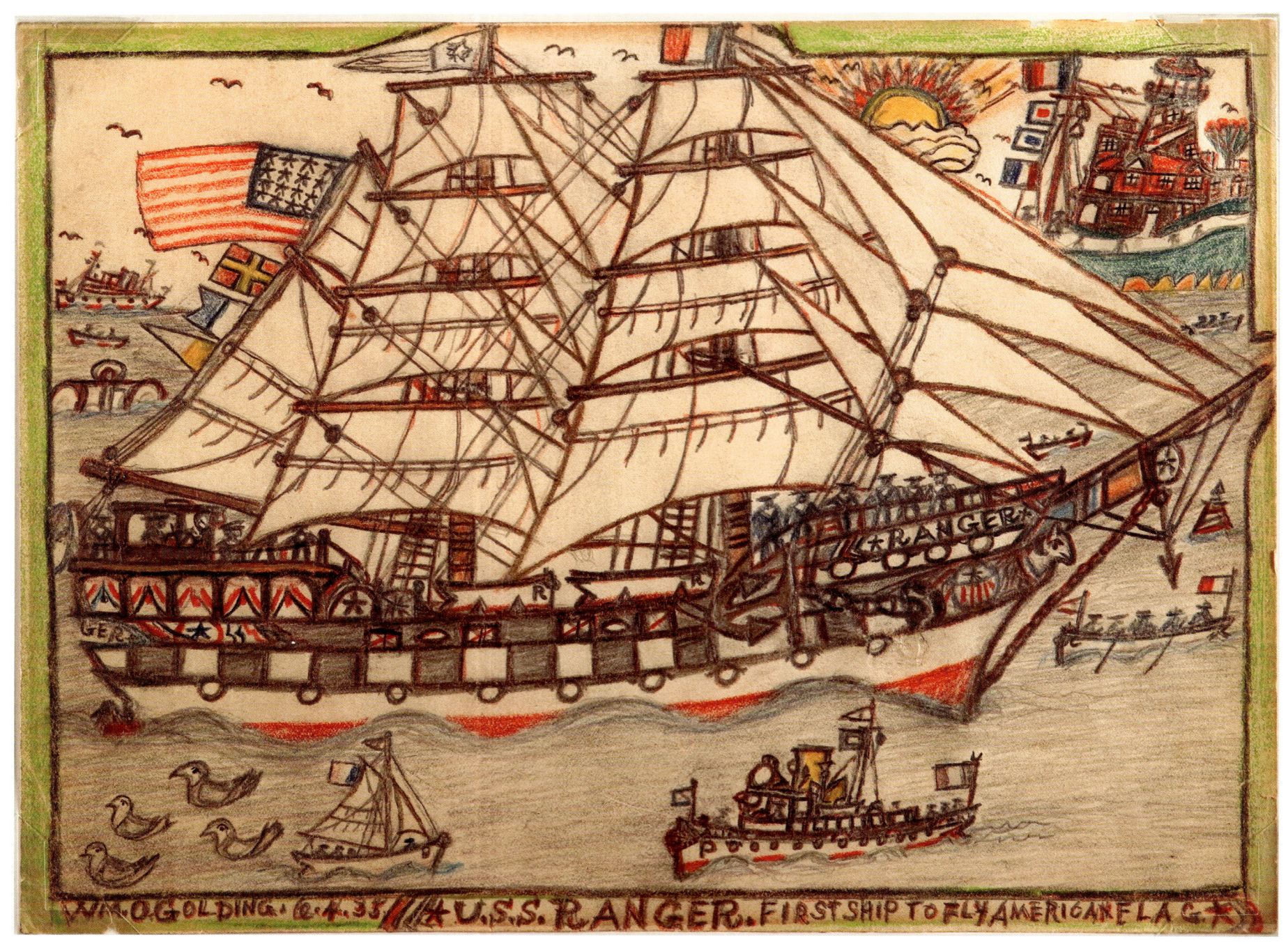

PLATE 5. *U.S.S. Ranger, First Ship to Fly American Flag, 1935*

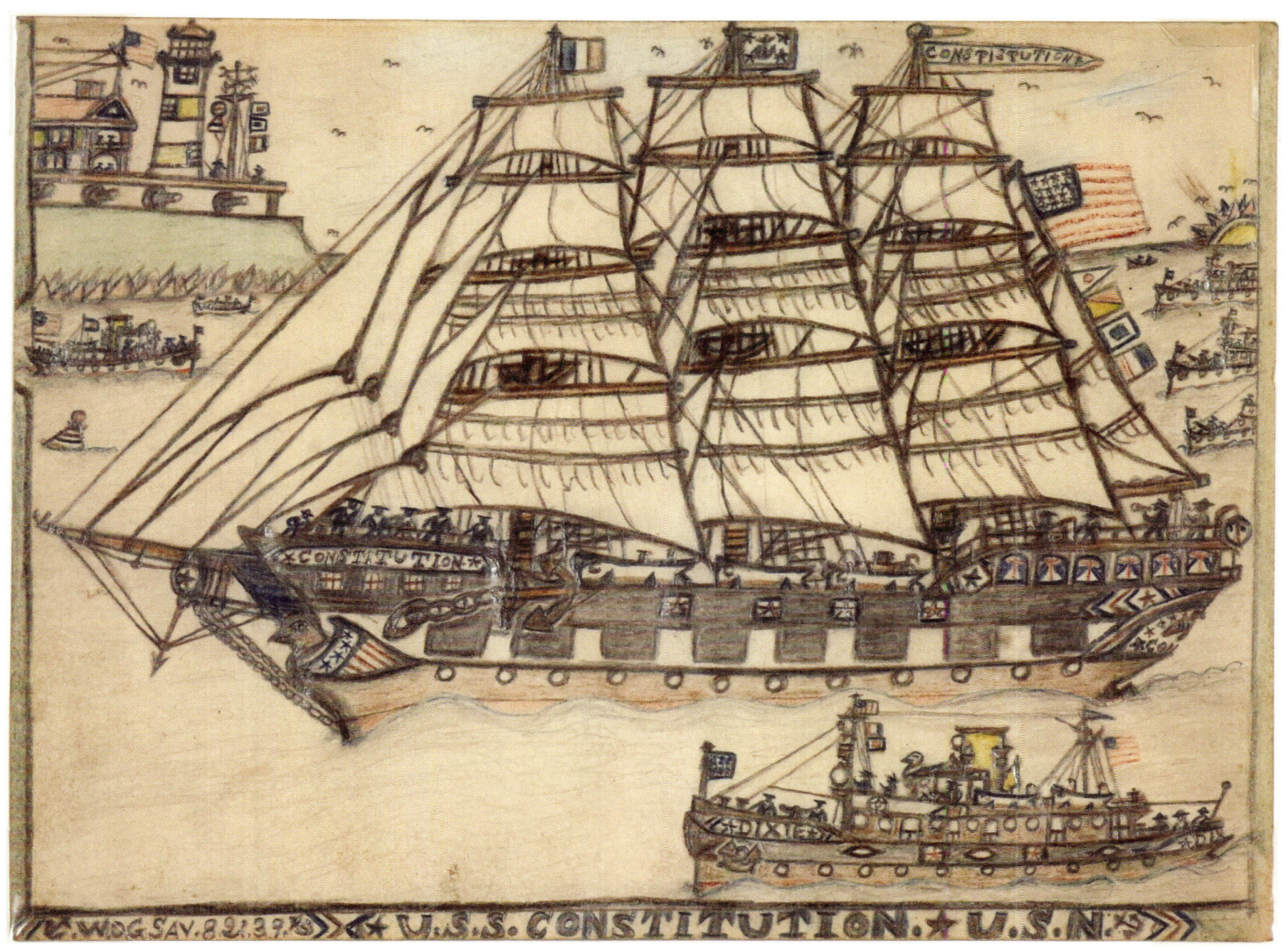

PLATE 6. *U.S.S. Constitution, U.S.N.,* 1939

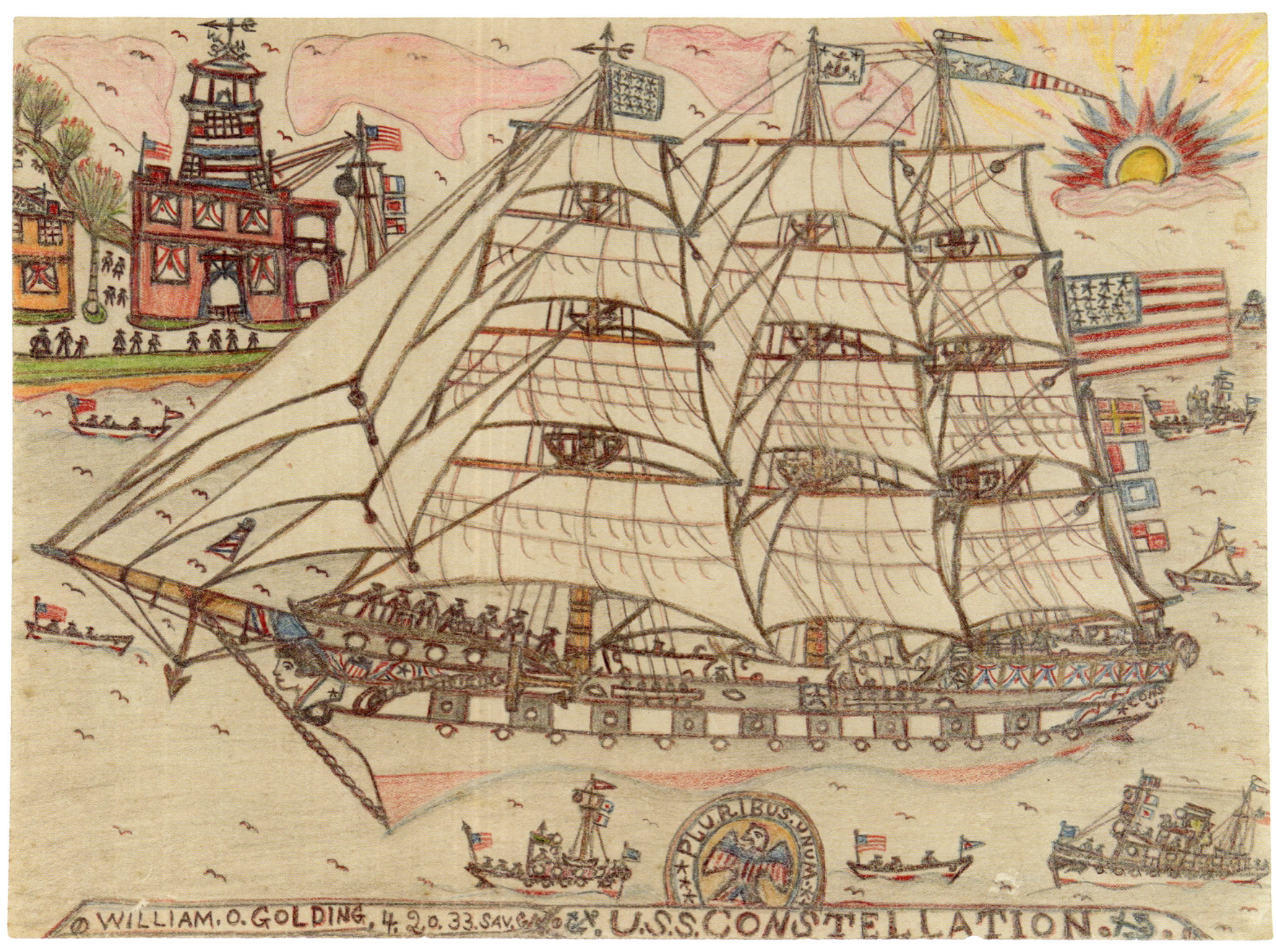

PLATE 7. *U.S.S. Constellation*, 1933

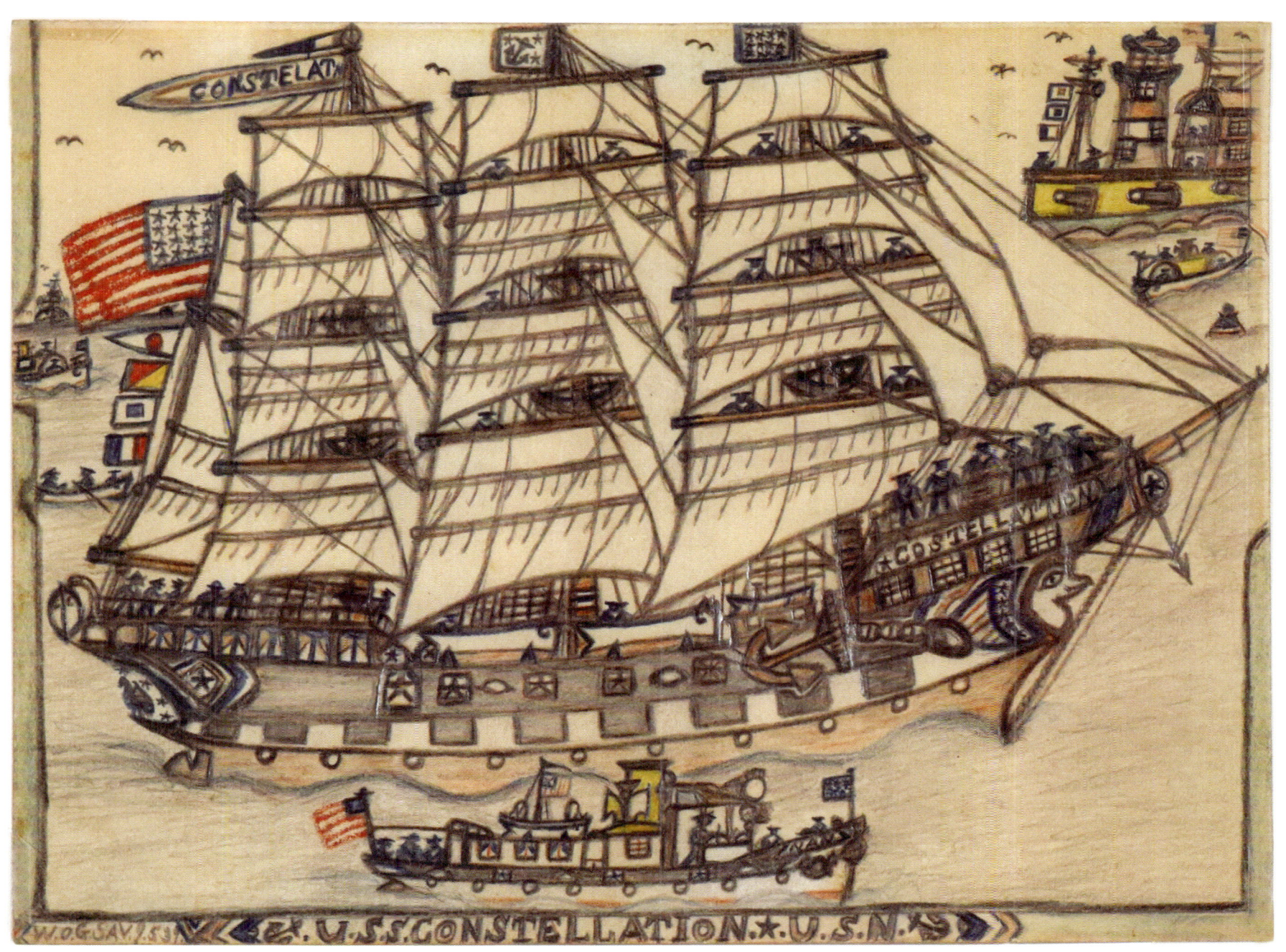

PLATE 8. *U.S.S. Constellation, U.S.N., 1939*

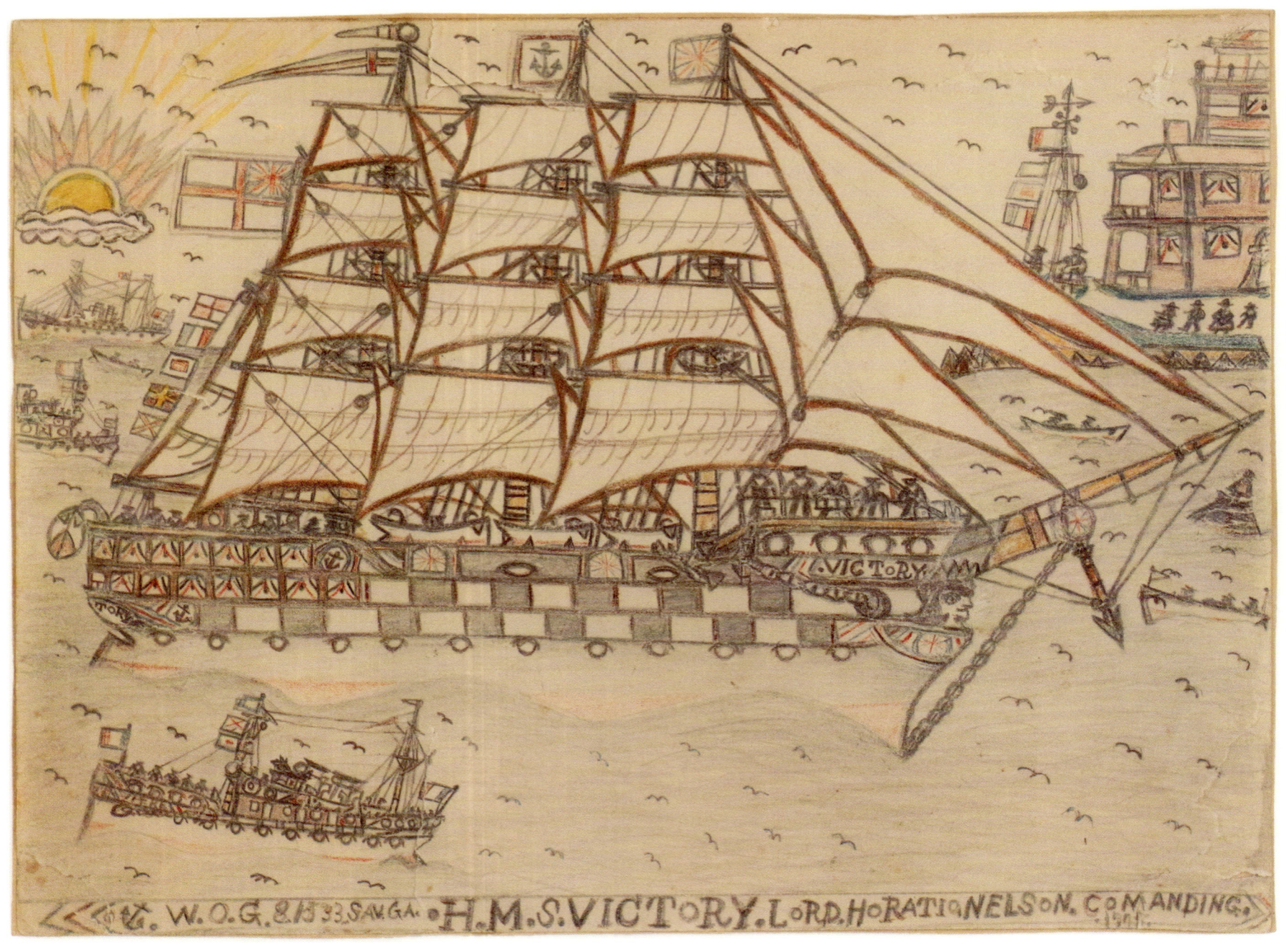

PLATE 9. *H.M.S. Victory, Lord Horatio Nelson Comanding*, 1933

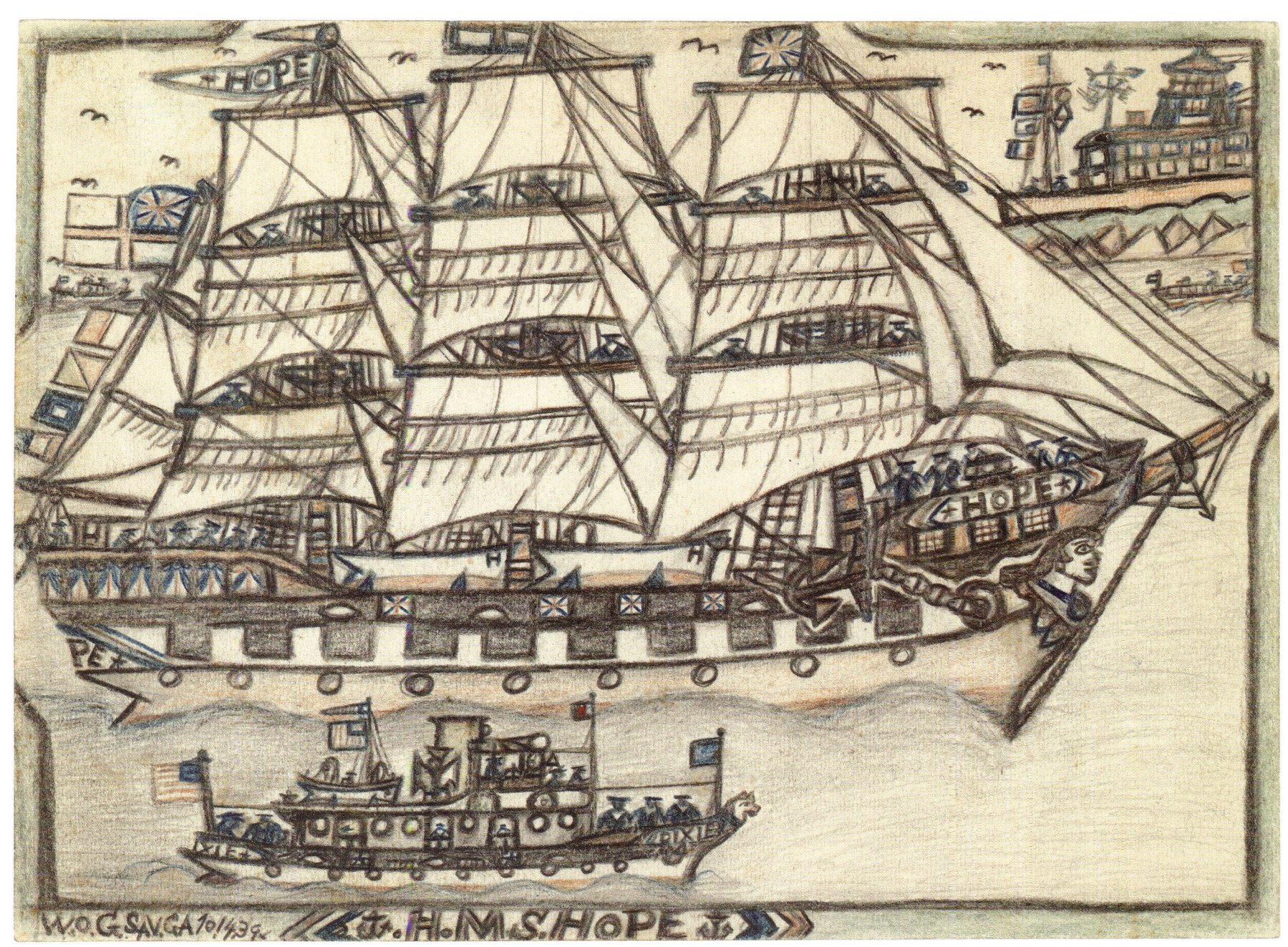

PLATE 10. *H.M.S. Hope, 1939*

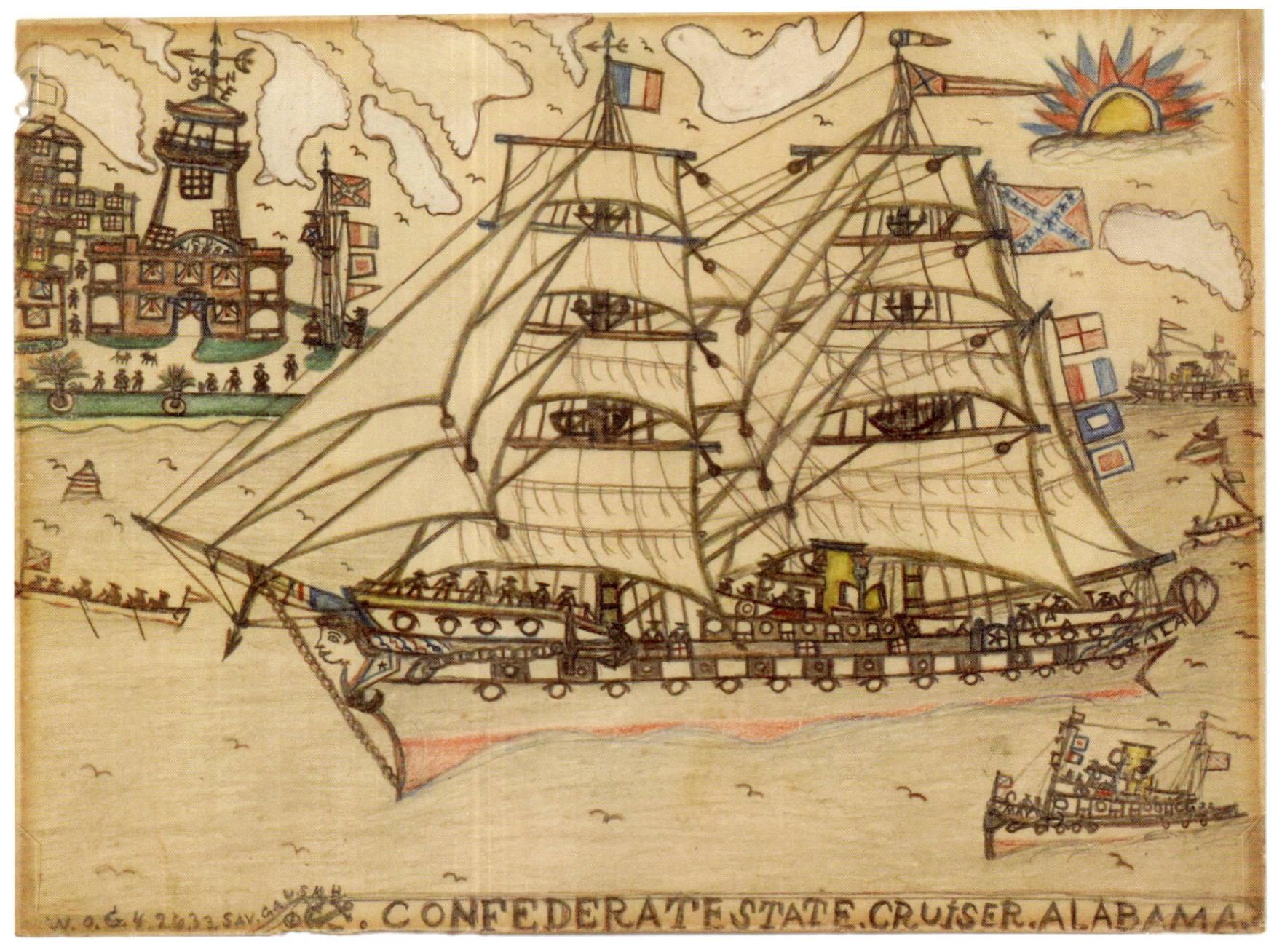

PLATE 11. *Confederate State Cruiser Alabama*, 1933

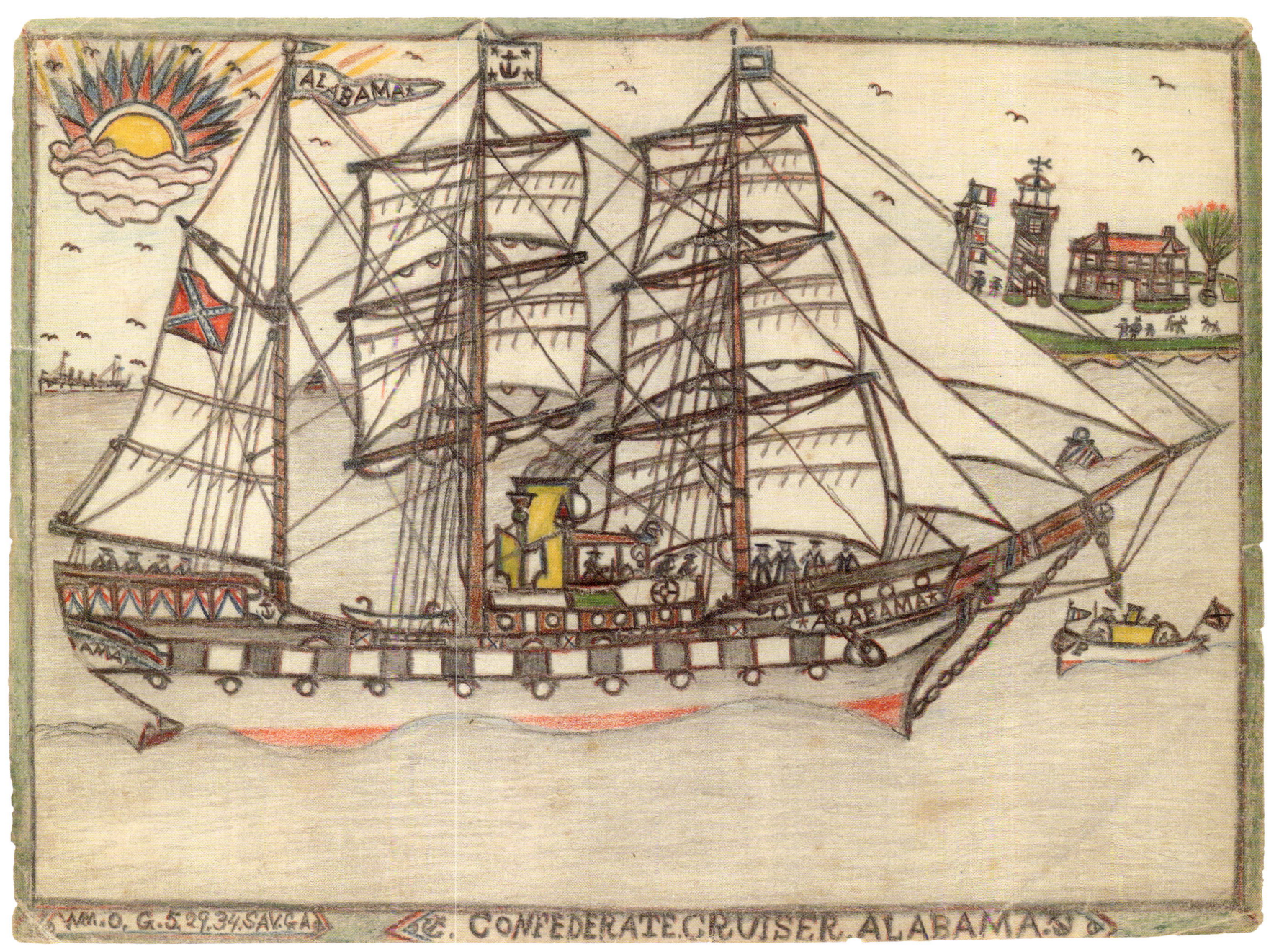

PLATE 12. *Confederate Cruiser Alabama*, 1934

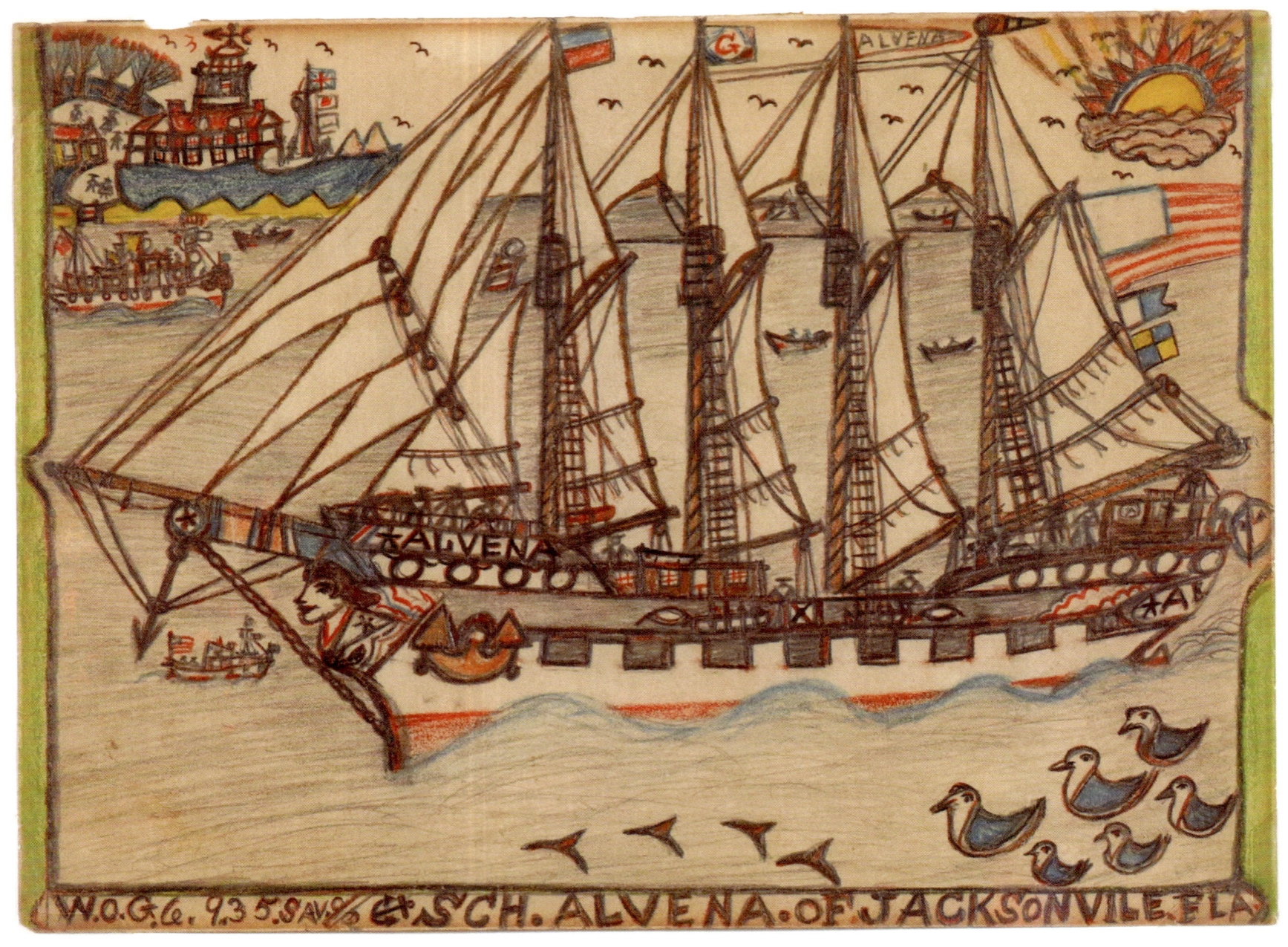

PLATE 13. *Sch. Alvena of Jacksonville, FLA.*, 1935

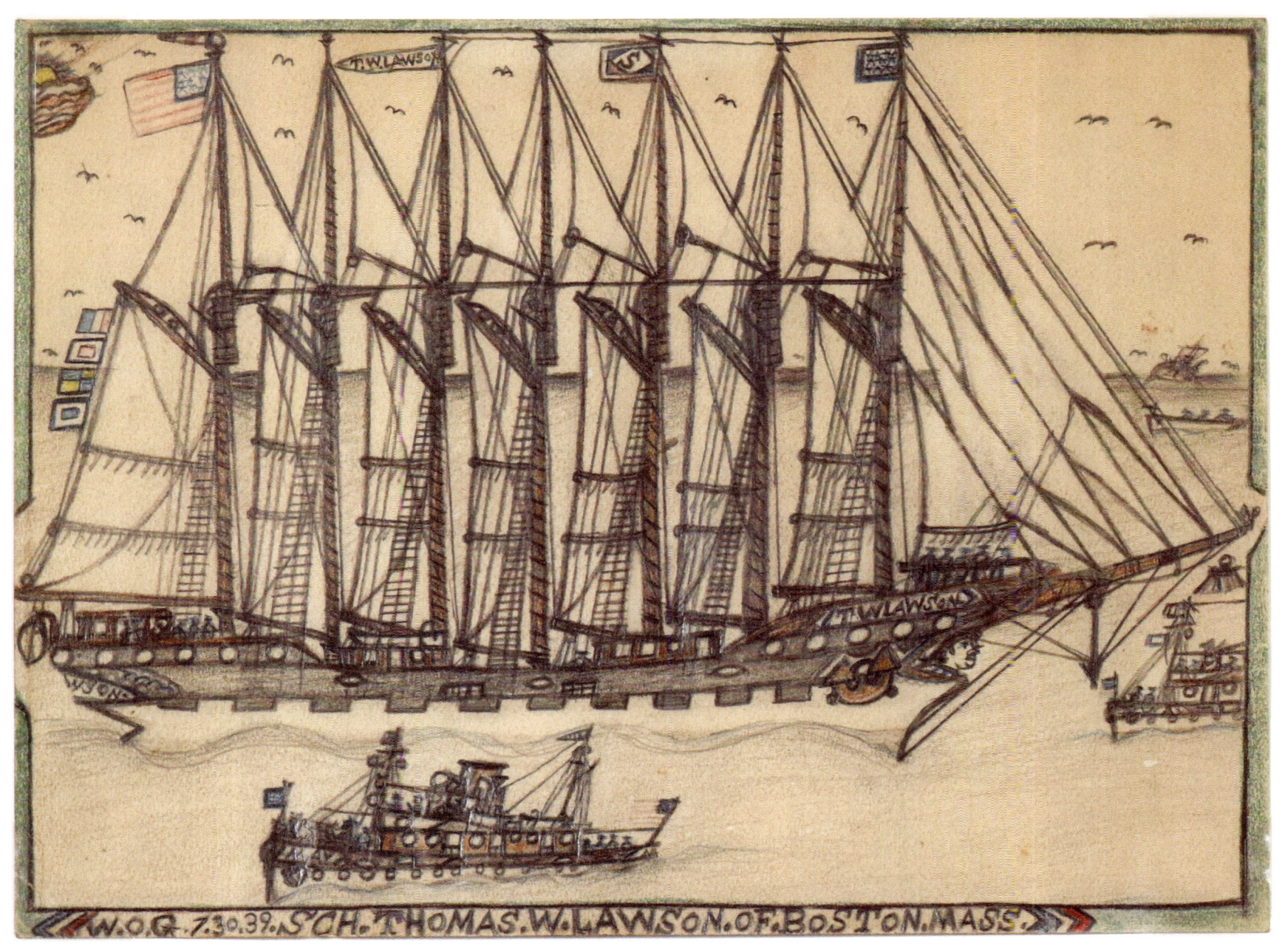

PLATE 14. *Sch. Thomas W. Lawson of Boston, Mass.*, 1939

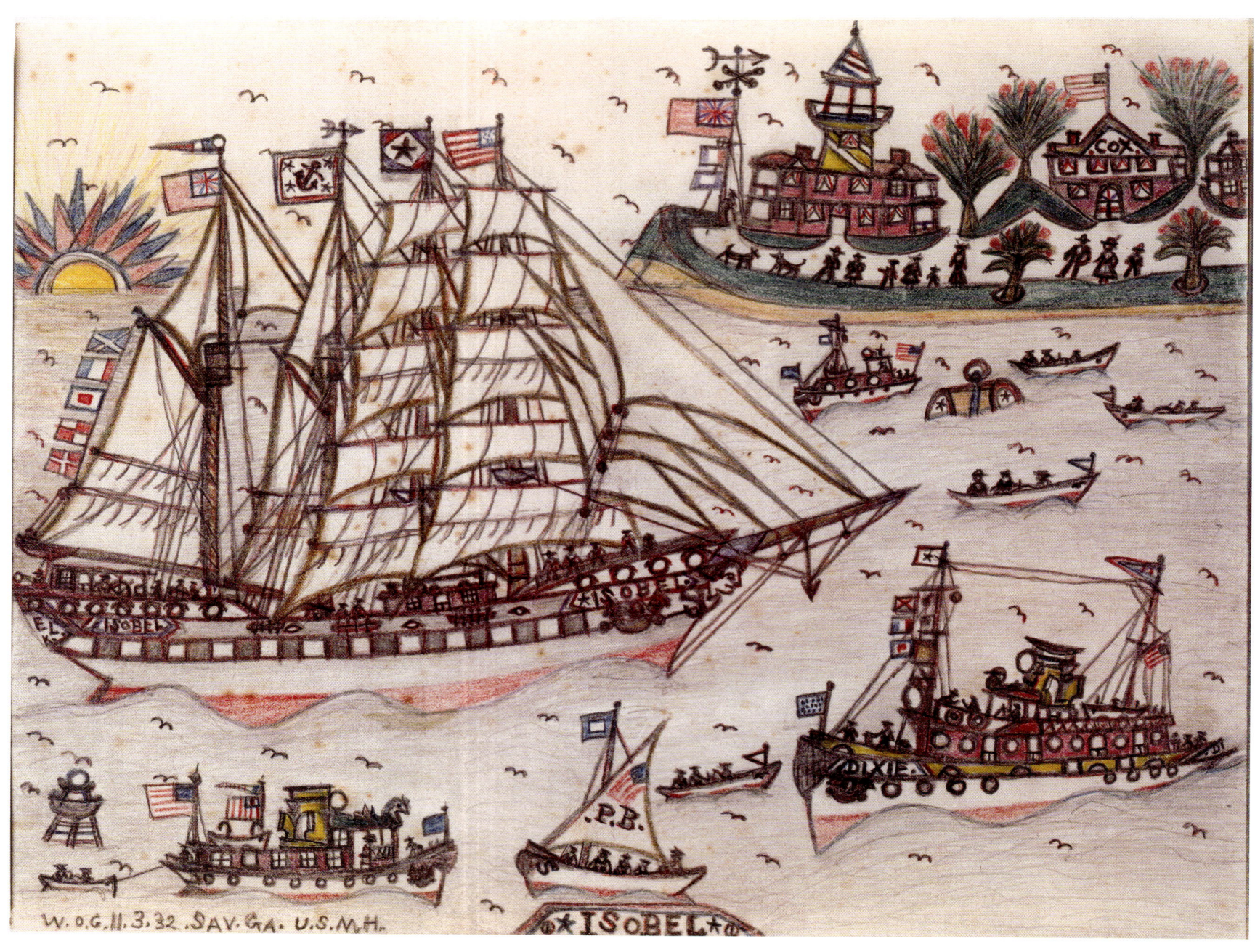

PLATE 15. *Isobel,* 1932

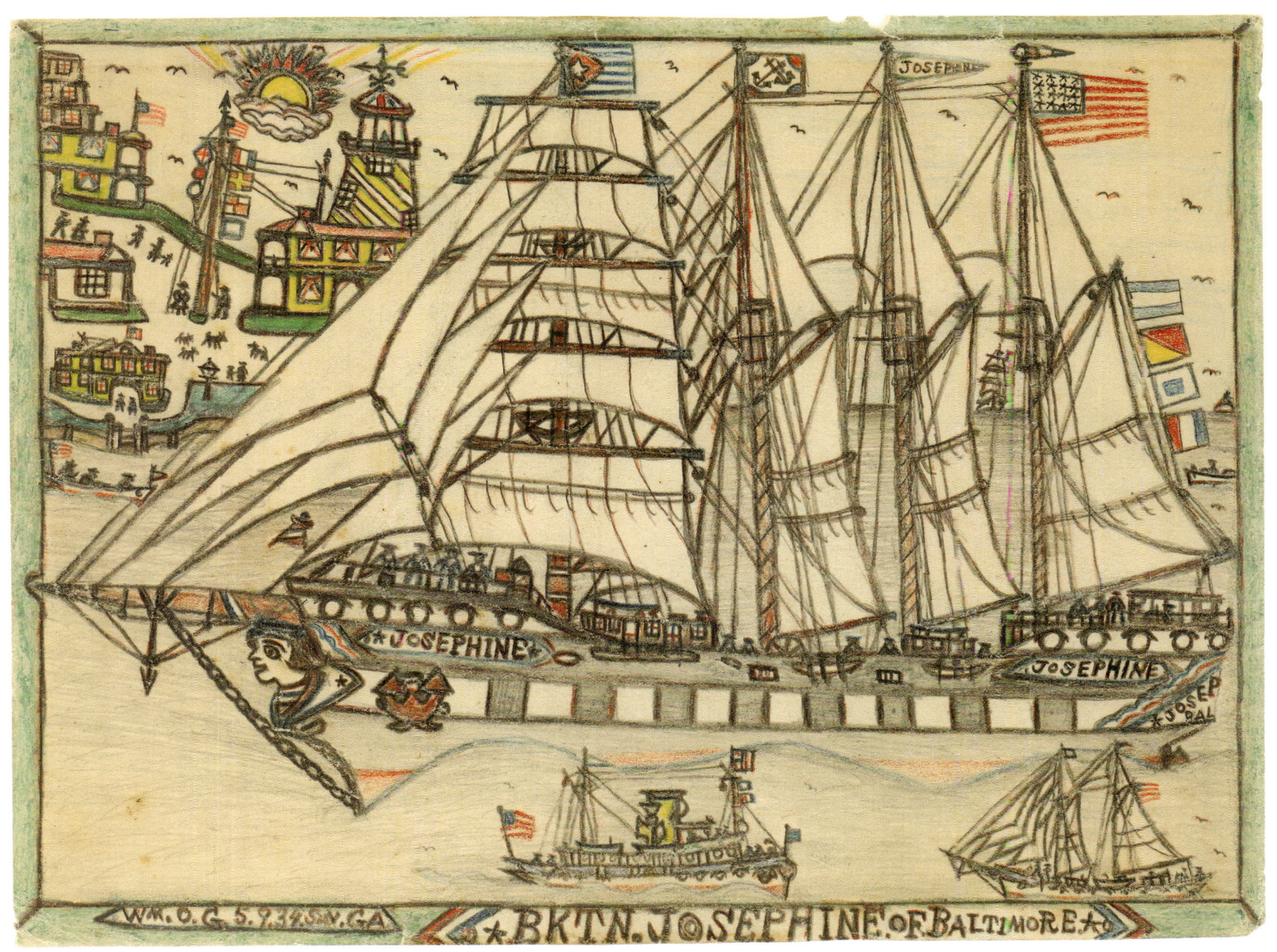

PLATE 16. *Bktn. Josephine of Baltimore*, 1934

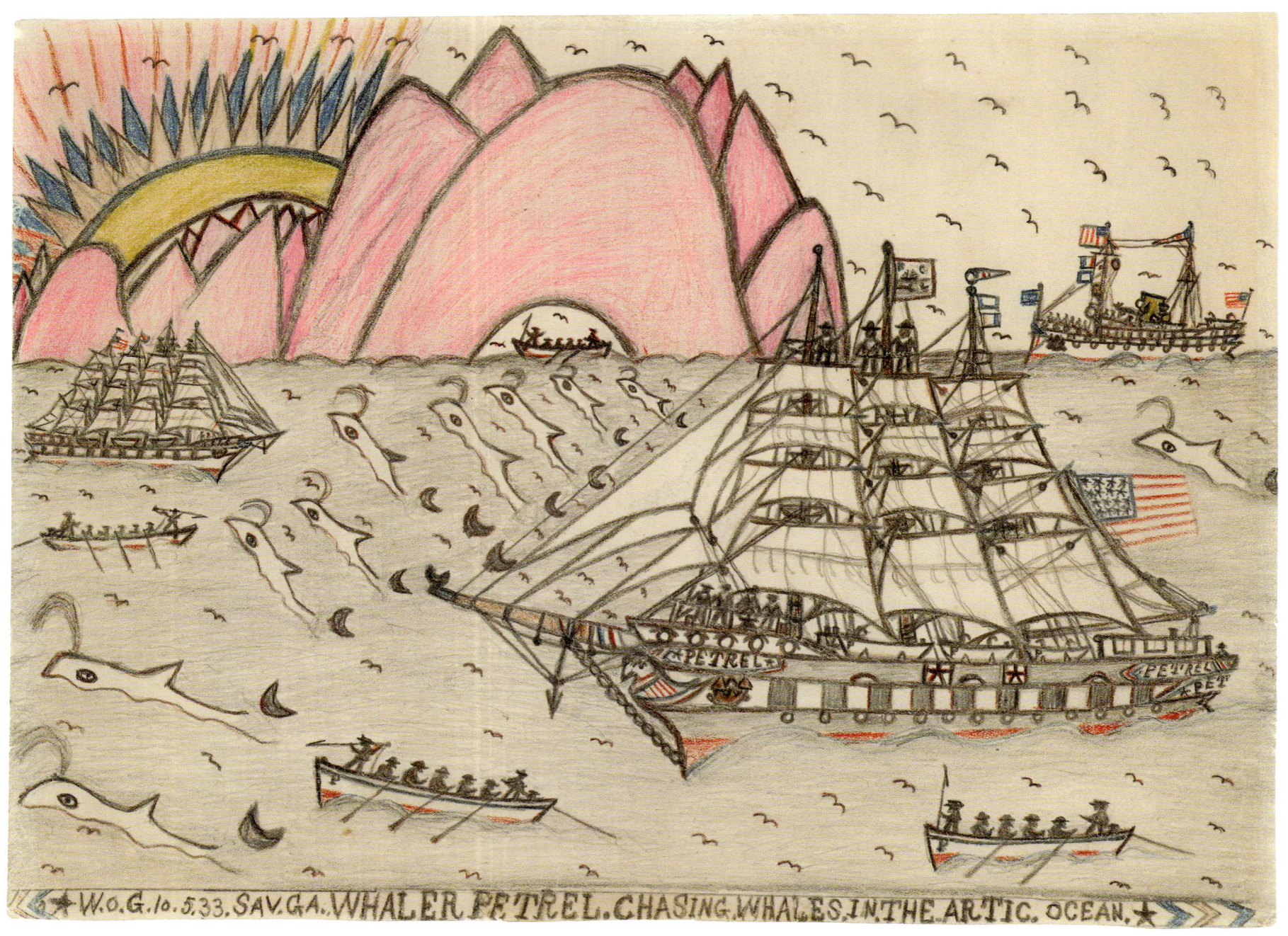

PLATE 17. *Whaler Petrel Chasing Whales in the Artic Ocean*, 1933

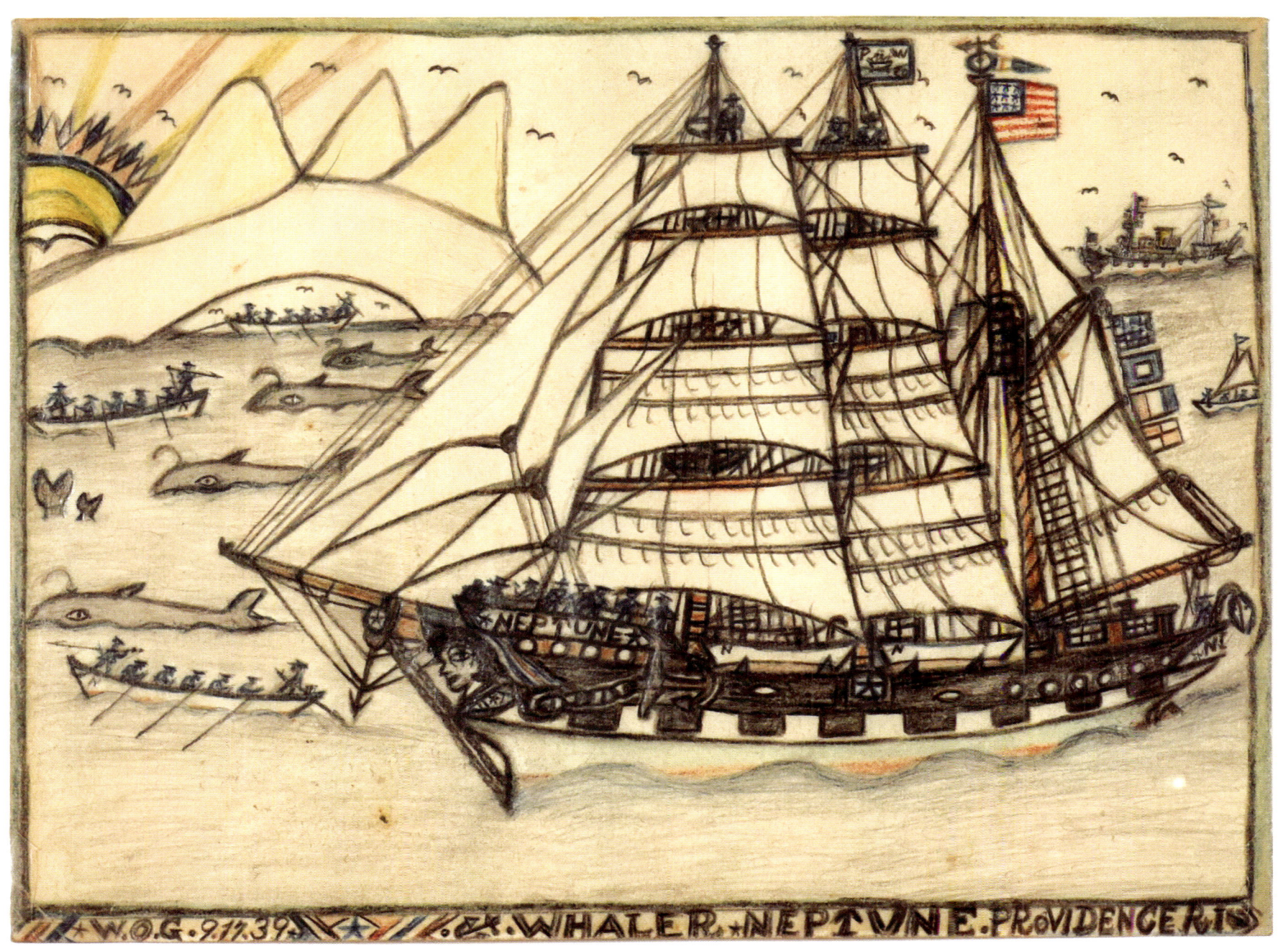

PLATE 18. *Whaler Neptune, Providence, R.I.,* 1939

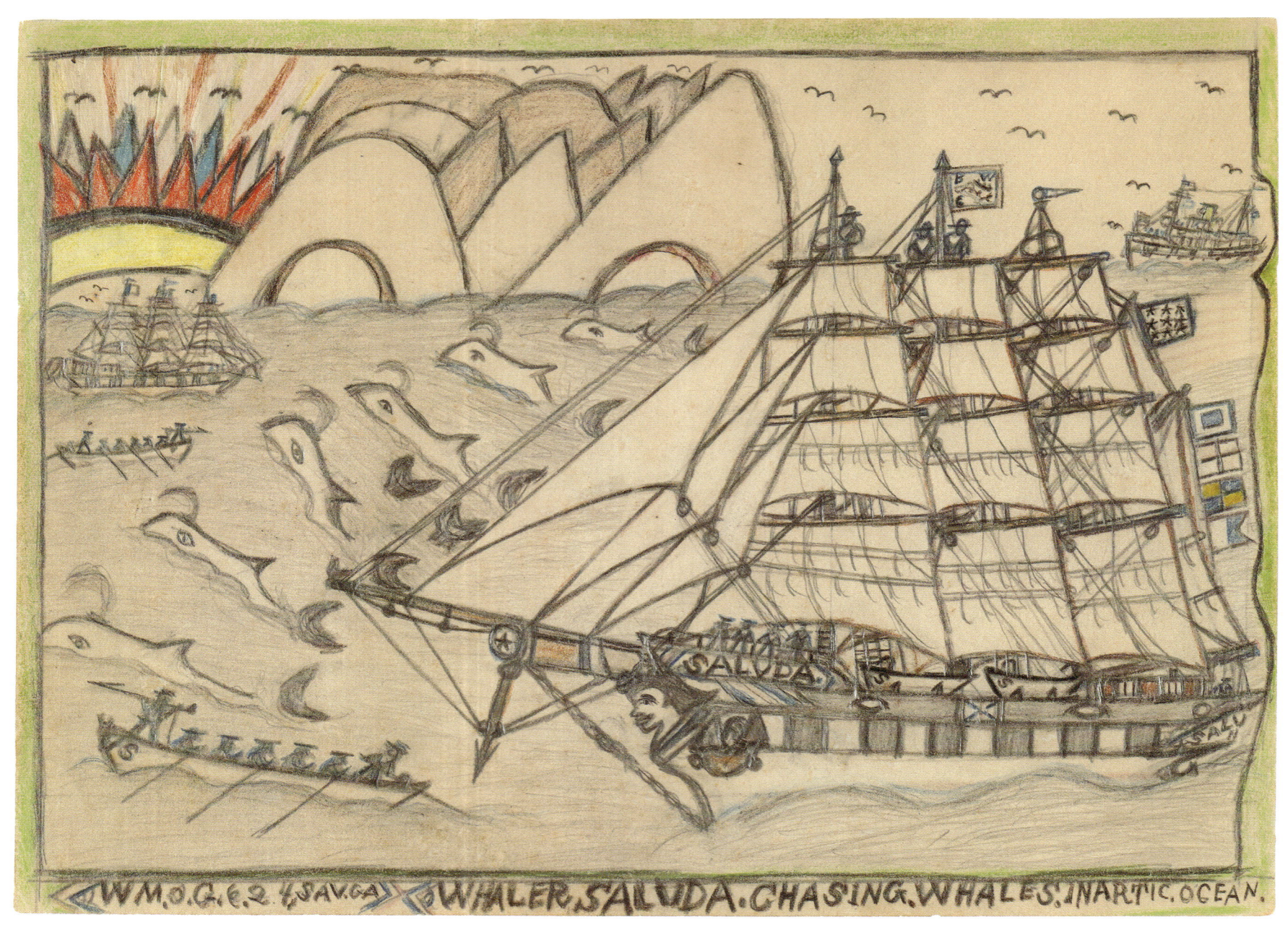

PLATE 19. *Whaler Saluda Chasing Whales in Artic Ocean*, n.d.

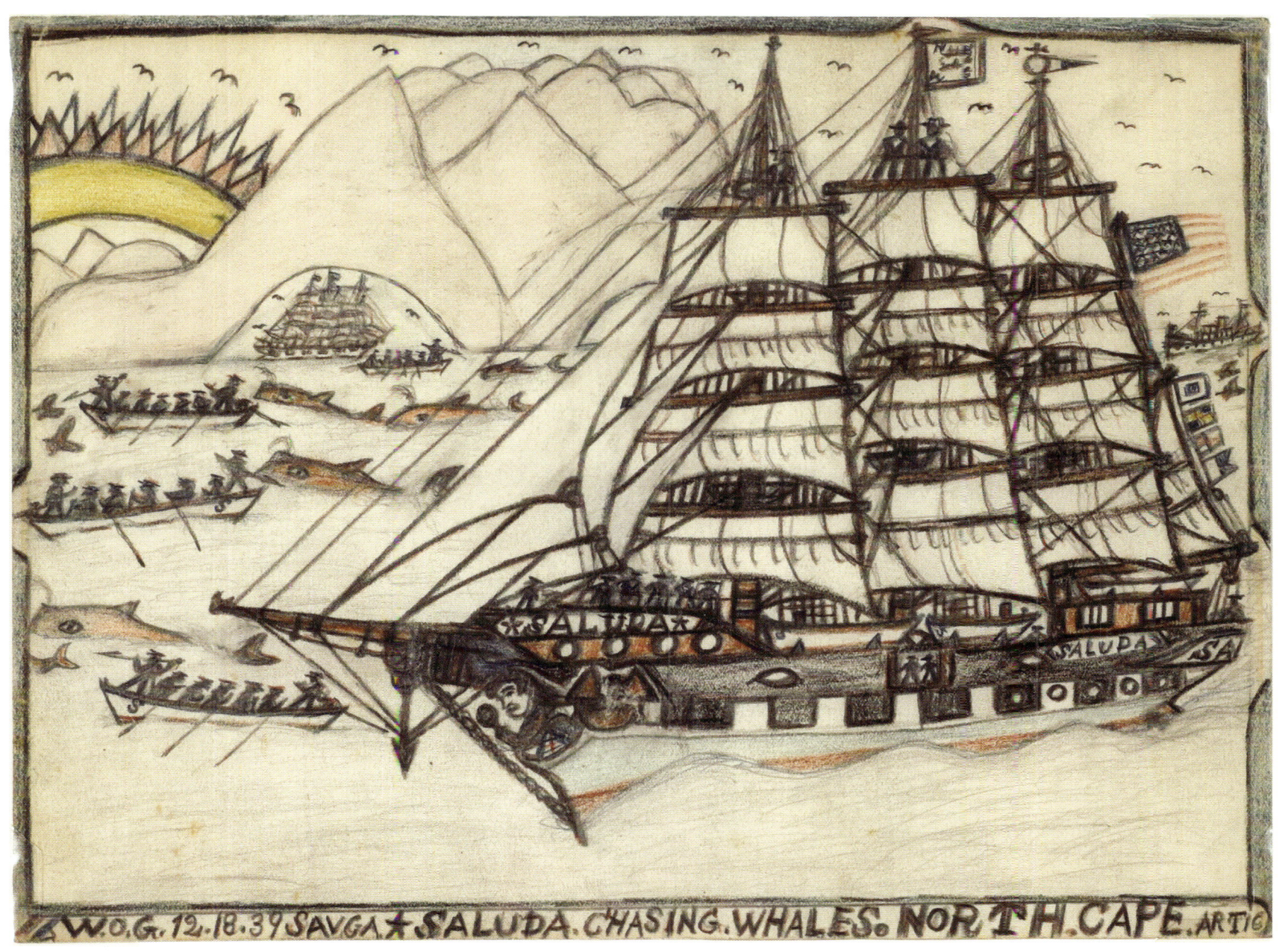

PLATE 20. *Saluda Chasing Whales, North Cape, Artic, 1939*

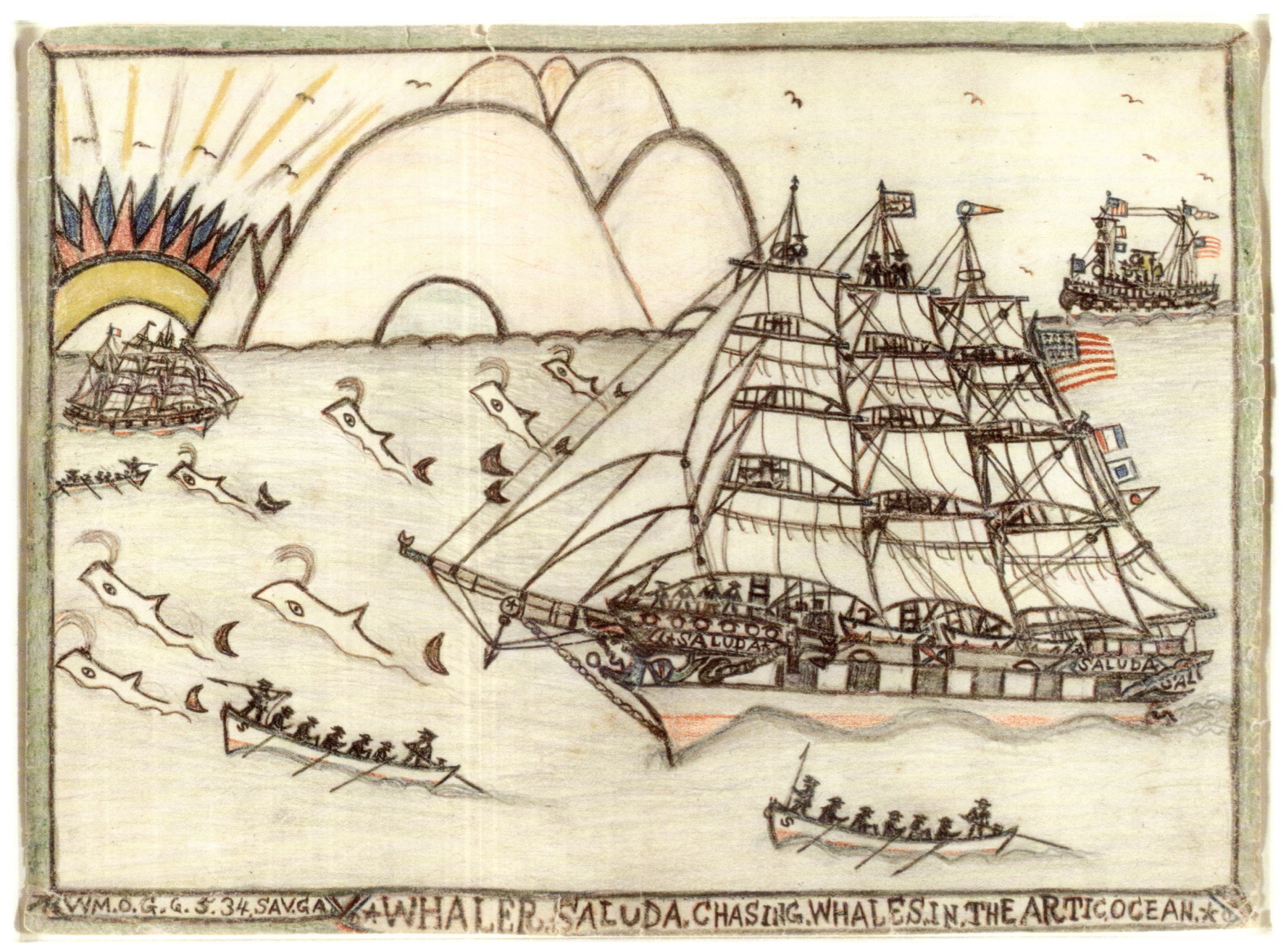

PLATE 21. *Whaler Saluda Chasing Whales in the Artic Ocean*, 1934

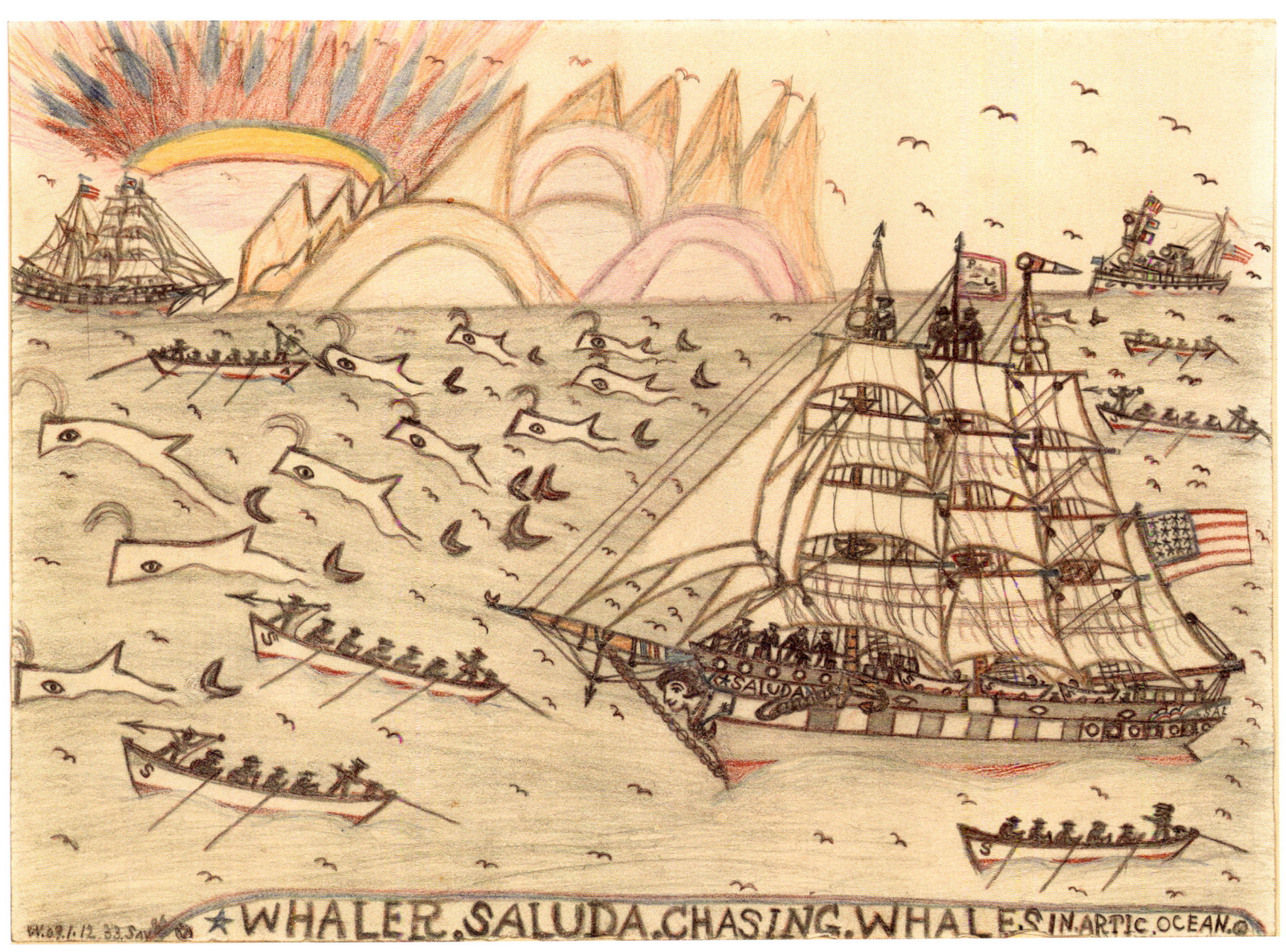

Whaler Saluda Chasing Whales in Artic Ocean, 1933
(not included in the exhibition)

STEAM YACHTS AND STEAM VESSELS

While sailing ships figure prominently in William O. Golden's art, his half century at sea was marked by the rise of the steam vessels that replaced them. Although Golden drew steam-powered warships, freighters, launches, tugs, and other watercraft, the large passenger steamships of the era are strangely absent in his work, save for cameos in images of other ships or ports. The most prevalent type of steam vessel in his oeuvre—and one with which he claimed a personal connection—was the steam yacht, appearing as the subject of some twenty drawings and shown as secondary craft in a dozen more. Originating in England in the 1820s, and increasing in number by the mid nineteenth century, steam yachts represented the pinnacle of luxury, attainable by only the wealthiest, and commissioned by the likes of Queen Victoria. In the United States, steam yachts appeared prior to the Civil War but enjoyed their heyday between the 1870s and World War I. [1] During these years, luxuriously appointed steam yachts became floating displays of ostentatious wealth for America's industrialists and business tycoons.

Golden could have easily observed steam yachts in various locations during his seagoing years, including large northeastern ports like New York, where owners would use the vessels to access their homes up the Hudson. The elegant craft could even be spotted on the Georgia coast, where members of the famed "millionaires club" an-

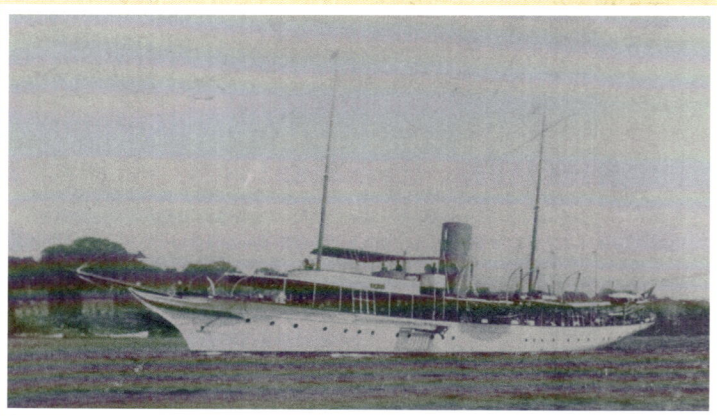

Fig. 1. Viking (American Steam Yacht, 1909), Halftone reproduction of a photograph of Viking in harbor, prior to World War I. This yacht was surveyed for possible Navy First World War service and assigned the Section Patrol registry number SP-618, but was not taken over. Original print in National Archives' Record Group 19-LCM. NH 102354. Courtesy the Naval History & Heritage Command.

chored near their Jekyll Island retreats. In one case, Golden depicted such a yacht passing Georgia's Sapelo Island lighthouse. Steam yachts were also pressed into military service during the Spanish-American War and World War I, periods when Golden was in the Navy and Merchant Marine and may have had the chance to observe them close at hand. [2]

If Golden served aboard a steam yacht, most of his subjects point to the period following the completion of his naval service in 1902. Margaret Screven Tuck stated that Golden claimed to have shipped on the *Warrior*, *Nourmahal*, and *Viking*, all steam yachts, with the caveat that he tended to exaggerate and may only have seen them. [3] All three were owned by some of America's wealthiest families. *The Warrior*, commissioned by F. W. Vanderbilt and launched in 1904, was later purchased by the British Royal Navy, becoming the HMS *Warrior* during World War I. Golden is not known to have depicted the *Warrior*, but he drew the other vessels named in Tuck's description. These include at least three drawings of the *Nourmahal*, in which Golden identifies the owner as John Jacob Astor, of *Titanic* fame. The Astors owned more than one yacht named *Nourmahal*, and John Jacob Astor was at one time owner of the first *Nourmahal*, which featured an elegantly tapered bow and bowsprit. Golden's drawings, however, more closely resemble a later *Nourmahal*, built in 1928 for William Vincent Astor. By the late 1920s Golden was already seeking treatment in Savannah, making it unlikely, though not impossible, that he served aboard that vessel. The steam yacht *Viking* seems a stronger possibility (Fig. 1). Like the *Nourmahal*, there was more than one iteration of the *Viking* yacht within the same family. Although a steam yacht named *Viking* built in 1883 was in use during the Spanish-American War, the *Viking* depicted by Golden (Pl.23) is likely one built in 1909. This particular drawing may have been a commission. Evidence survives of the purchase of this work by the *Viking*'s owner, George F. Baker, Jr., of New York, scion of New York banking and railroad magnate George F. Baker. The younger Baker was serious about seagoing. While many steam-yacht owners were content to use their opulent vessels for comfortable commutes, Baker commissioned a second *Viking* in 1929 to allow for deep-sea fishing and pleasure excursions throughout the world. Margaret Stiles apparently enlisted her niece, then Margaret Screven Tuck, and her husband A. J. M. Tuck, to coordinate a sale of a group of Golden's works to Baker. Margaret Tuck's biographical statement on Golden remained attached to the back of the commissioned drawing, which was also accompanied by a letter from A. J. M. Tuck to Baker. Tuck mentions that Golden "does not know who his benefactor is," perhaps signaling the artist's familiarity with Baker [4] Golden further notes Baker as owner of the *Viking* in the title of the work.

In other steam-yacht drawings, Golden namechecks prominent individuals as owners, including J. P. Morgan, William Vanderbilt, and others, some possibly misidentified. In addition to those already named, many steam yachts Golden drew—*Mermaid, Petrel, Seneca*—were real vessels. As with his sailing ships, certain features are repeated in his steam yachts, indicating that these representations are perhaps based more upon memory of the type than documentation of specific vessels.

Some steam yachts Golden drew are difficult to locate in records, offering the possibility that some emerged from his imagination. In an unusual example, Golden created a steam yacht as a form of self-portrait, choosing this vessel type to embody his own experience (Fig. 2). In the 1936 drawing, Golden does not depict a real-world vessel; rather, he renders a steam yacht that he names the *Wm O. Golden* (Pl. 22). Perhaps Golden was projecting a personal fantasy that one day a ship would bear his name. Close reading suggests that

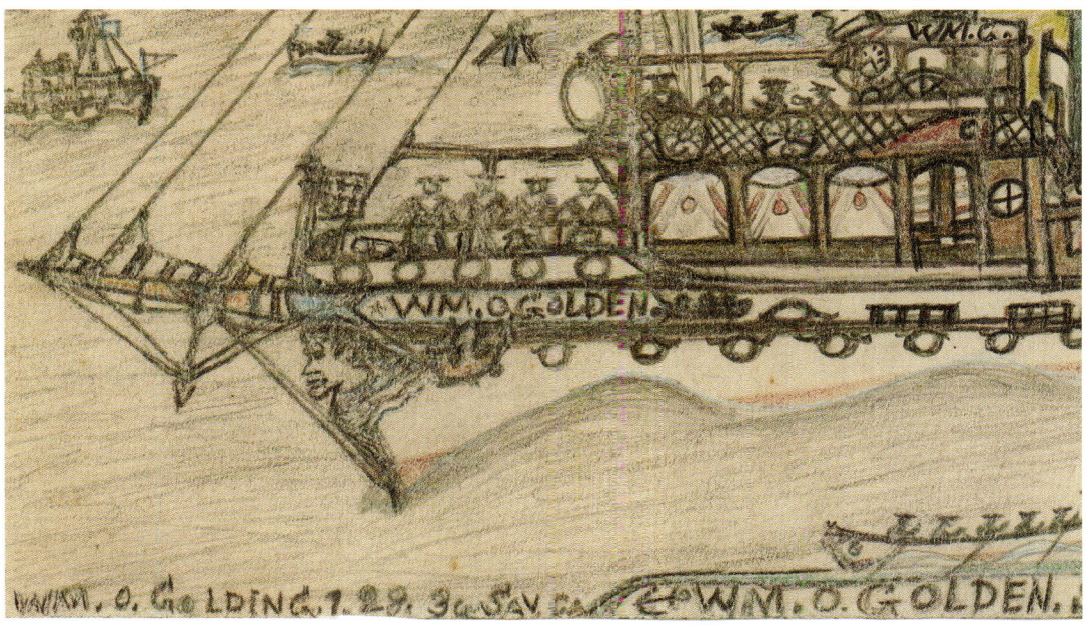

Fig. 2. *William O. Golding, Wm. O. Golden, 1936, Telfair Museums* (detail, Pl. 22).

the vessel may even represent the artist himself. Most compellingly, the yacht's figurehead depicts a man wearing what seems to be a sailor's uniform. The figure's hair appears curly and his skin tone is shaded. Given that other vessels drawn by Golden include figureheads that reflect the name of the ship—embodied by a man, woman, or even a bird—it seems highly likely that Golden is presenting the viewer with his self-portrait. Various versions of Golden's name and initials are peppered throughout the vessel, from the stern plate to the nautical signal flags that spell out an abbreviation of his name. Many small watercraft appearing in the periphery of the image also bear Golden's initials. In the background, he includes familiar elements from other works that reflect his personal experiences, including a lighthouse, an armed fortification, and a pagoda. Golden's mixtures of past and present, of fact, memory, and fantasy, all seemingly converge in this one astonishing image, which functions as a statement of identity and metaphor for his life as a seaman. —*H.D.*

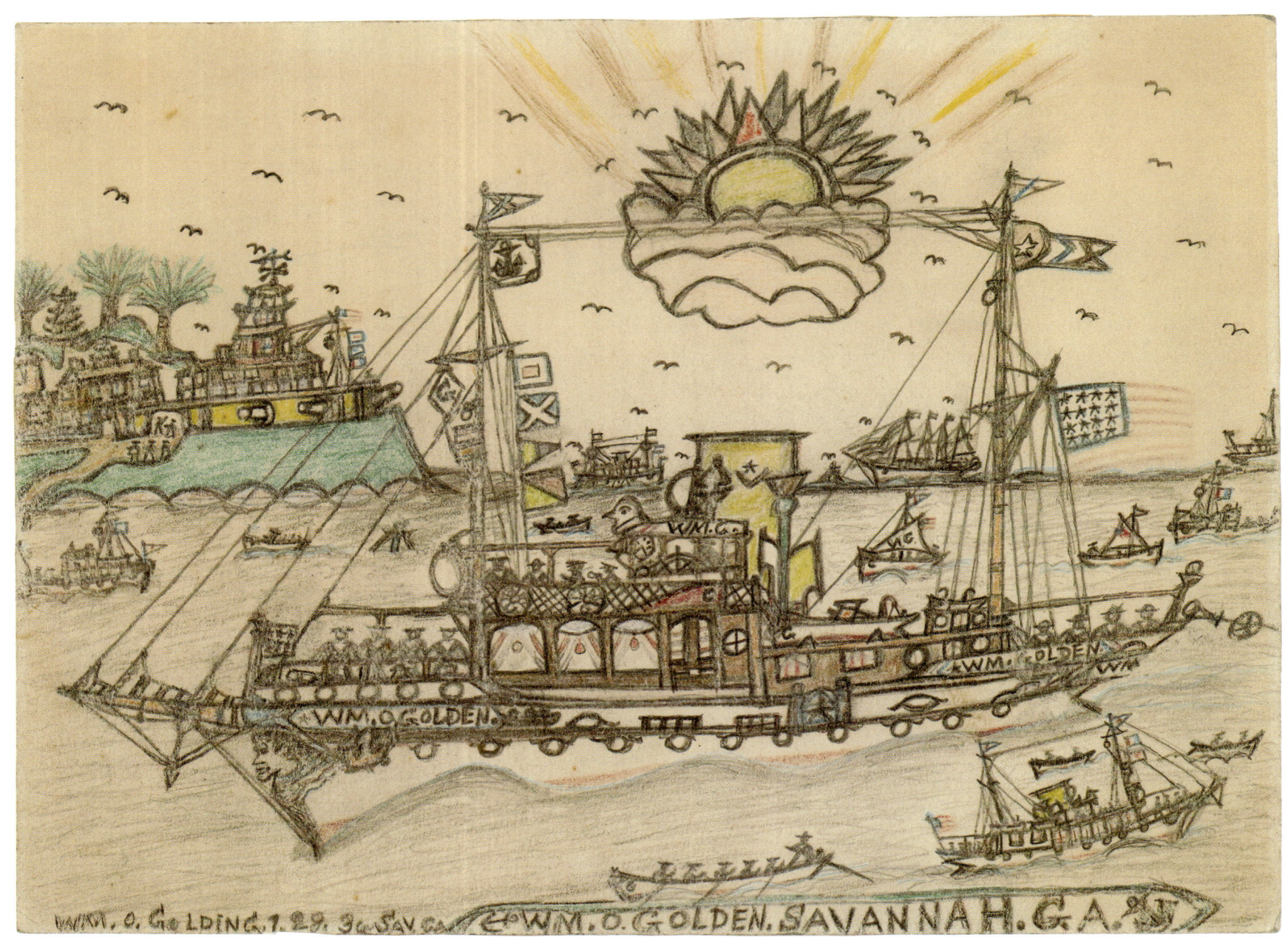

PLATE 22. *Wm. O. Golden, 1936*

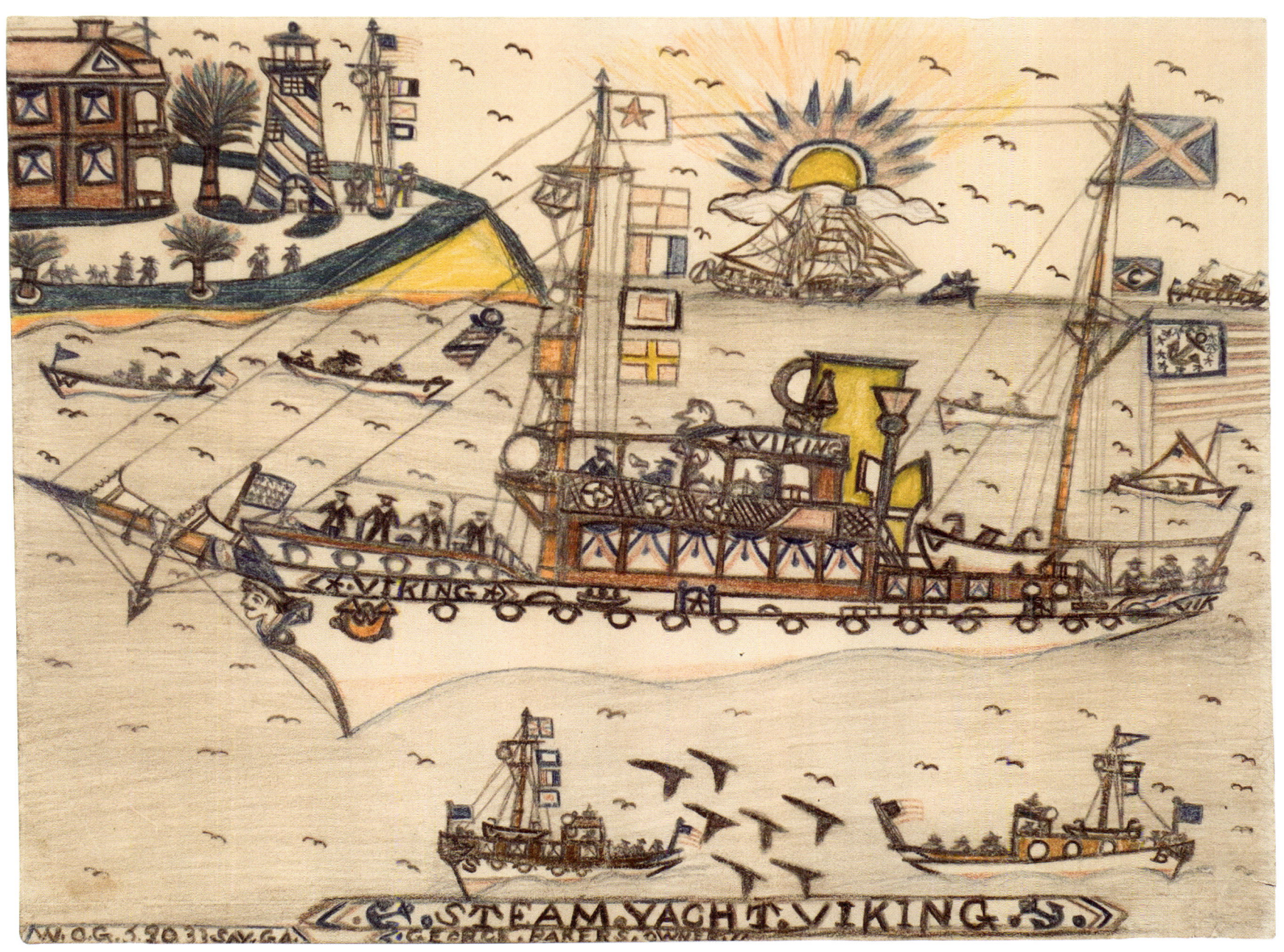

PLATE 23. *Steam Yacht Viking*, George Bakers, Owner, 1933

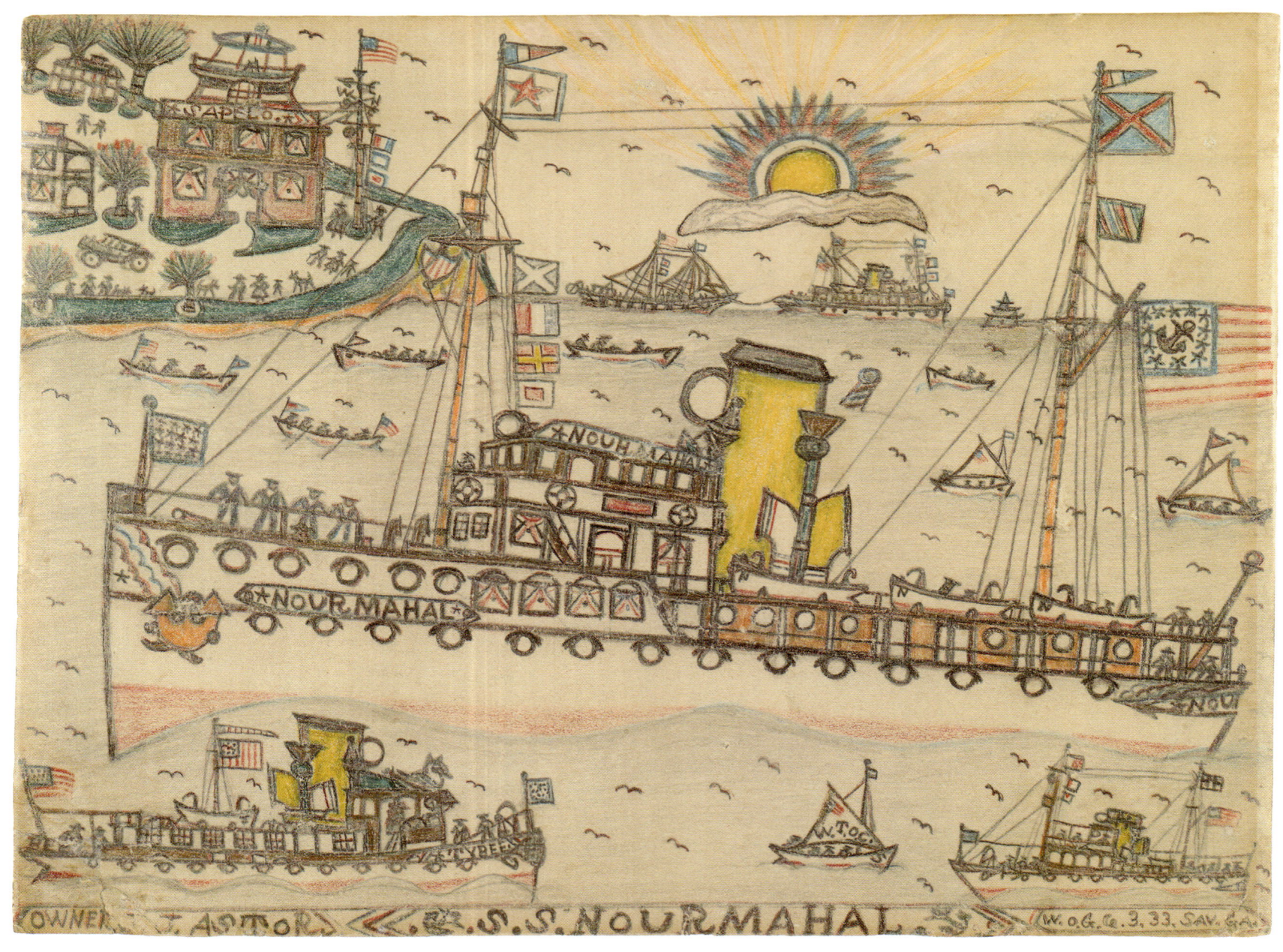

PLATE 24. *S.S. Nourmahal*, Owner J. J. Astor, 1933

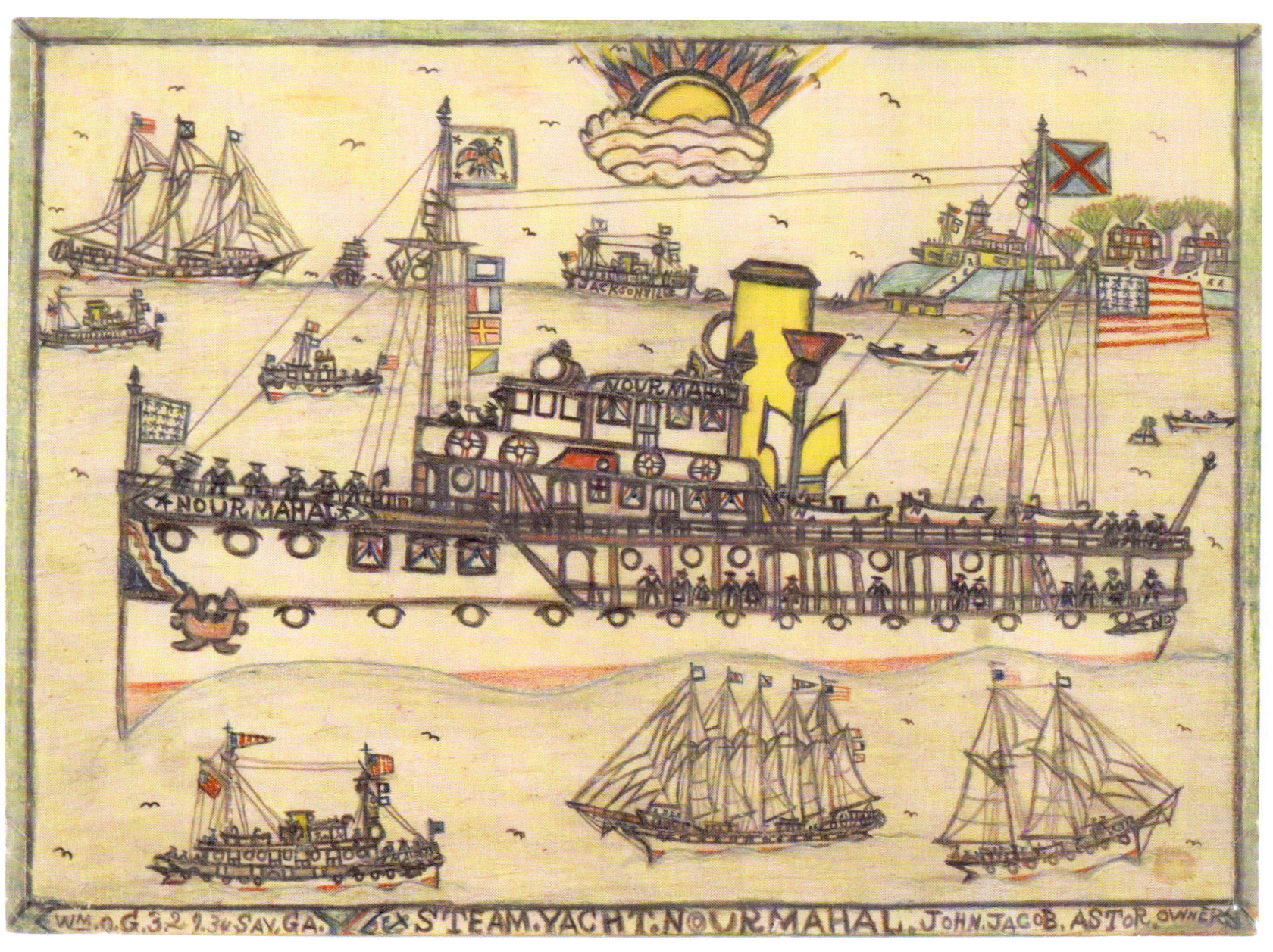

PLATE 25. *Steam Yacht Nourmahal, John Jacob Astor, Owners, 1934*

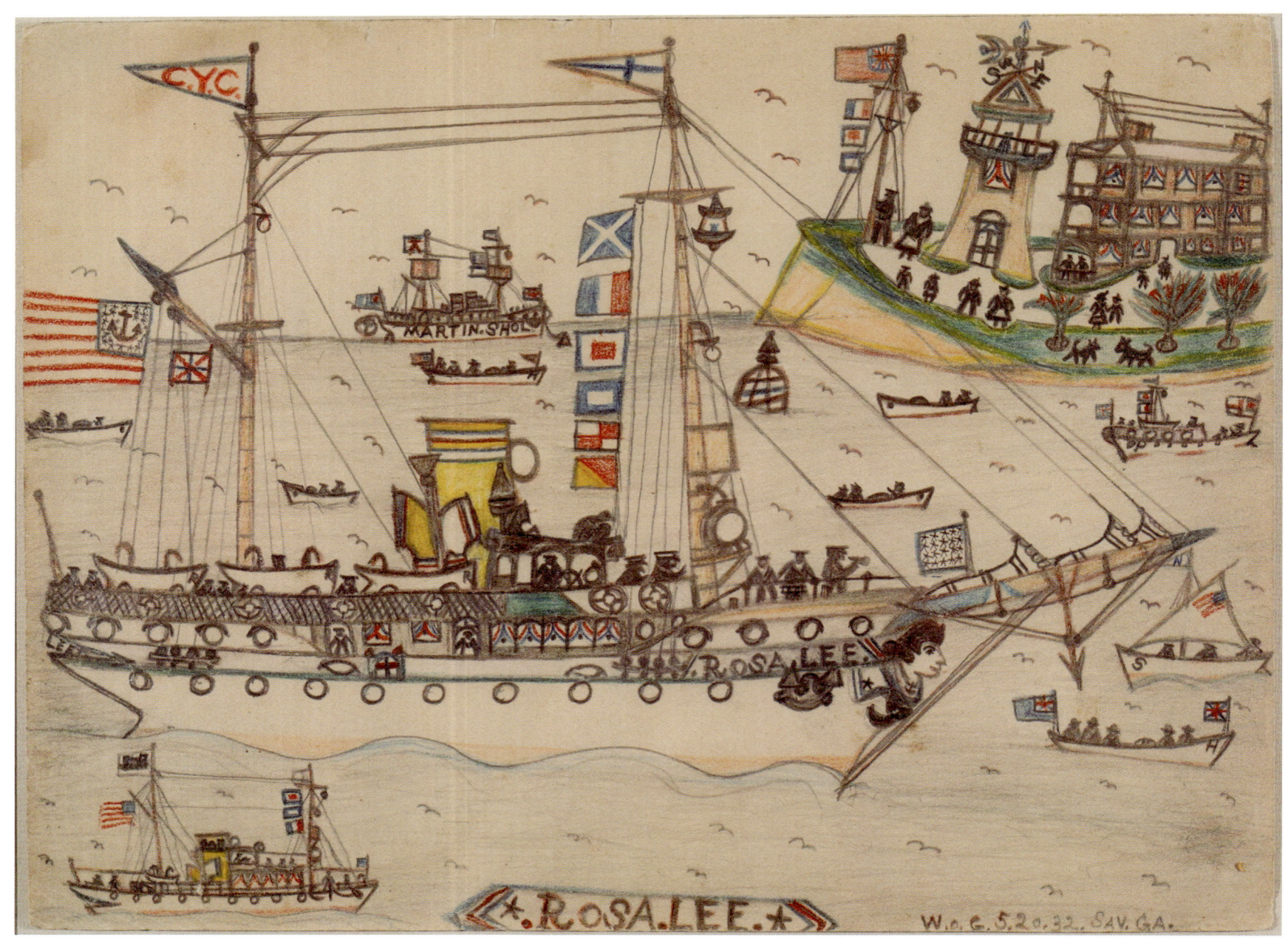

PLATE 26. *Rosa Lee*, 1932

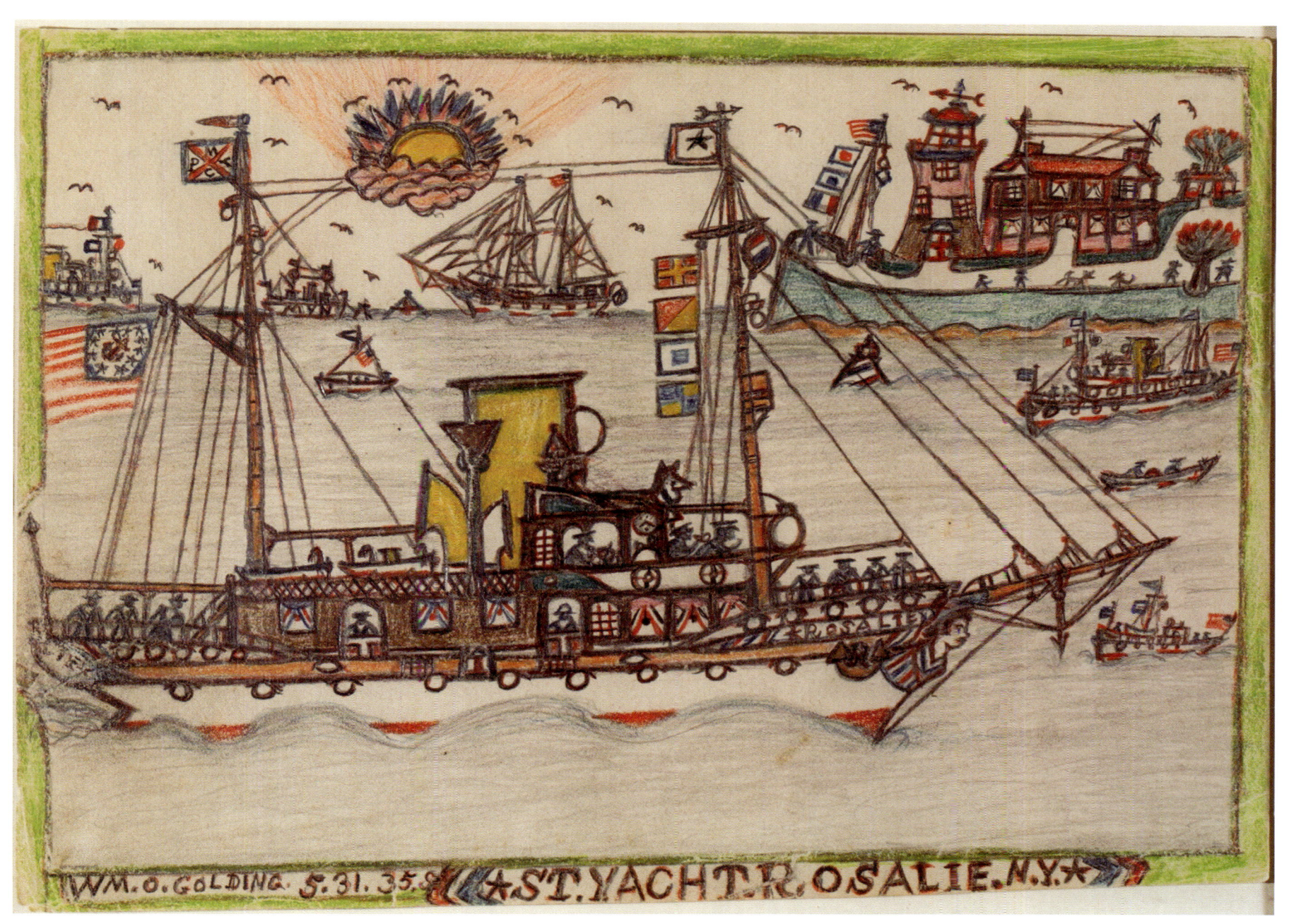

PLATE 27. *St. Yacht Rosalie, N.Y.*, 1935

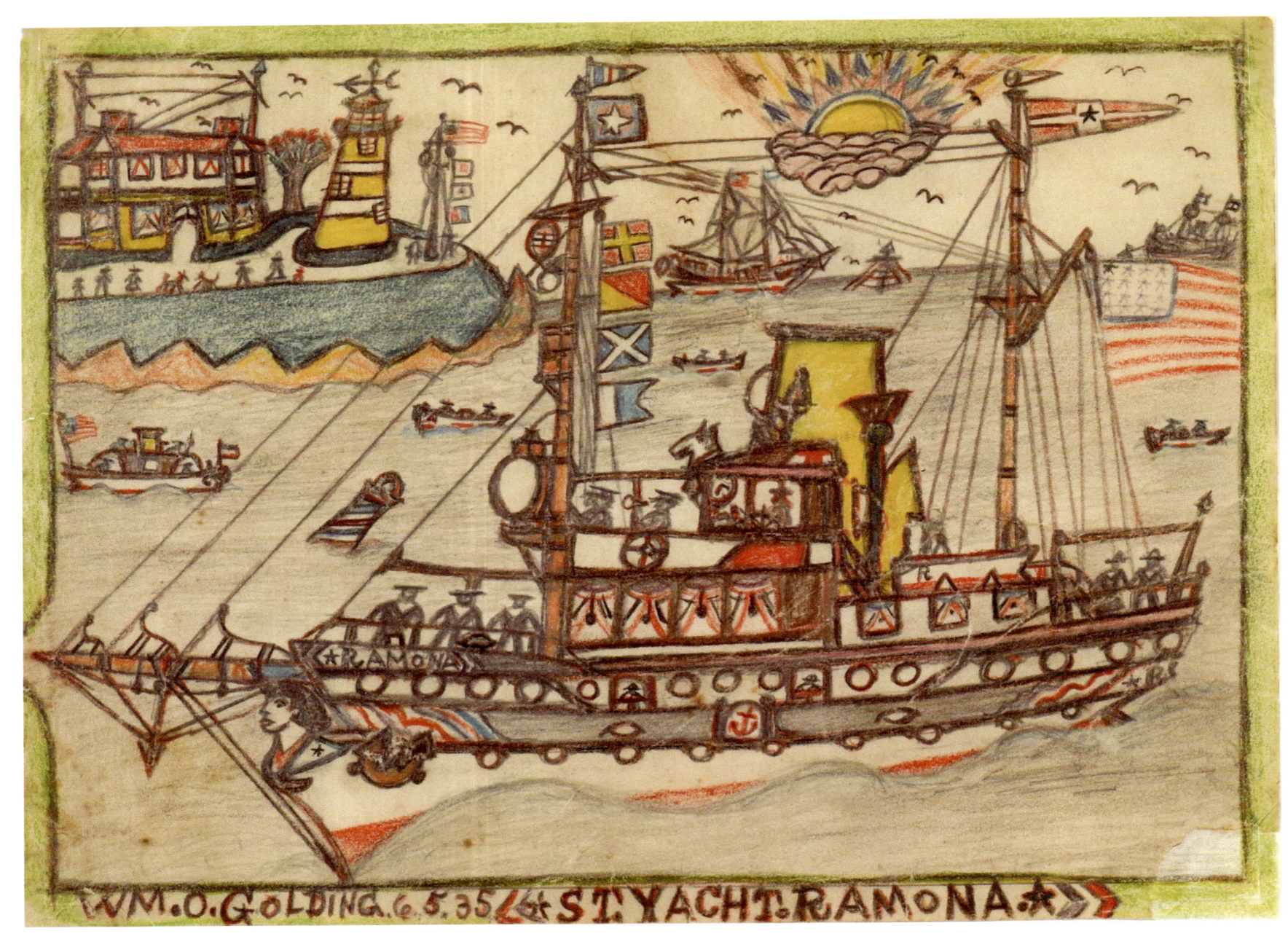

PLATE 28. *St. Yacht Ramona*, 1935

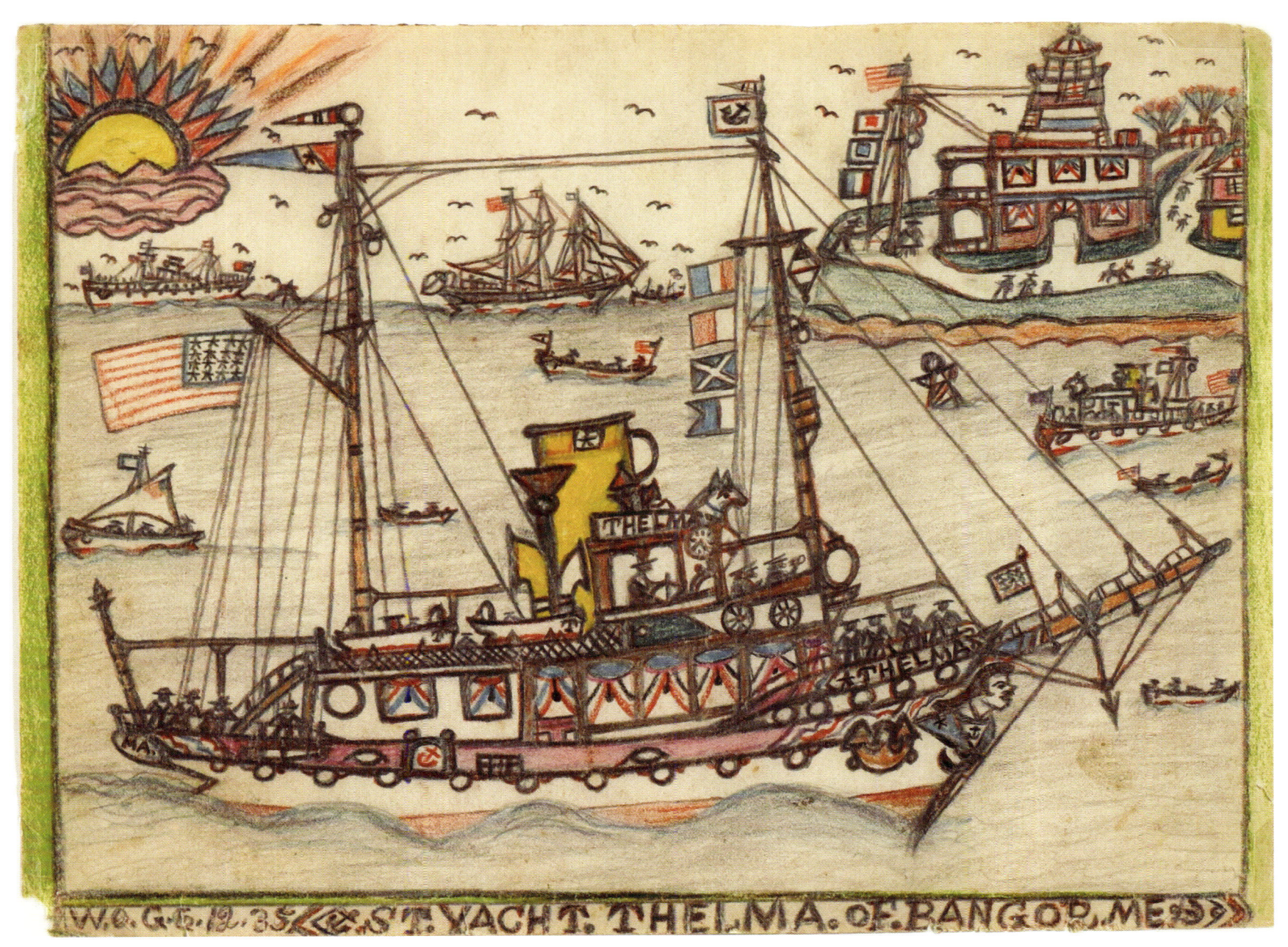

PLATE 29. *St. Yacht Thelma of Bangor, ME*, 1935

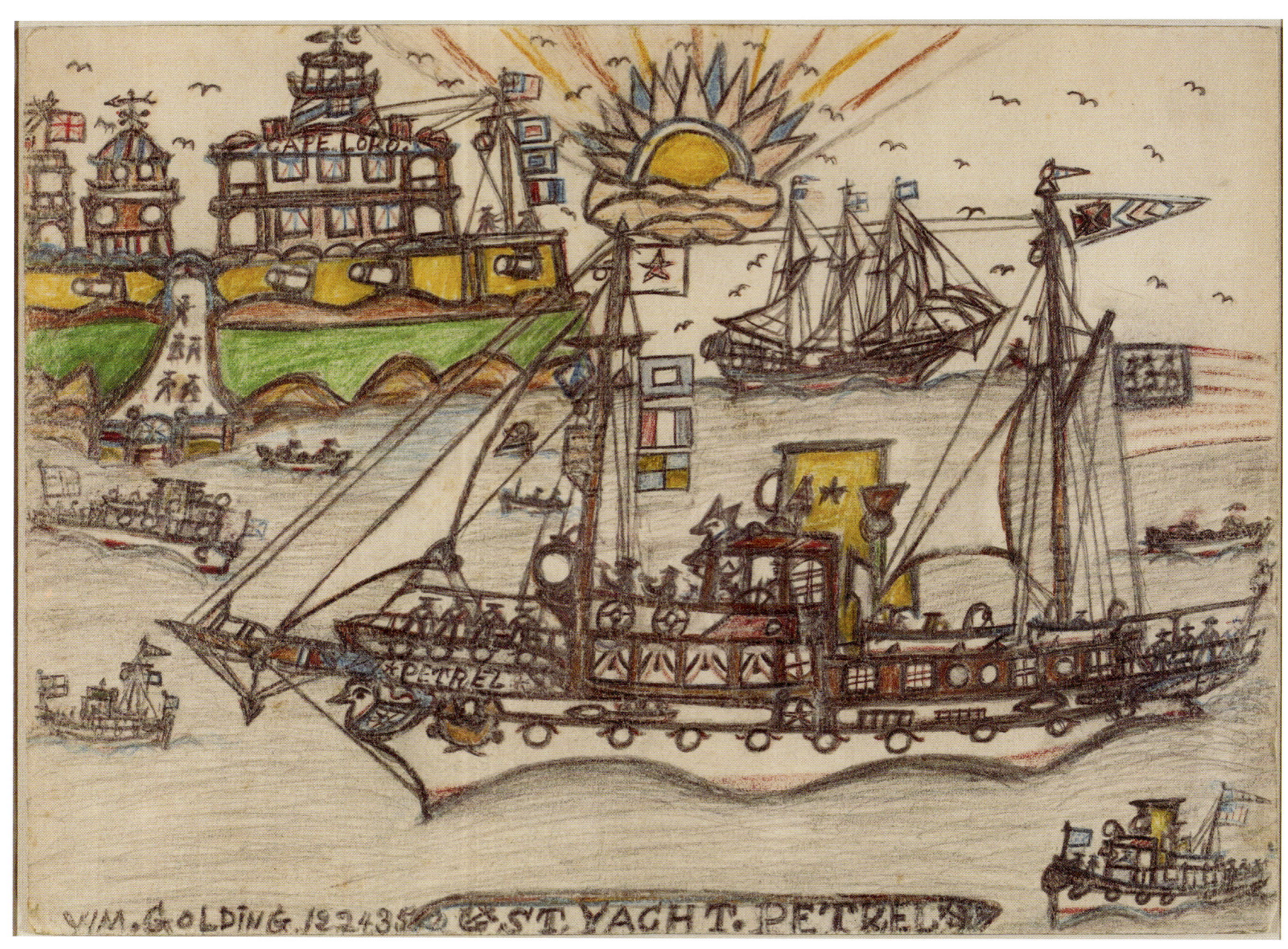

PLATE 30. *St. Yacht Petrel, 1935*

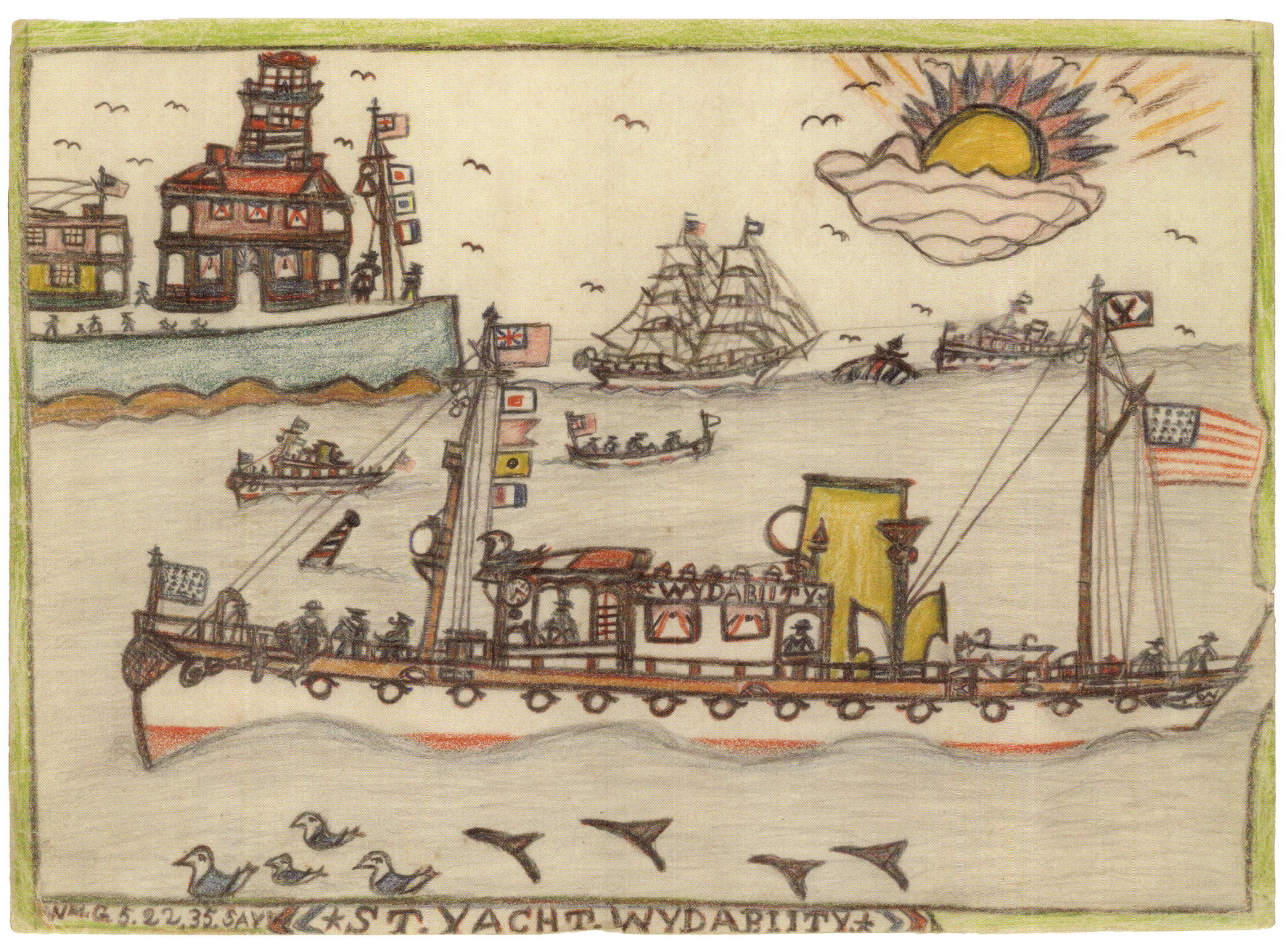

PLATE 31. *St. Yacht Wydabiity, 1935*

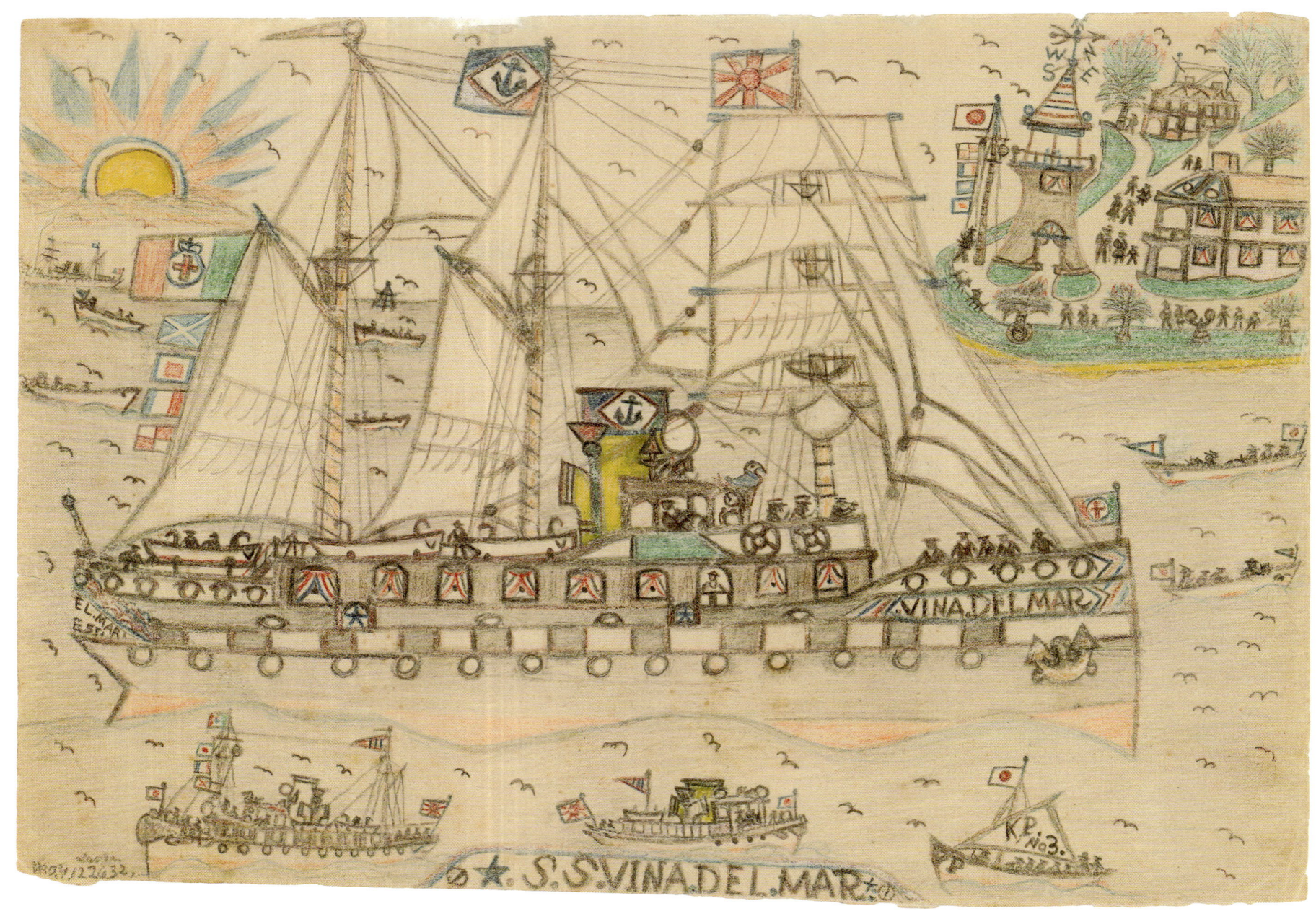

PLATE 32. S.S. *Vina Del Mar*, 1932

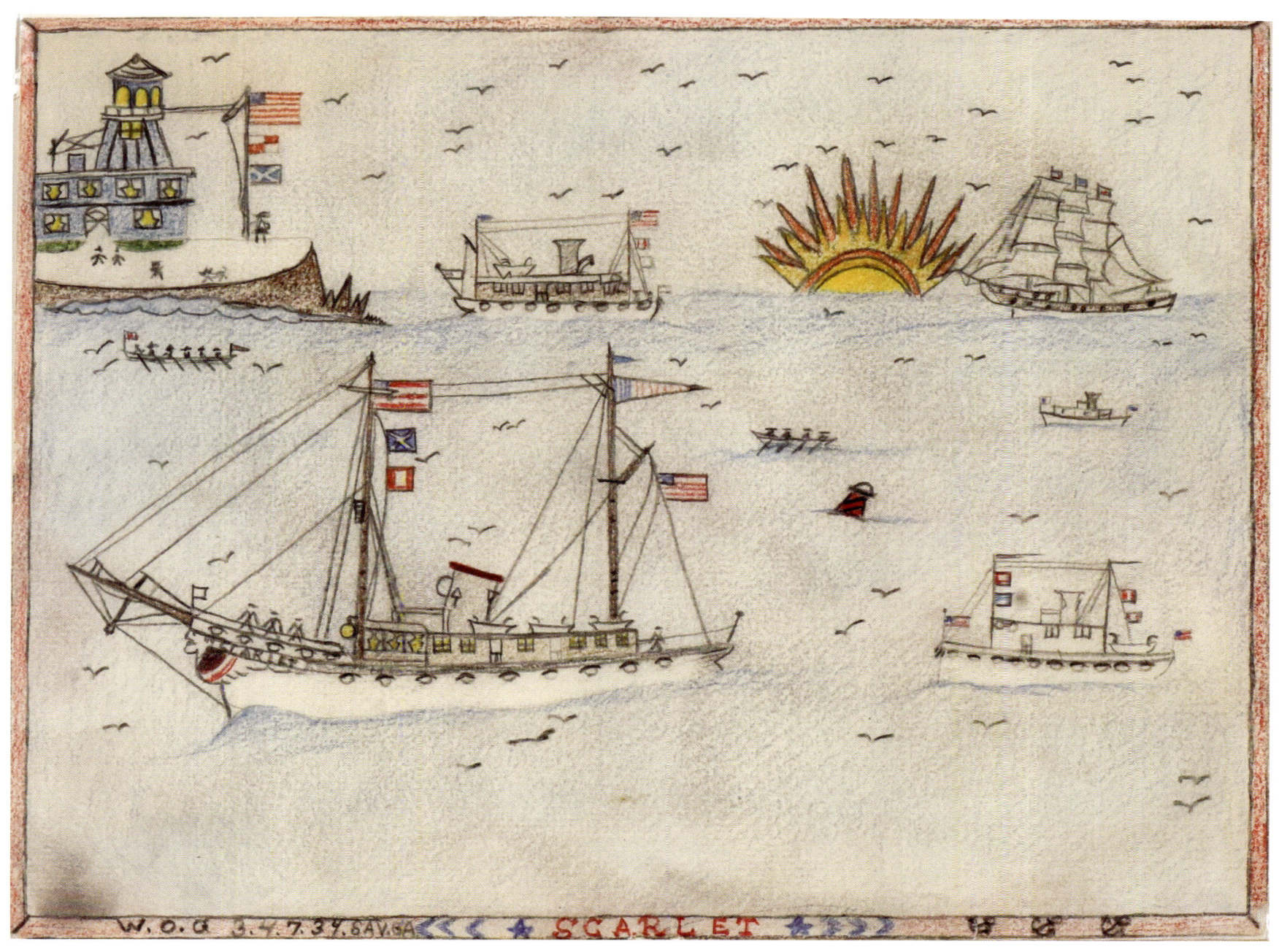

PLATE 33. *Scarlet*, 1934

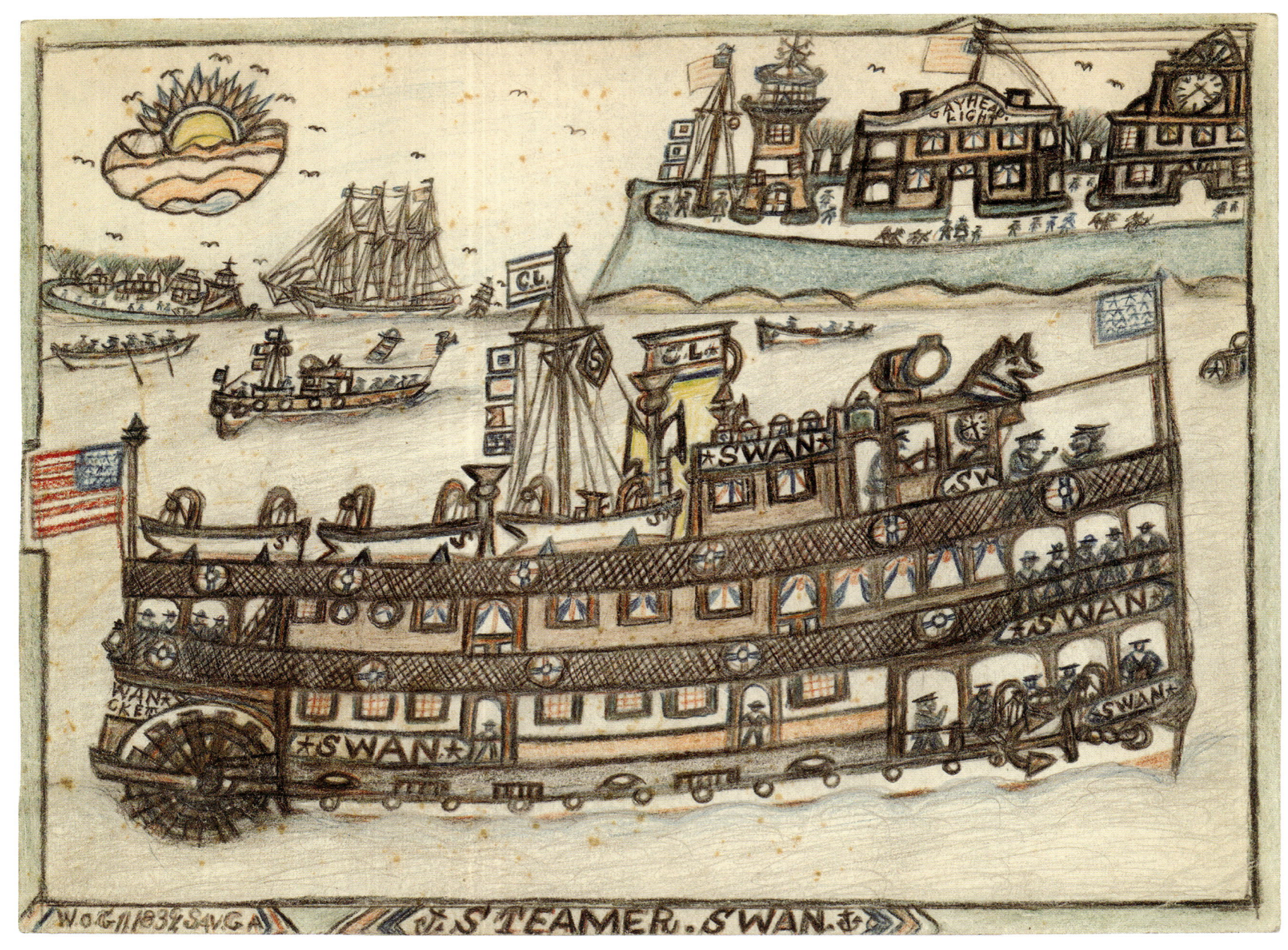

PLATE 34. *Steamer Swan*, 1939

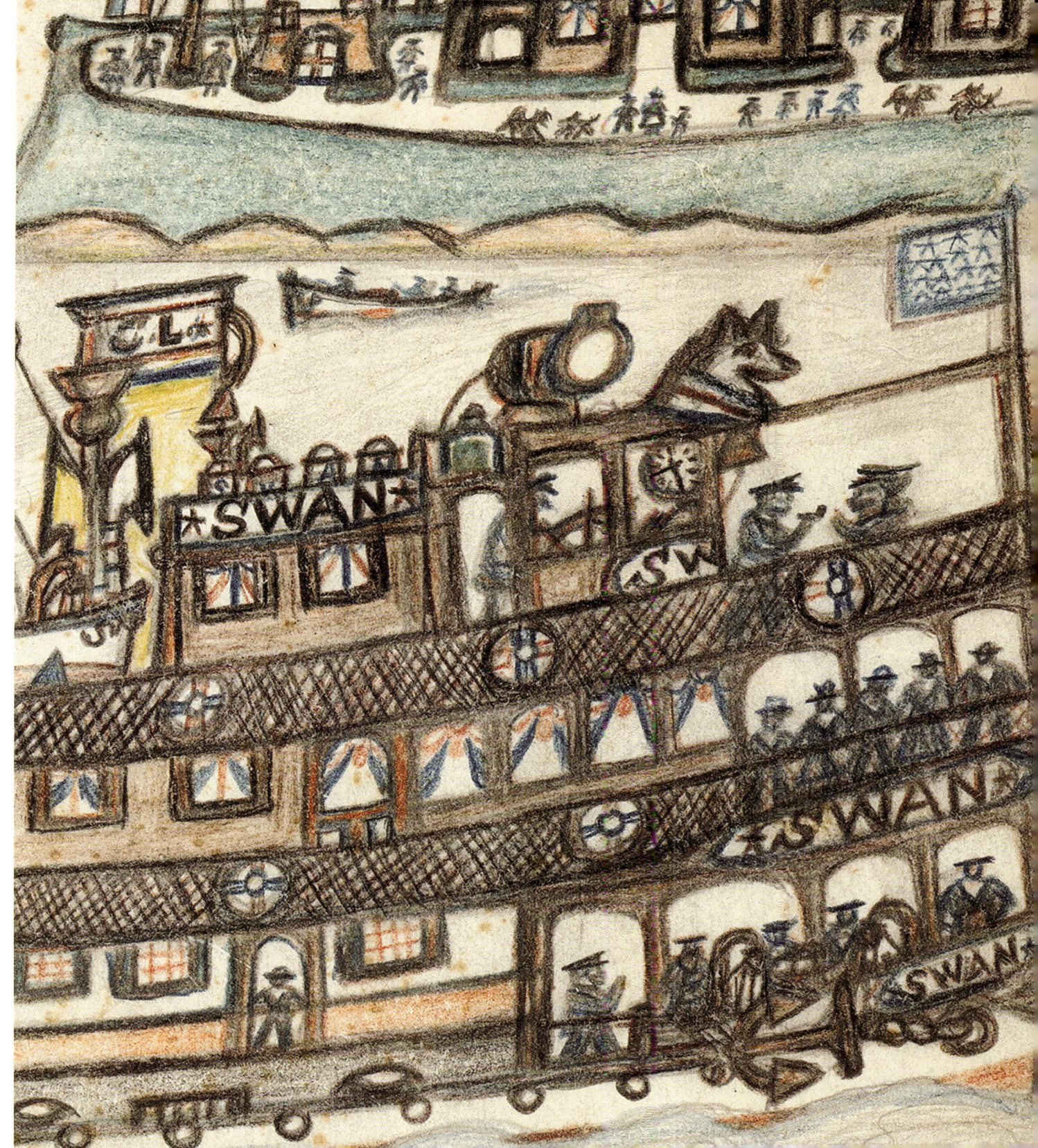

Detail. *Steamer Swan*

THE ATLANTIC: CANADA TO CAPE HORN

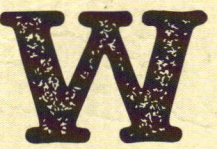illiam O. Golden wrote that he had traveled "all over the world from North, South, East, and West and plenty of ports in the Seven (7) Seas from England to China, Japan, India, Australia, Africa, West Indies, Central America, South America." [1] Encouraged by Margaret Stiles, he created fanciful views of landmarks and ports throughout the world. Beginning in the North Atlantic, it is possible to follow his images of locations from coastal Canada and the Eastern Seaboard of the United States, south to the Caribbean, and around Cape Horn to the Pacific.

Whether or not Golden left Savannah on a ship from Nova Scotia, his drawings indicate familiarity with ports, vessels, and landmarks in Atlantic Canada. His drawings of the *Wandering Jew*, the ship he said had abducted him, show the vessel flying a British Canadian flag and identify the vessel's home port as Liverpool, Nova Scotia. A vessel of that name, however, does not appear in Canadian shipping databases. Other references to Nova Scotia and Newfoundland do appear in his work. A 1939 drawing features the yacht *Muriel* (Pl. 3), which he also identifies as hailing from Liverpool. A 1935 drawing entitled *Table Island, N.S.* (Pl. 35) depicts a small island sporting a literally tabletop-shaped mountain. The work may refer to Table Head, Glace Bay, part of Cape Breton Island, Nova Scotia, famous as the site of the first transatlantic wireless telegraph message transmission in 1902. [2] Golden drew Cape Breton in two additional drawings misidentified as Newfoundland, understandable if he was drawing decades later from memory. In his 1935 Cape Breton drawing (Pl. 37), a five-masted British Canadian schooner named *Sarah* sails through the foreground. A land mass is dominated by a lighthouse and a building marked with the initials *V.R.*, perhaps representing the royal cypher *Victoria Regina*, for Queen Victoria. A later drawing of Cape Breton is quite different, with a lighthouse relegated to an upper corner and

greater attention devoted to two sailing vessels: an American barkentine named *Maud* and a French bark he identifies as *Gipsy*.

Golden depicted Newfoundland in the drawings *Belle Island, Newfoundland* from 1934 and *Belle Isle* from 1936. *Belle Island* could refer to one of two possible locations, neither a close match to Golden's image, which may include relocated or imagined buildings. Bell Island, Newfoundland and Labrador, was the site of mining operations in the 1890s. [3] Belle Isle, north of Newfoundland, is largely uninhabited today but was home to a light station in Golden's time. One drawing (Pl. 36) includes numerous buildings, among them a light station, a "Bel Hotel" and "American Bar" with a date of 1881, a church, drugstore, café, and a civic building with a clock tower. Another Belle Isle image is even more elaborate, depicting a lively port and town, a lighthouse, fortifications, and a hilltop building Golden identifies as a "laboratory." Whether Golden sailed on Canadian vessels or merely visited Nova Scotia and Newfoundland, he clearly embellished his memories of these locales.

From Atlantic Canada one may follow Golden through his drawings down the US East Coast. Golden shipped on merchant vessels out of New York in the 1910s and 20s but apparently never drew New York's harbors. He did, however, draw steam yachts identified with New York and Northeastern yacht clubs, and other ships hailing from Northeastern ports, including Bangor and Bath, Maine; Boston, Massachusetts; and Providence, Rhode Island. More frequently he drew harbors and navigational landmarks along the Eastern Seaboard, such as Gay Head (now Aquinnah), Massachusetts; Barnegat, New Jersey; Cape Henlopen, Delaware; Cape Fear, Cape Lookout, and Bodie Island, all in North Carolina; and, of course, Savannah. Of these locations, only Gay Head and Savannah appear in multiple works. His three drawings of Gay Head on Martha's Vineyard are wildly different from one another, all seeming to show the area's clay cliffs but with buildings and establishments that were not built on the cliffs proper, perhaps meant to represent buildings and communities nearby. In a fourth drawing, Golden identifies a Gay Head lighthouse in the background of a portrait of a paddle-wheel steamer, an abbreviated *Nantucket* appearing on the stern plate (Pl. 34).

Light stations feature more prominently in Golden's colorful *Off Barnegat* (Pl. 42) and his interpretation of Cape Henlopen on the Delaware Bay. The latter historic lighthouse (isolated, in reality) is shown adjacent to a bustling community perhaps meant to represent nearby Lewes, which the artist has taken the liberty of relocating so that it fits

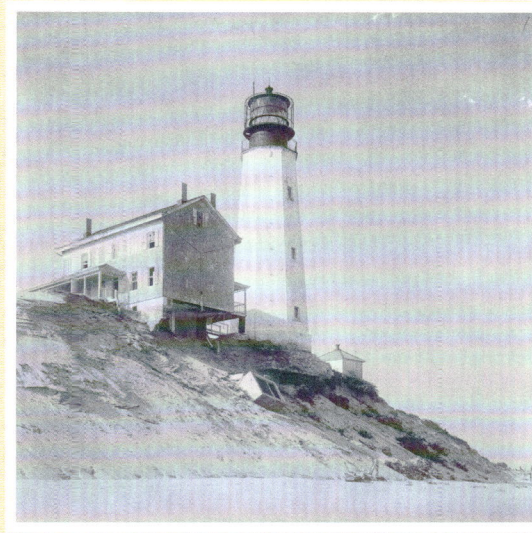

Fig. 1. *Cape Henlopen Lighthouse from southeast, 1926. Photographer: Hammond, Roydon L., RG 1380 006 Board of Agriculture Glass Negative Collection. Courtesy Delaware Public Archives.*

into his view (Fig.1). Views of Cape Fear and Cape Lookout in North Carolina have not been located; drawings of his home port of Savannah are discussed elsewhere in this catalogue.

Golden mentioned that he had visited the West Indies, and in one of his only three known drawings from 1937, he depicted the harbor of Port of Spain in the then-British colony of Trinidad, now Trinidad and Tobago (Pl. 44). Golden's Port of Spain includes buildings ranging from a "Seaview Hotel" to a church sited on a hillside sloping down to the harbor, where British vessels ply the waters. Farther south still, Golden drew the lonelier British outpost of Saint Helena, famous as the site of Napoleon Bonaparte's exile in 1815. In his drawings of Saint Helena (Pl. 45) Golden depicts a chapel or tomb emblazoned with the name of Napoleon. Even though the former emperor's remains were removed to France less than twenty years after his death, Napoleon's former residence there and the parklike location of his original resting

place remain under French ownership.

At the southernmost point of South America lies Cape Horn, the long-feared rocky landmark that was an essential route for sail and steam vessels of Golden's day seeking passage between the Atlantic and Pacific. The passage around Cape Horn was crucial to commercial shipping for centuries, even with its gale force winds, occasional rogue 100-foot waves, and the very real threat of loss of ships and human lives. The development of a transcontinental railroad, the Suez Canal, and eventually the Panama Canal, caused the gradual decline of the Cape Horn route. Golden claimed, somewhat incredibly, that he had rounded "Cape Horn 23 times, Cape of Good Hope 25 or 30 times." [4] This may have been an exaggeration, but seamen like Golden regarded any rounding of the Horn as a milestone. Despite Golden's written mention of a vessel "lost with all hands off the Horn," his drawings of the cape are cheerfully imaginative (Pls. 46, 47). In both, Golden shows a full-rigged ship about to round the rocky, mountainous Horn from the upper right, while a steam vessel proceeds past the cape heralded by a pod of spouting whales. On the promontory of Cape Horn, Golden lets his imagination fly. Men, women, dogs, and birds walk paved pathways. At the water's edge a boathouse beckons to passing ships, promising safe harbor, while under looming mountains, a building identified as a post office offers a place for sailors to mail loved ones about their perilous voyage. Together the two images are beautiful, mythic expressions of the hopes of a sailor facing one of the planet's most feared passages. —H.D.

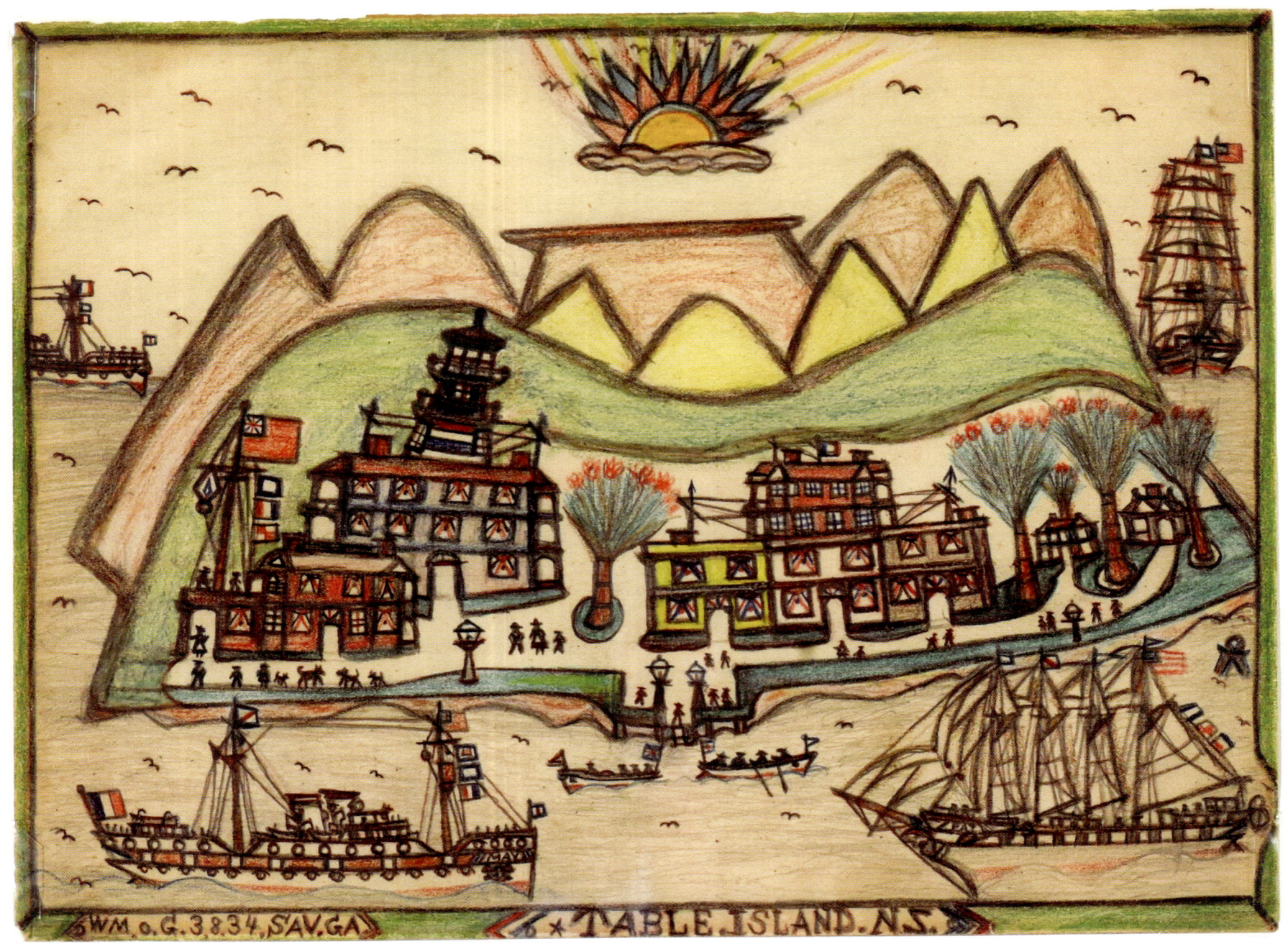

PLATE 35. *Table Island, N.S.*, 1934

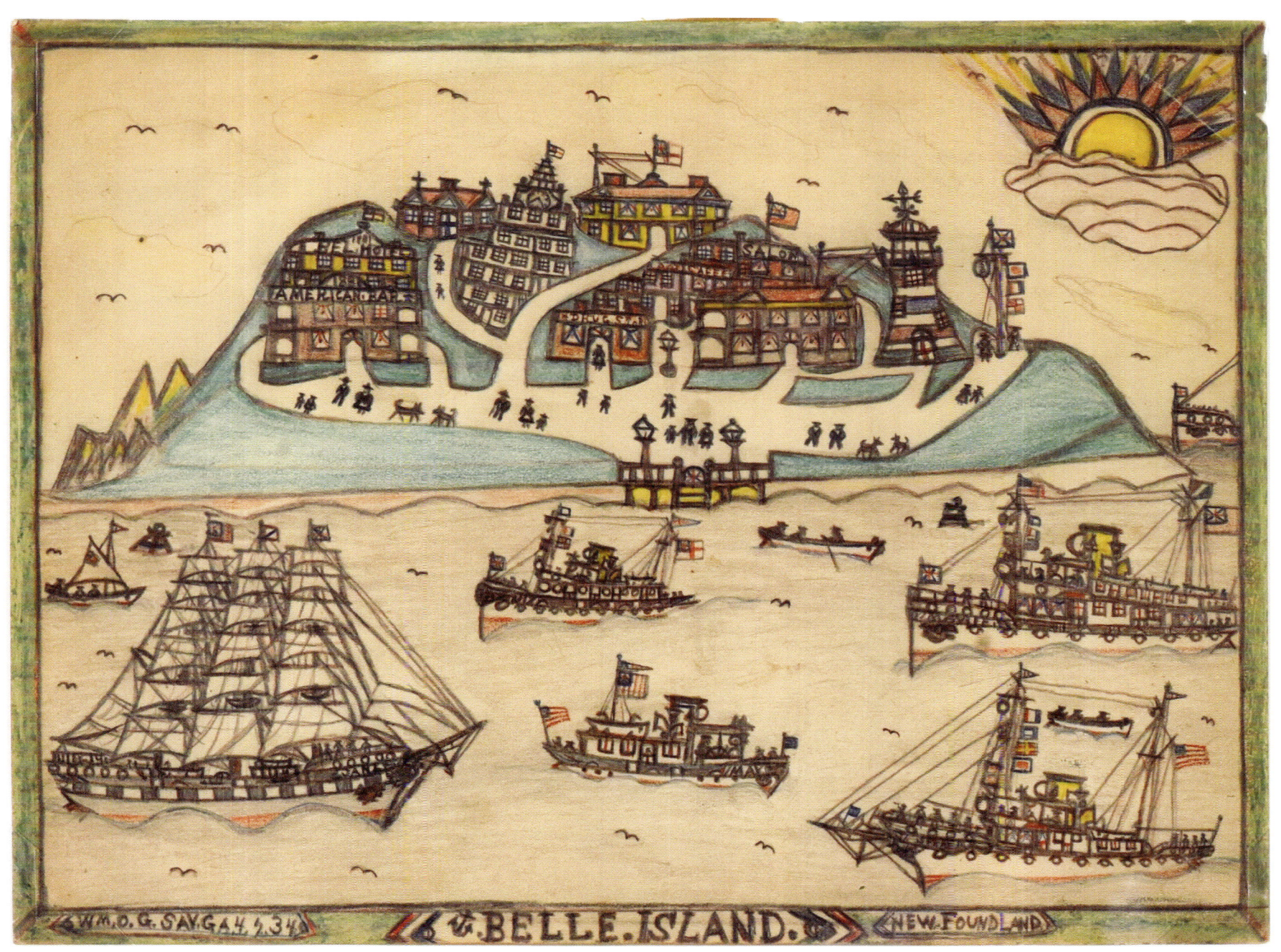

PLATE 36. *Belle Island, Newfoundland, 1934*

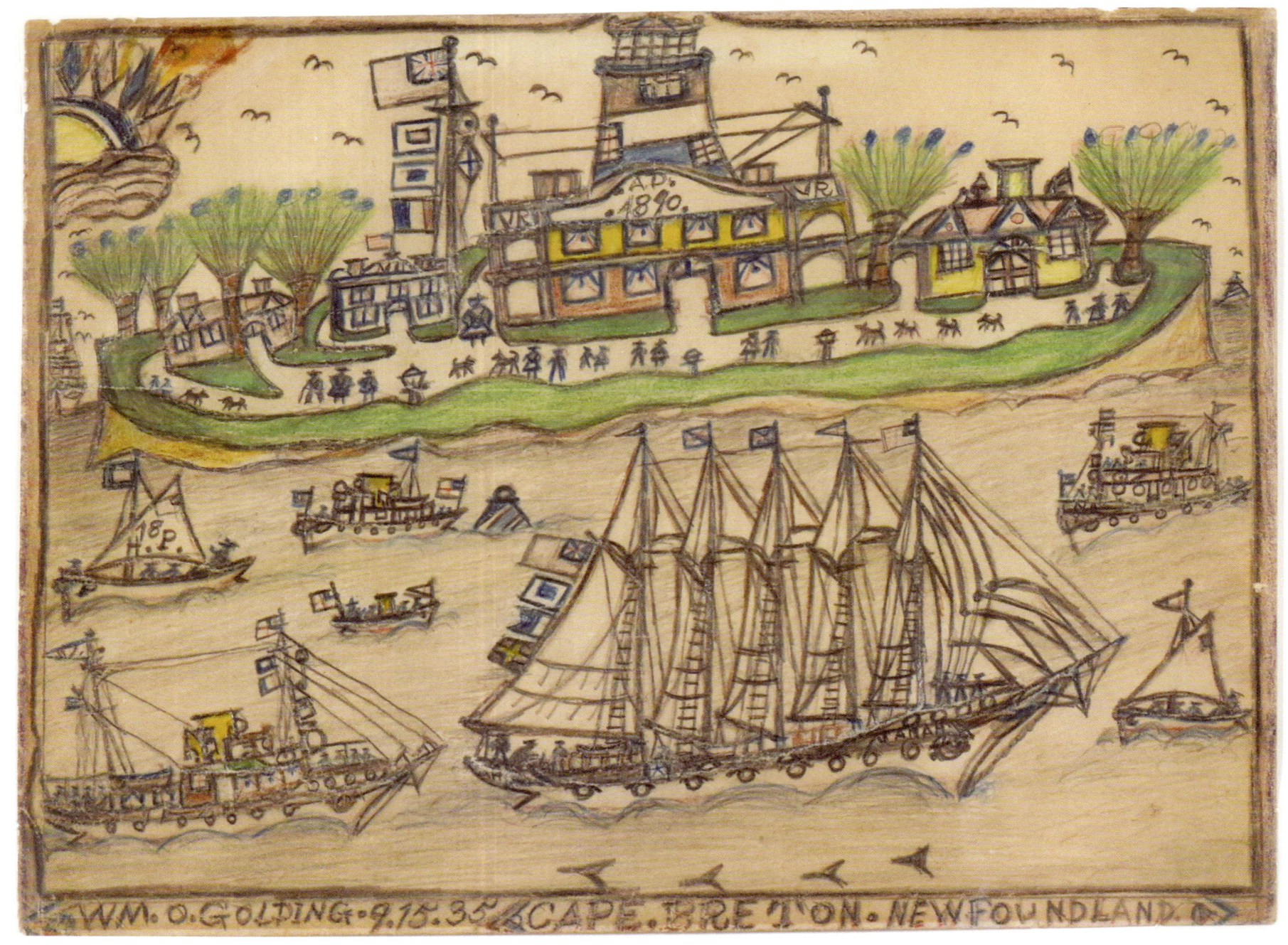

PLATE 37. Cape Breton, Newfoundland, 1935

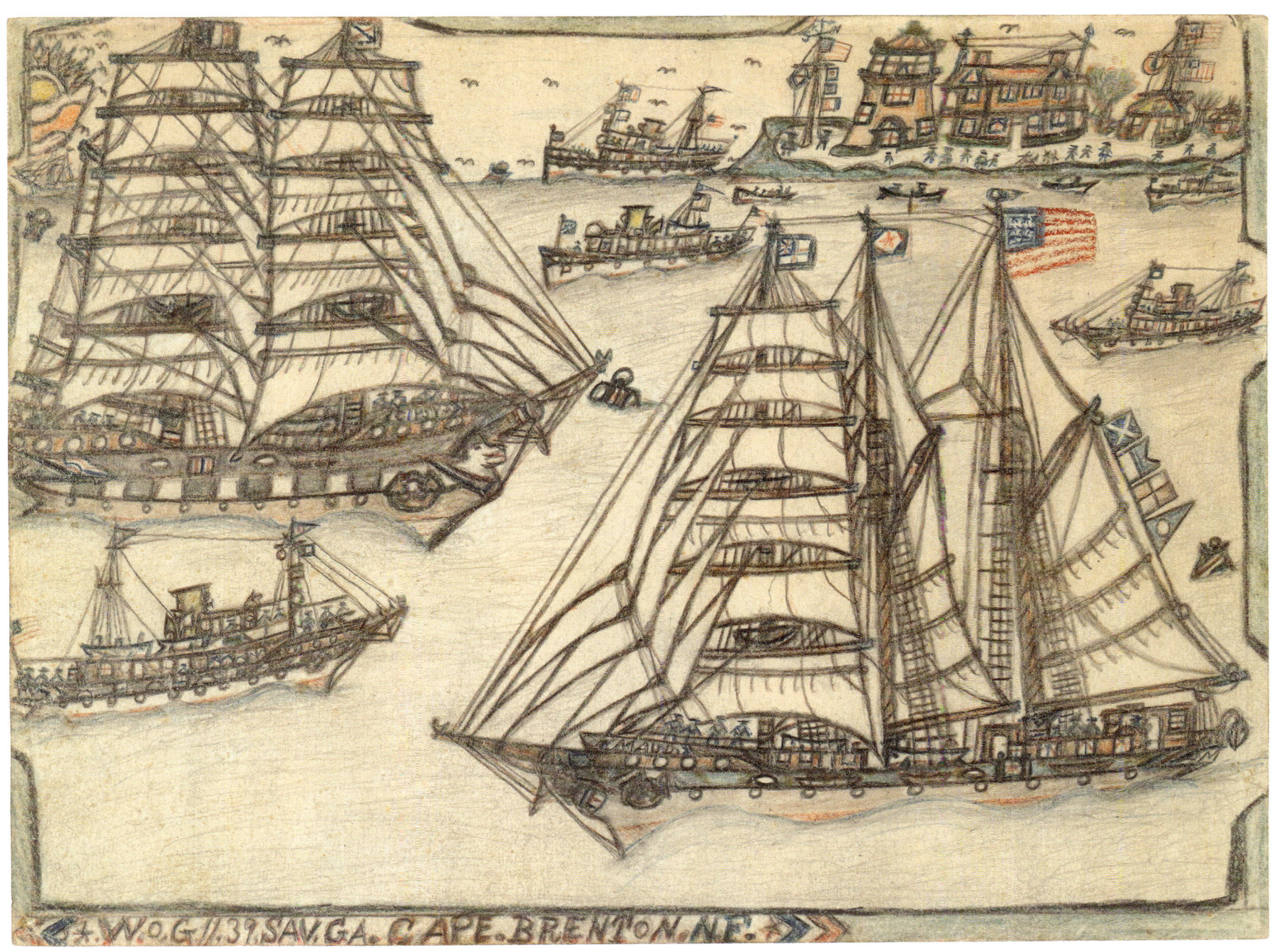

PLATE 38. *Cape Brenton, NF, 1939*

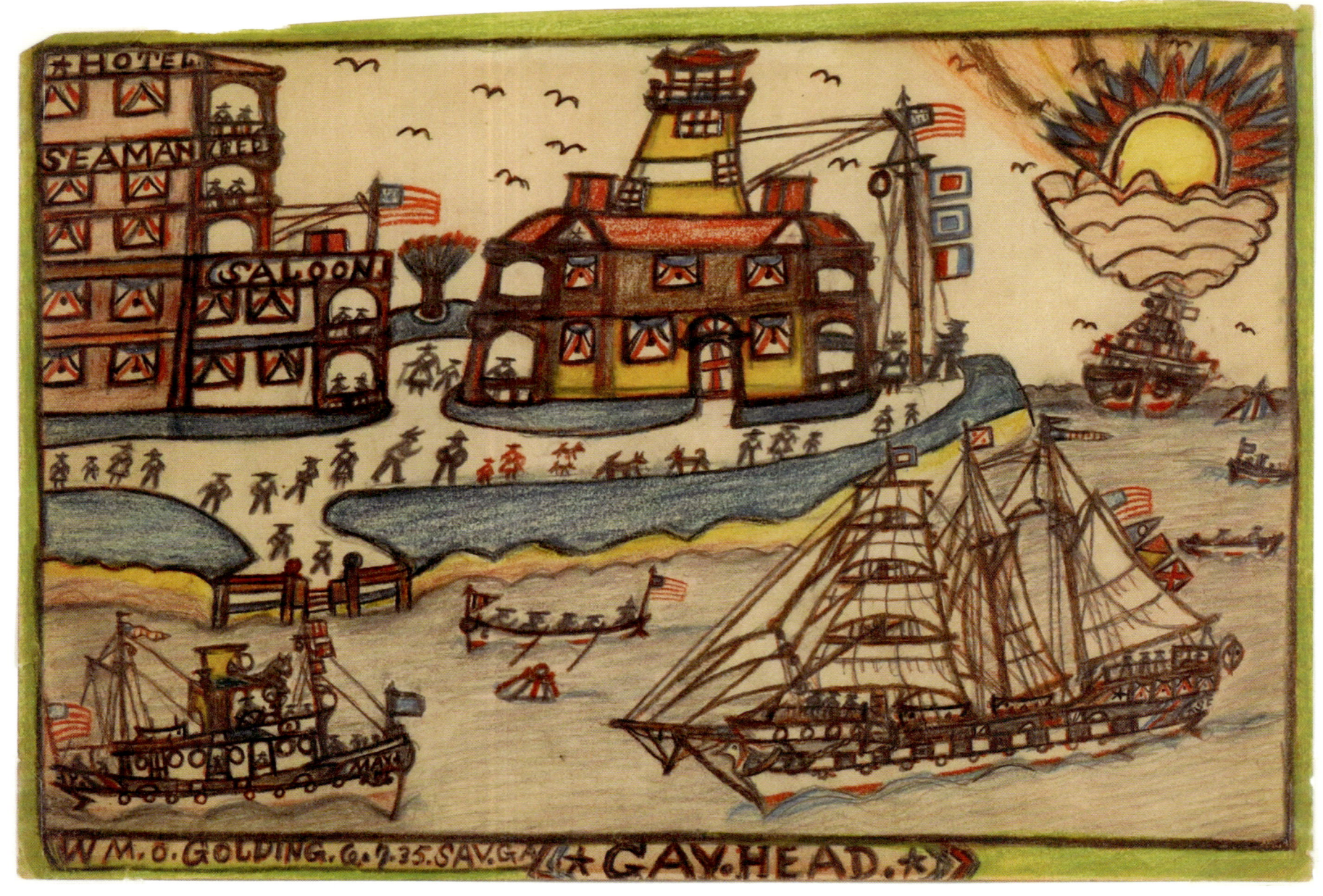

PLATE 39. *Gay Head, 1935*

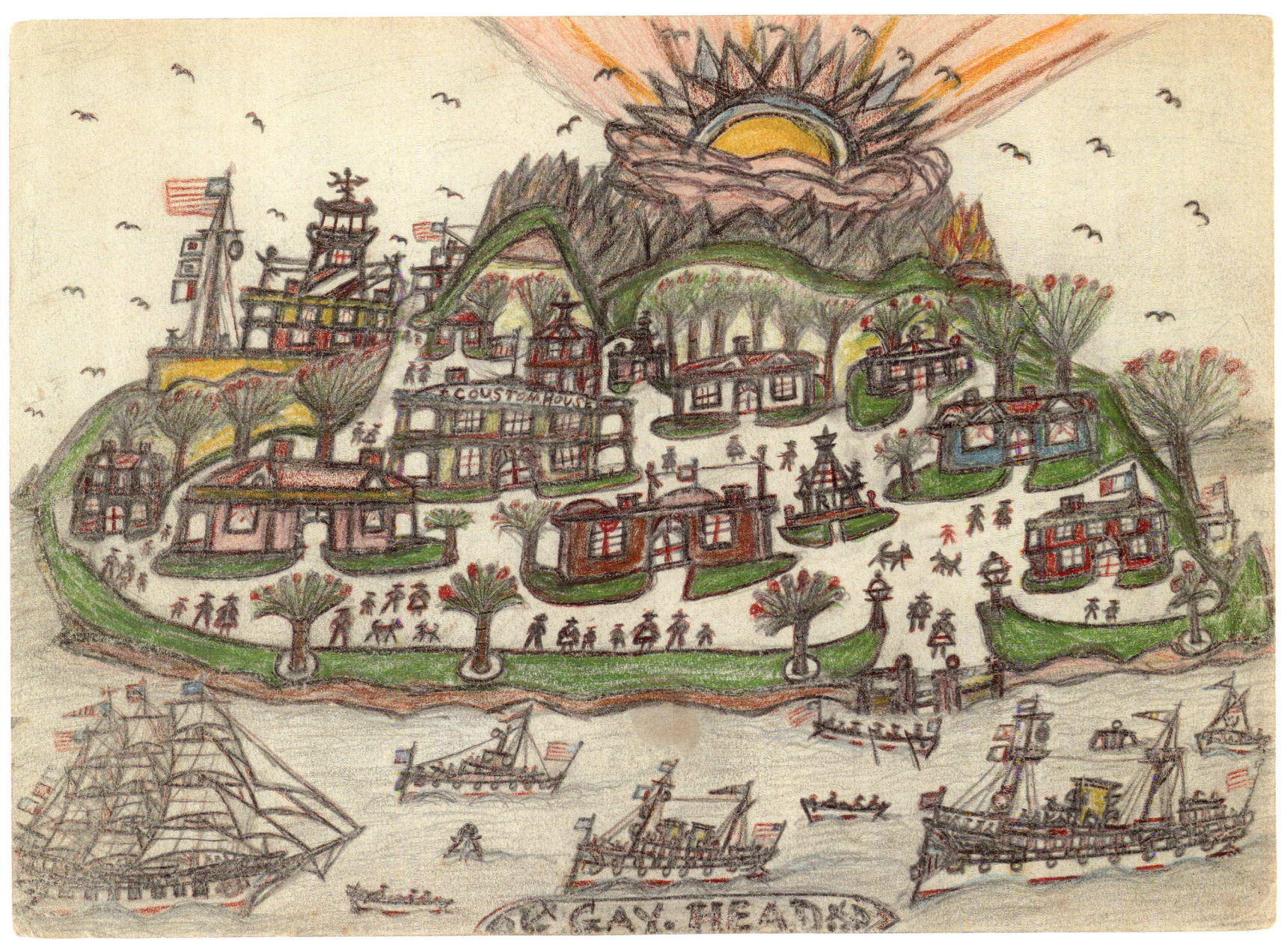

PLATE 40. *Gay Head,* n.d

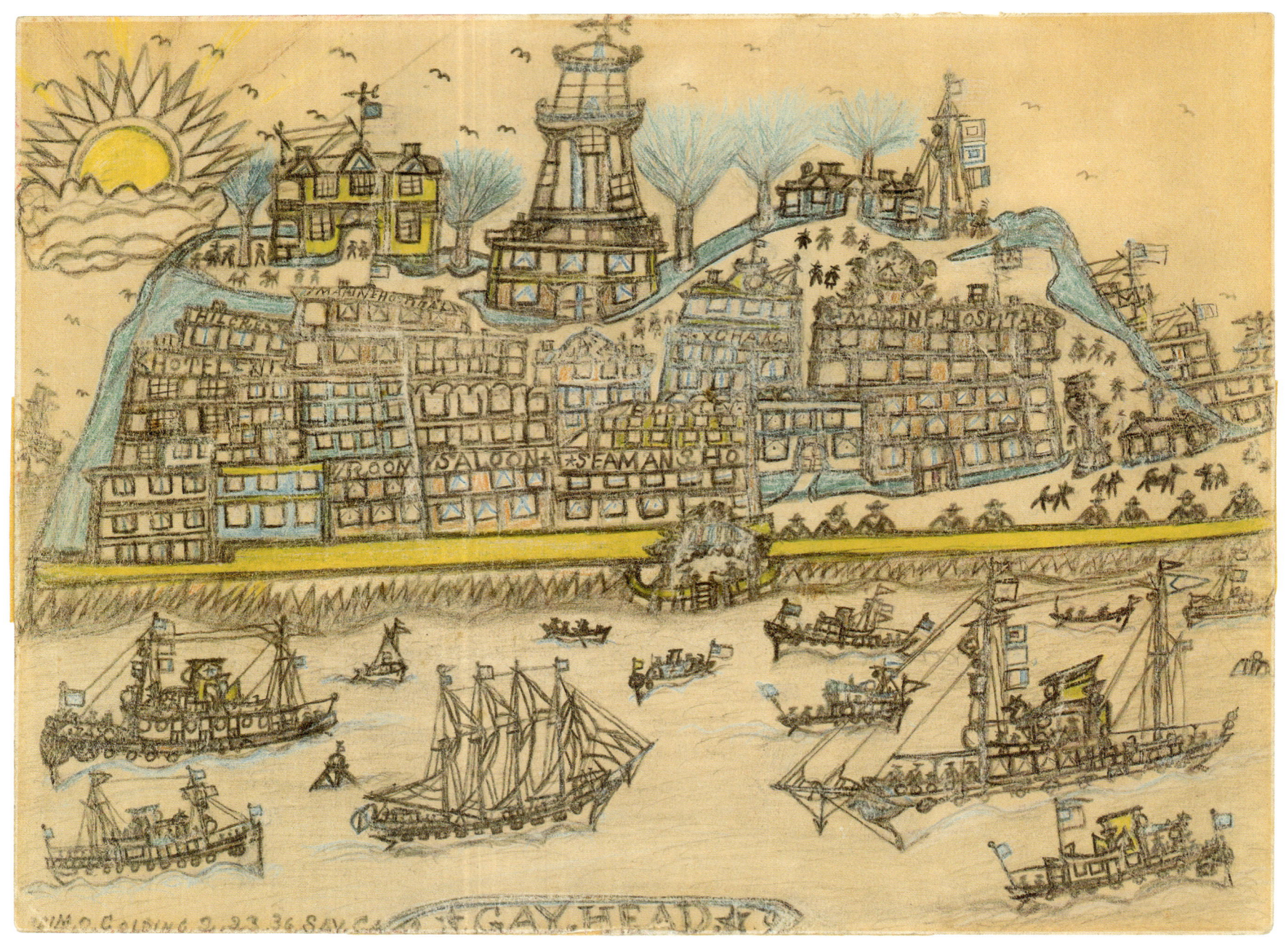

PLATE 41. *Gay Head, 1936*

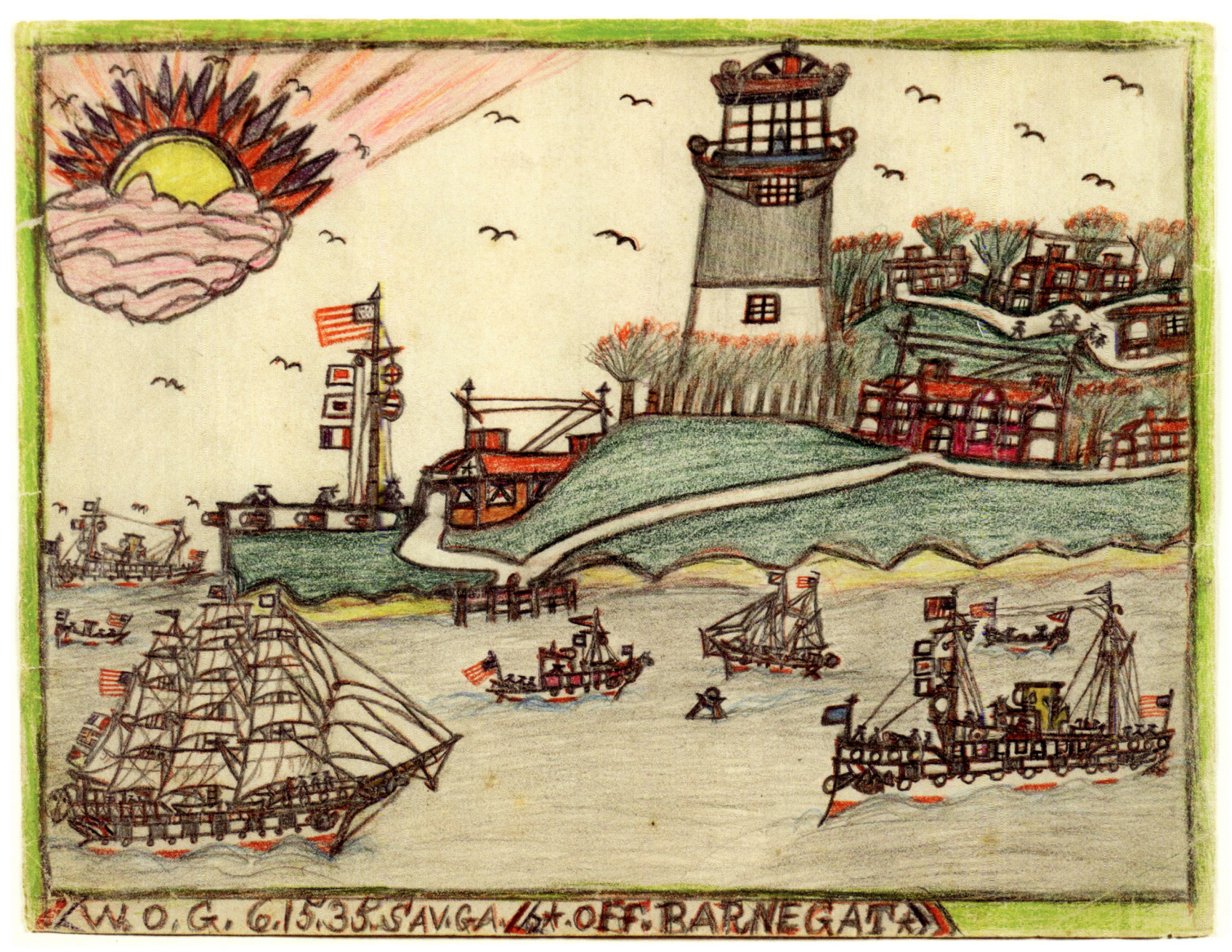

PLATE 42. *Off Barnegat*, 1935

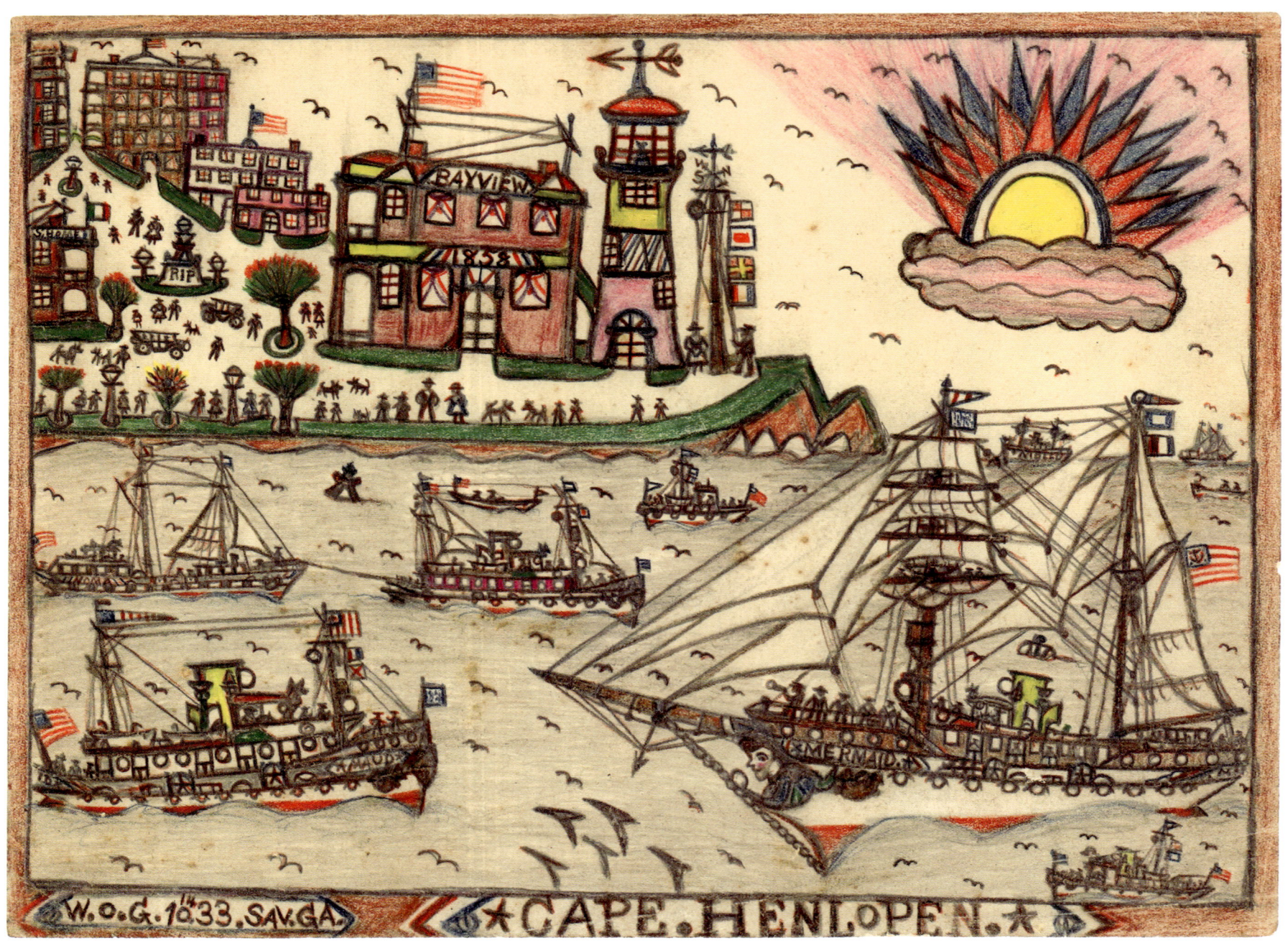

PLATE 43. *Cape Henlopen, 1933*

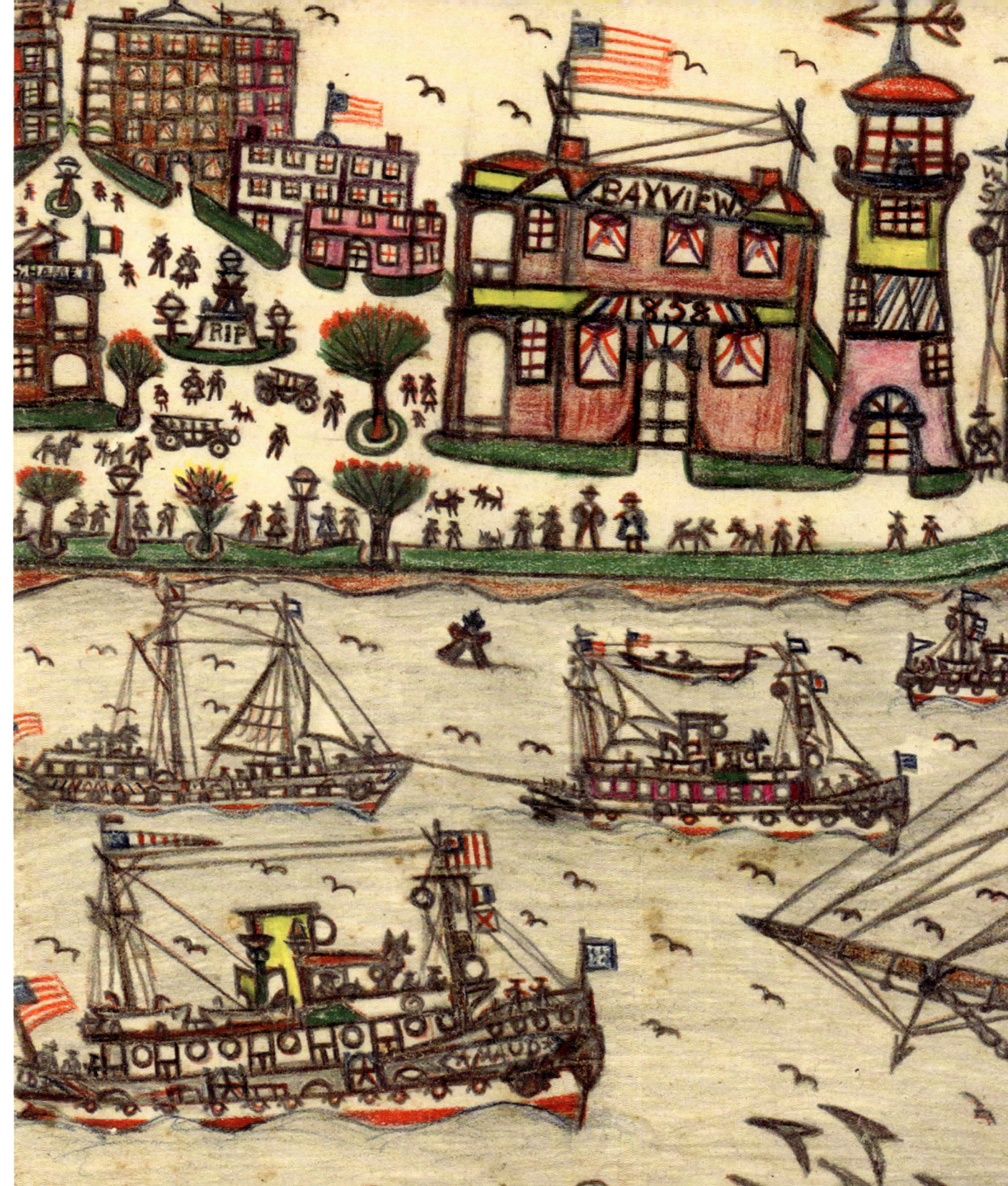

Detail. *Cape Henlopen*

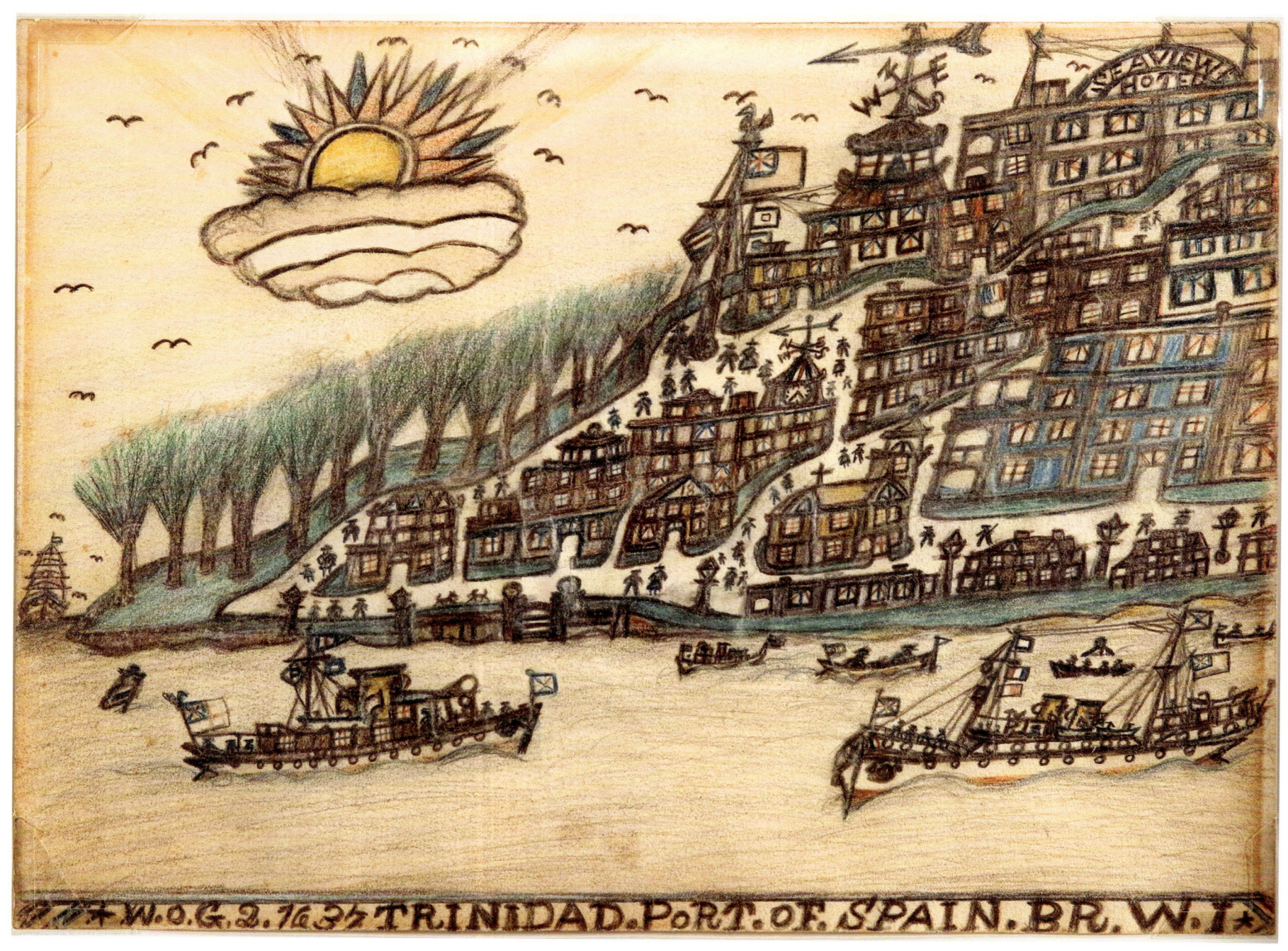

PLATE 44. *Trinidad, Port of Spain, Br. W. I.*, 1937

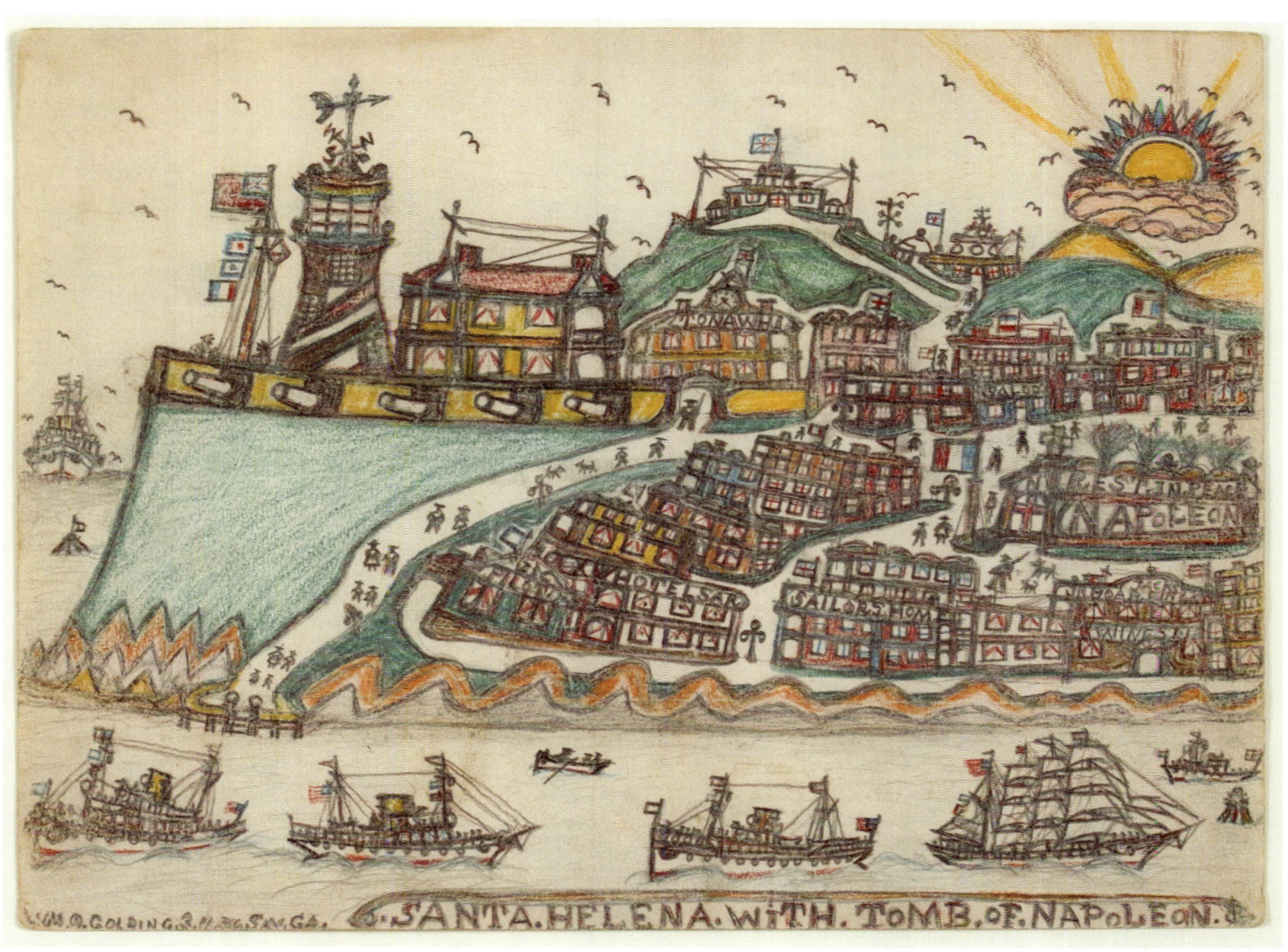

PLATE 45. *Santa Helena with Tomb of Napoleon*, 1936

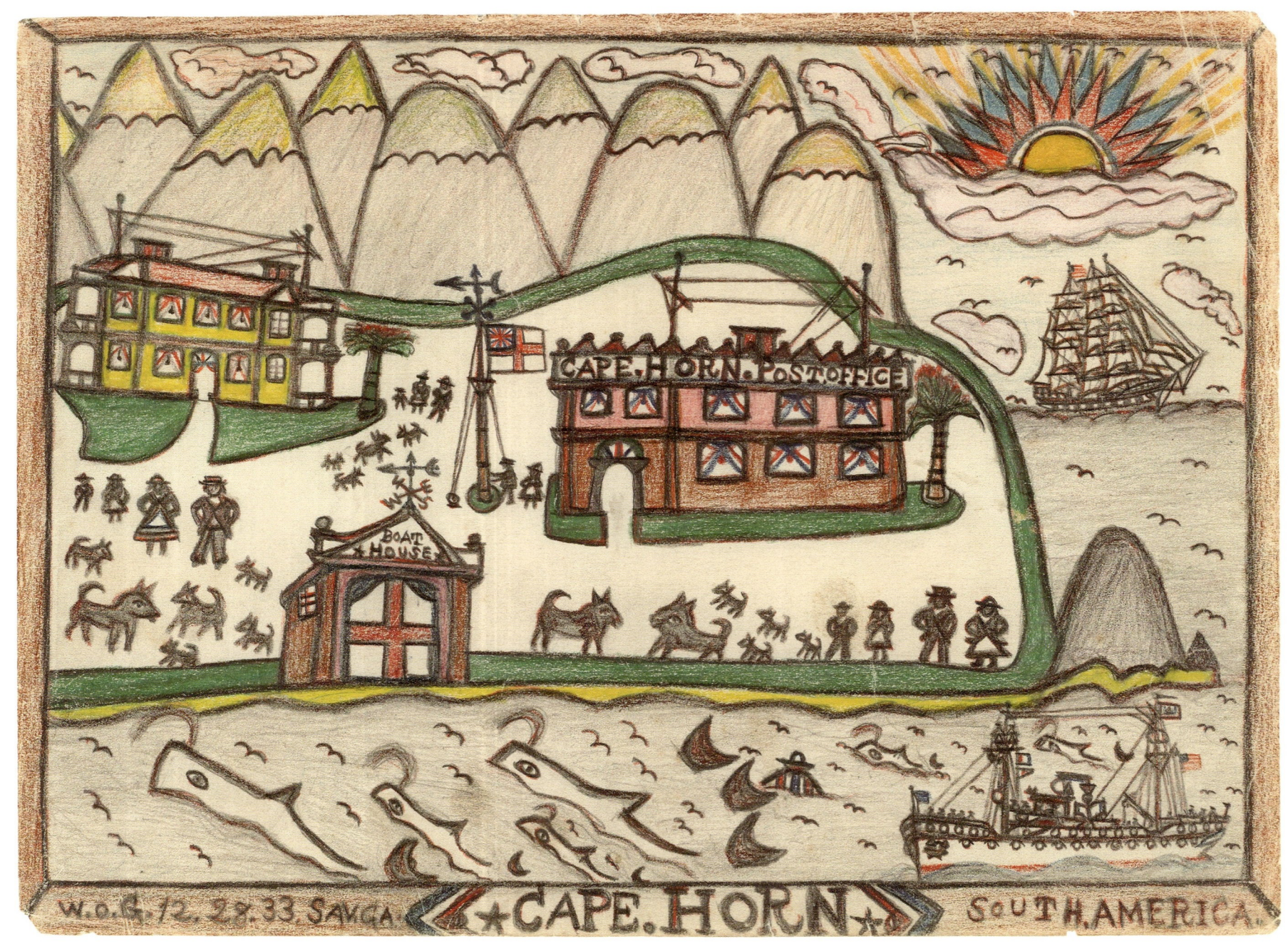

PLATE 46. *Cape Horn, South America, 1933*

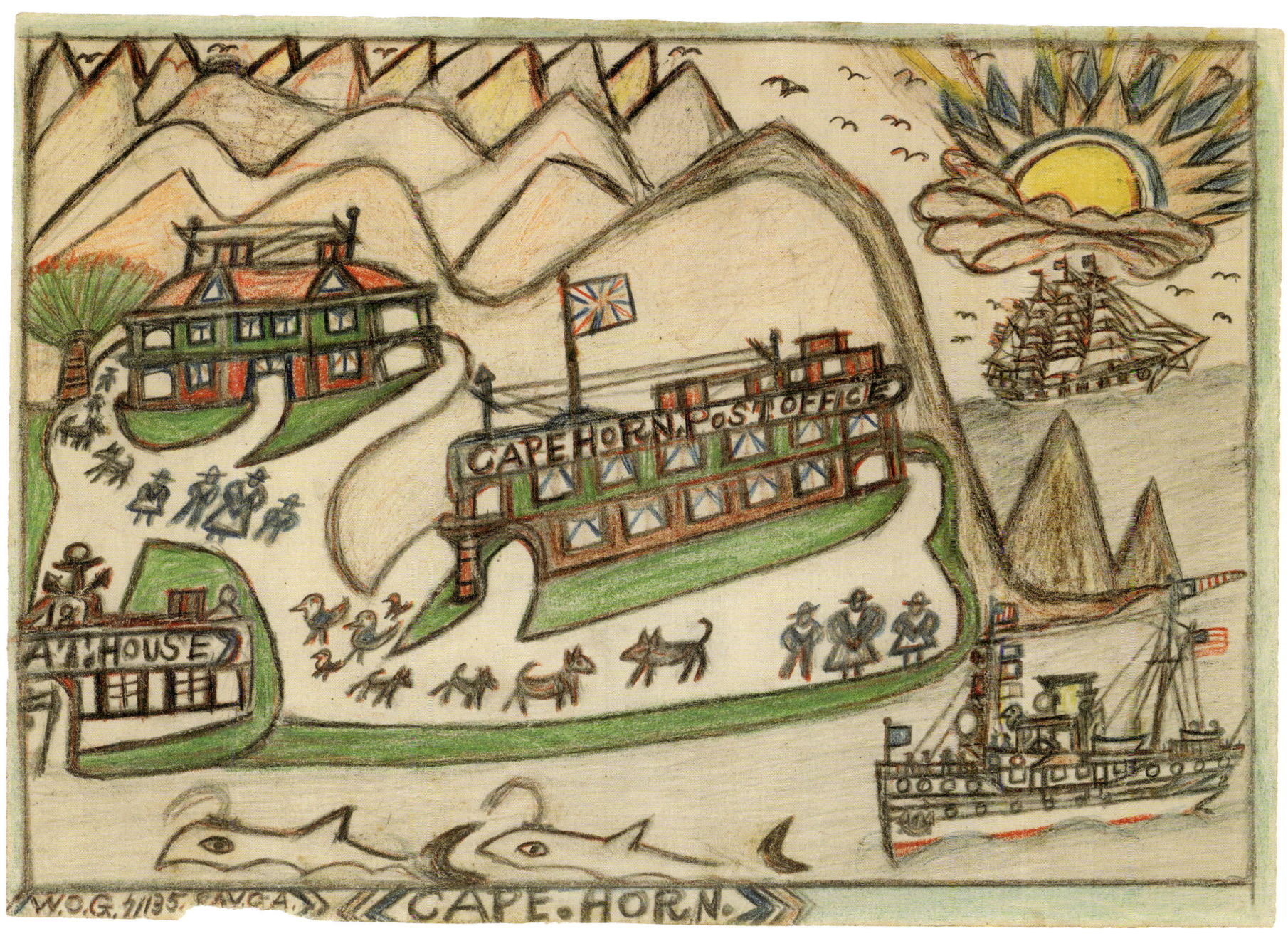

PLATE 47. Cape Horn, 1935

THE PACIFIC: CHINA AND INTERNATIONAL PORTS

The majority of William O. Golden's harbor views focus on China and former Western colonial ports in the Pacific and Asia, his maritime years encompassing a significant period of imperialist ambition and colonial rule in the region. In addition to British colonies and possessions in the Atlantic, Golden drew French-controlled colonial territories in the Pacific, including Vietnam (then Indochina) and Tahiti. Golden implied that he had visited these places, apologizing to Margaret Stiles that he could not draw her suggested subjects of Bali and Hawaii because he had never seen them, drawing Tahiti and Gibraltar instead. [1] His view of Tahiti from 1935 (Pl. 48) differs from many of his port subjects in that no steam vessels are present in the harbor. Instead, fully-rigged tall sailing ships appear in the harbor and on the horizon, complemented by Tahitian canoes with their distinctive profiles and inverted triangular sails. Colonial houses and buildings fill the greenery surrounding the harbor on the drawing's right side. In what almost resembles a snippet out of a romantic painting, a pair of human figures at the bottom look out over the harbor from a small promontory surmounted by a cross. By contrast, Golden's view of Saigon appears to reflect his Navy years, as a squadron of American warships cruises in from the lower right border to meet approaching French warships. This complex and dynamic composition contains no less than seventeen detailed renderings in miniature of sail and steam vessels with some rowboats thrown in for good measure. Golden identifies Saigon as "China," understandable as it was then part of French Indochina, specifically Cochinchina, adding that it is "under French protection," indicating awareness of the European powers that held sway in many of the places that he drew. A drawing of Penang, however, places the longtime Malaysian trading hub, then controlled by the British, in "Java, Dutch East Indies." Golden even includes Dutch flags in the image, calling into question whether he actually visited or if the locations were mixed in his memory, a tendency that occurs in several works.

The majority of Golden's Pacific port views, at least nine, are located in China, which appears to have held special significance for him. The locations he depicted were all at one time part of the system of treaty ports stretching up the coast of China and major river systems, established by western powers, usually by force or threat, to open these locations to trade, often against the interests of the Chinese. Several ports Golden drew (Hong Kong, Canton, Foochow) were among the first such treaty ports created by the Treaty of Nanking in 1842, which transferred Hong Kong to British rule. Decades later, Golden's years at sea encompassed a time of continued transformation and turmoil in East Asia, with Western imperialists—including an increasingly ambitious US and regional powers like Japan and Russia—jockeying for economic interest in China. Golden's naval service also overlapped with American involvement in the Boxer Rebellion and "China relief expedition," although there is no obvious connection in his drawings. Certain details point to Golden's presence in China in the 1890s, during his Navy years. In images of the Chinese cities of Foochow (Fuzhou) (Pl. 52), "Yunnan Island" (possibly Yunnan-Fu or Pakhoi), and Canton (Guangzhou) (Pl. 51), Golden depicts light and signal stations hoisting the yellow dragon flag or ensign of the Qing Dynasty. The version of the flag that Golden drew, featuring a blue dragon on yellow ground, was used between 1889 and 1912. The flag also appears flying over a waterfront building in Golden's 1933 image of Chefoo. A great many details in his Chinese port scenes reflect the presence of Western powers, though not always remembered accurately. A French flag flies over fortifications in Golden's 1933 view of British-controlled Foochow, while American,

French, and Japanese vessels patrol the harbor. A drawing from the same year of Macau (Pl. 50) includes various buildings flying flags of the US, France, the Netherlands, England, and Japan though the flag of the Portuguese, who then controlled Macau, does not appear. In the harbor, a French warship is joined by an American tug-like vessel and a Japanese ship. Although most of Golden's views of Chinese treaty ports do not show harbors patrolled by military vessels, several do include images of warships and fortifications.

Despite the long gap between his experiences and his commitment of the same to paper, Golden does give us the flavor of the ports, the features and businesses that stood out to him. Some of these may be invention or details borrowed from other locales for the sake of making an interesting drawing, while other details can be confirmed today. Although some features carry over from scene to scene, like the ubiquitous sailors' hotels and bars, Golden's view of Hong Kong (Pl. 53) includes establishments that still seem to match up to contemporary reality, including the Victoria Hotel, City Hall, and Bank of England buildings (Fig. 1). Other landmarks appear to be transposed from one Chinese port to another. His 1935 drawing of Foochow includes a "Peak Hotel" and the distinctive tramway leading up to it, very real features that were located in Hong Kong. [2] These mixed locations do not impair our enjoyment of Golden's images, which are impressions of place based on memory, not documentation.

Golden returned to some Chinese subjects more than once. In addition to two views of Foochow, he made three drawings of Chefoo (Yantai) spread out over his years of art production. His drawings of Chefoo are among the densest of his port views. In all three, Golden depicts a church he names "St. Paul's." A church with a squat tower does appear in late-nineteenth-century views of the Chefoo waterfront, though Golden's depictions are not consistent.

He may in fact have misremembered the name, which could have derived from a famous landmark, the ruins of the massive St. Paul's Jesuit church in Macau.

Whether he visited China as a merchant seaman or while serving in the US Navy, Golden consistently represents businesses and establishments arrayed along the "bund" or waterfront commercial strips common to the treaty ports. In some of these enclaves, foreigners were more prevalent than Chinese. As always, Golden tended to represent the places most familiar to sailors, primarily boardinghouses and bars, along with custom houses, churches, ship chandleries, and, occasionally, other distinctive landmarks, making these lively port views among his most colorful and elaborate compositions. —H.D.

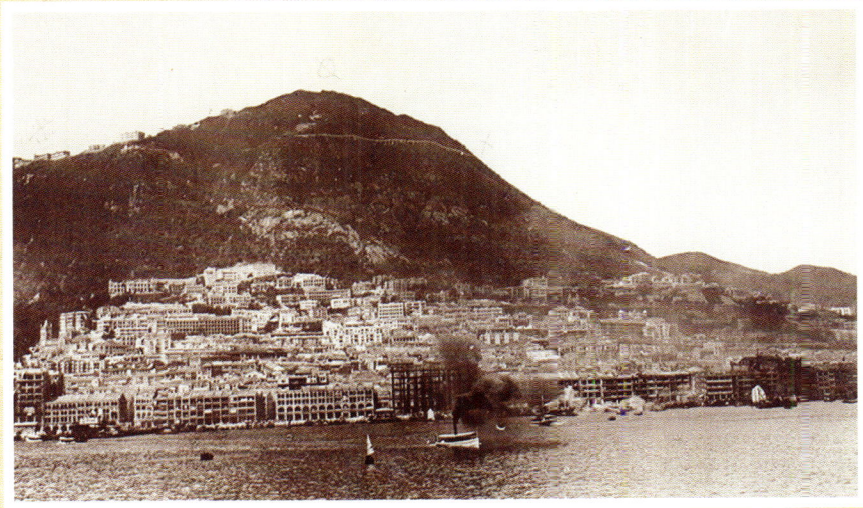

Fig. 1. *Denis Henry Hazell (British, 1897-1970), Central Hong Kong and Victoria Peak, Viewed from the Harbour, published in Picturesque Hong Kong (Ye Olde Printerie Ltd., Hong Kong), approximately 1925. Courtesy Special Collections, University of Bristol Library. (www.hpcbristol.net)*

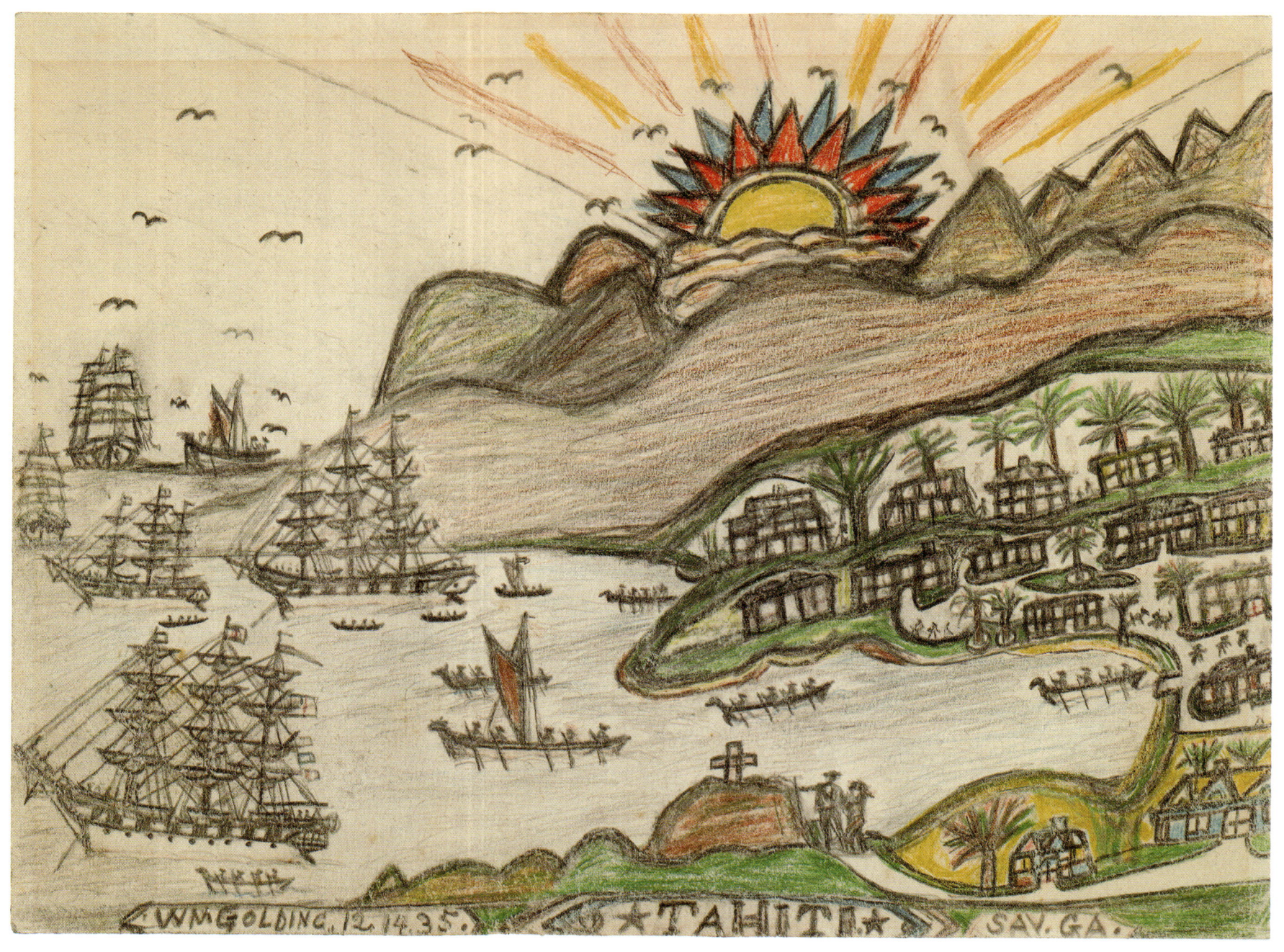

PLATE 48. *Tahiti, 1935*

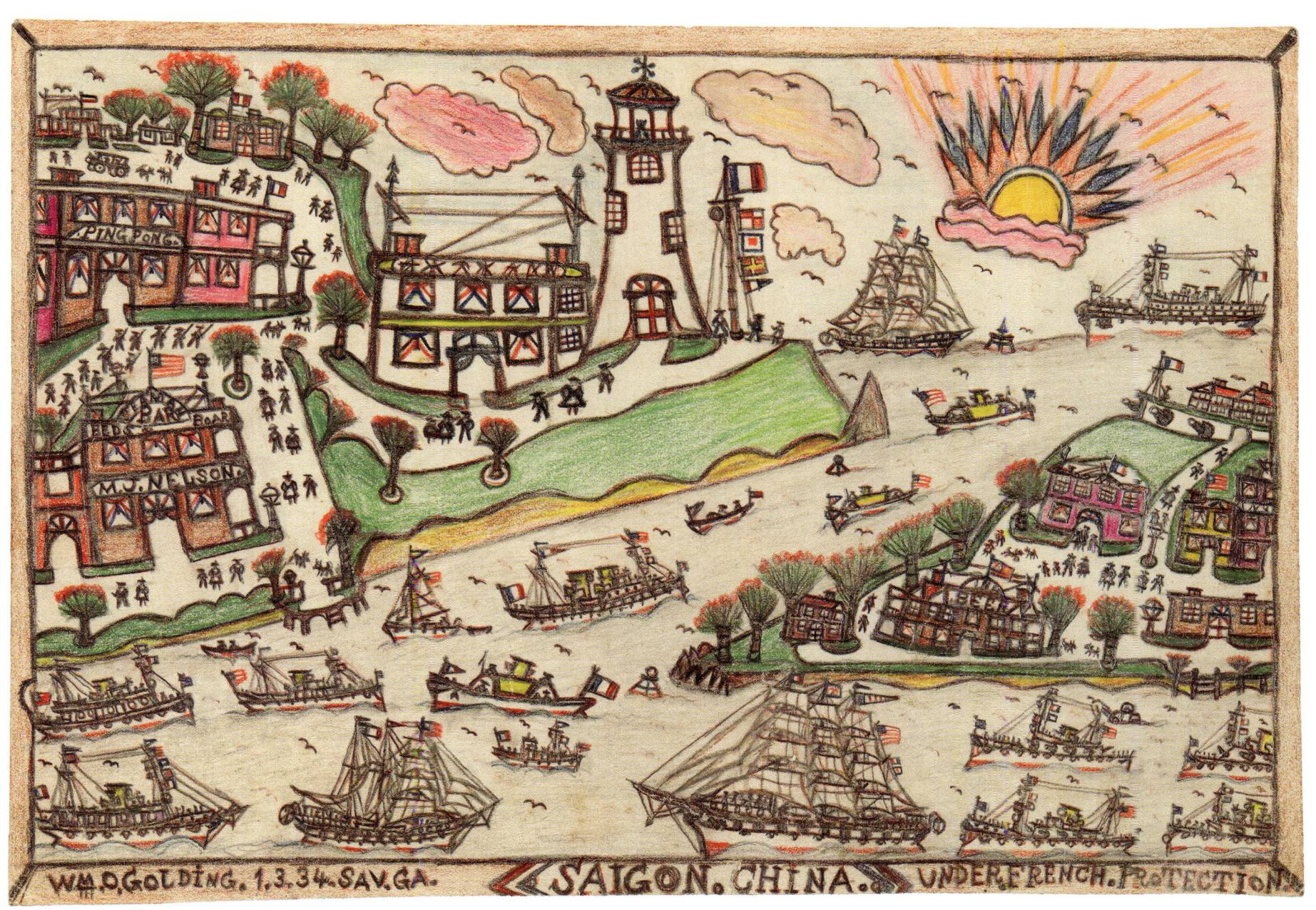

PLATE 49. *Saigon, China, Under French Protection*, 1934

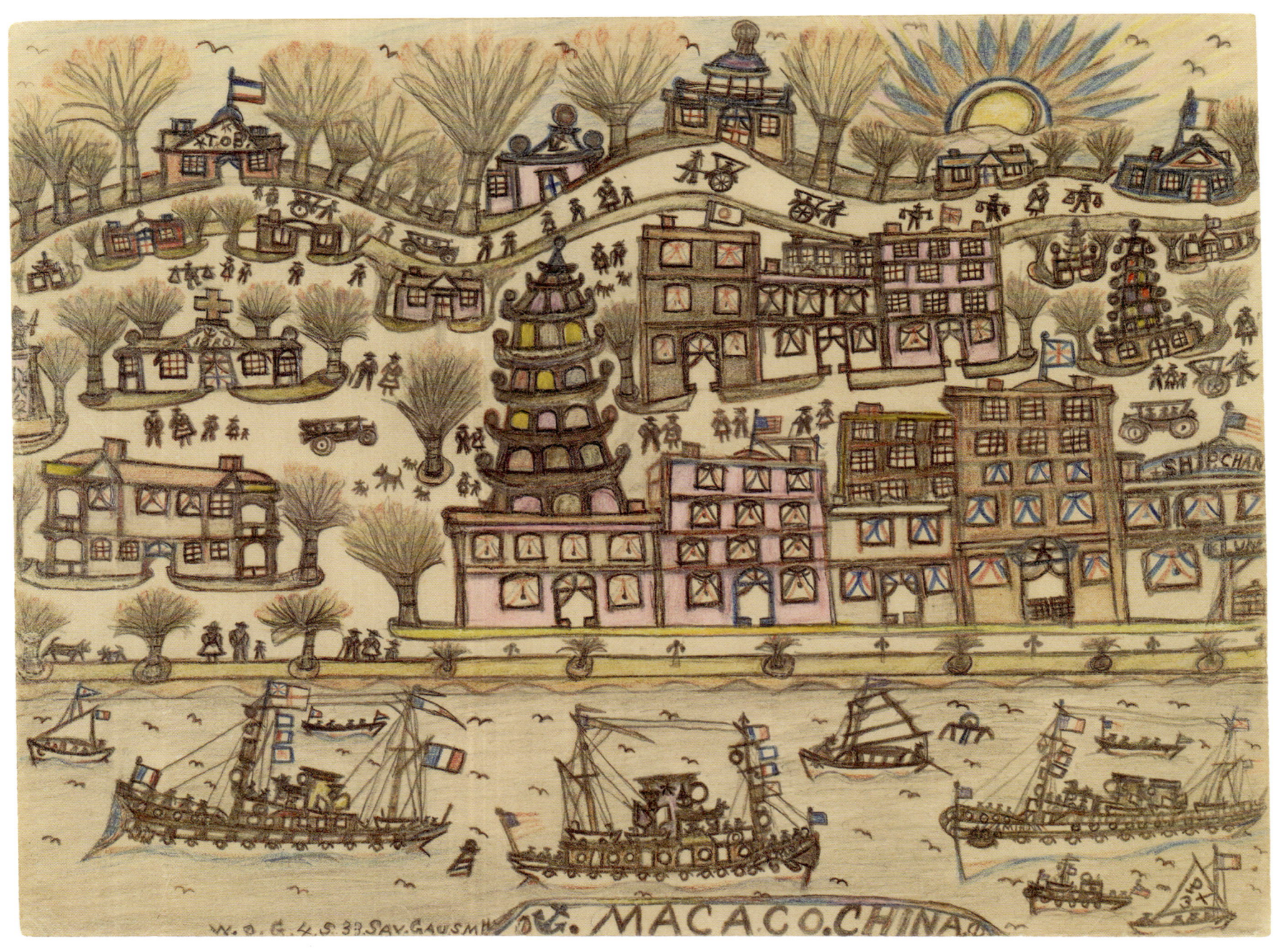

PLATE 50. *Macaco, China*, 1933

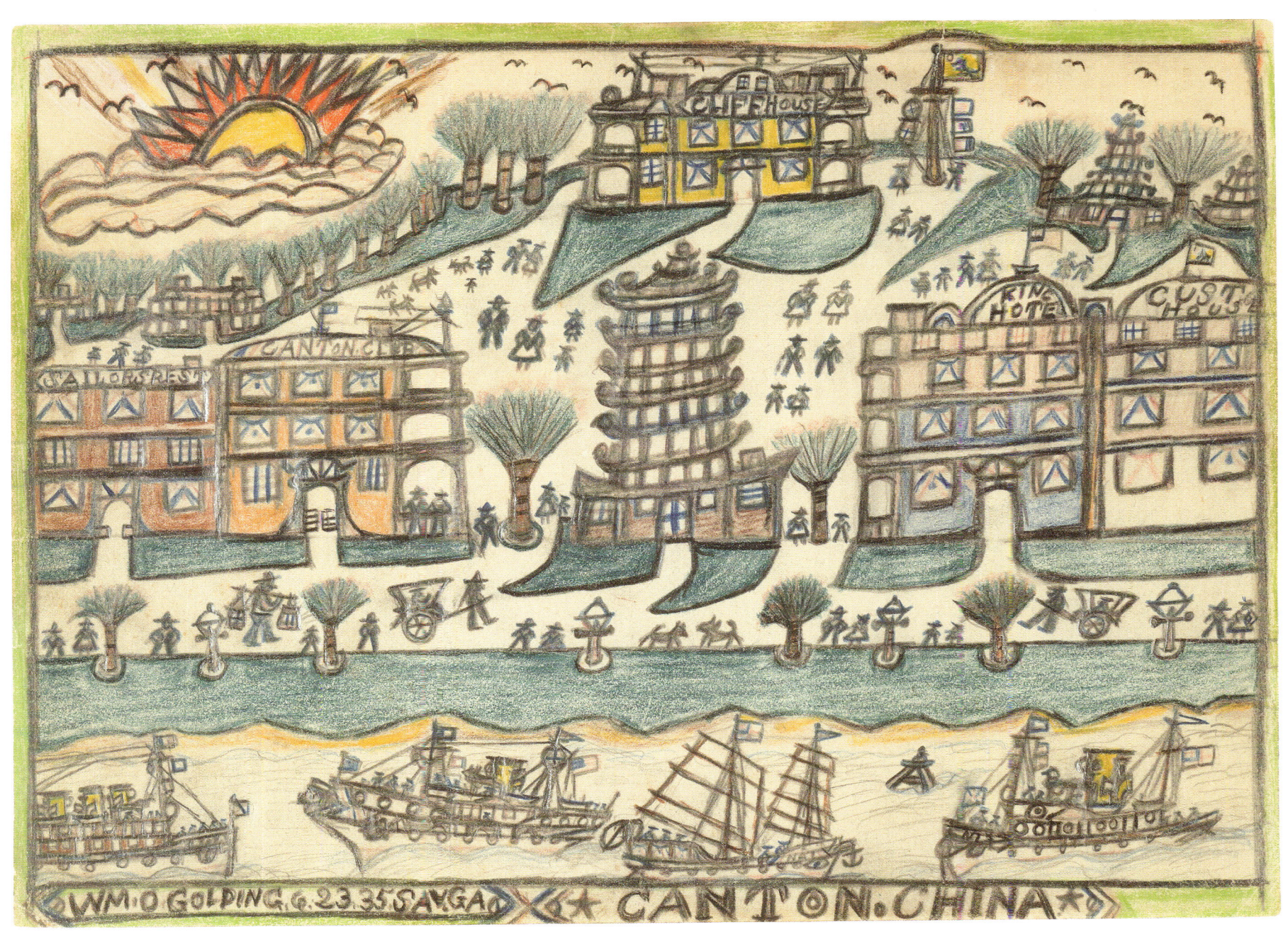

PLATE 51. *Canton, China, 1935*

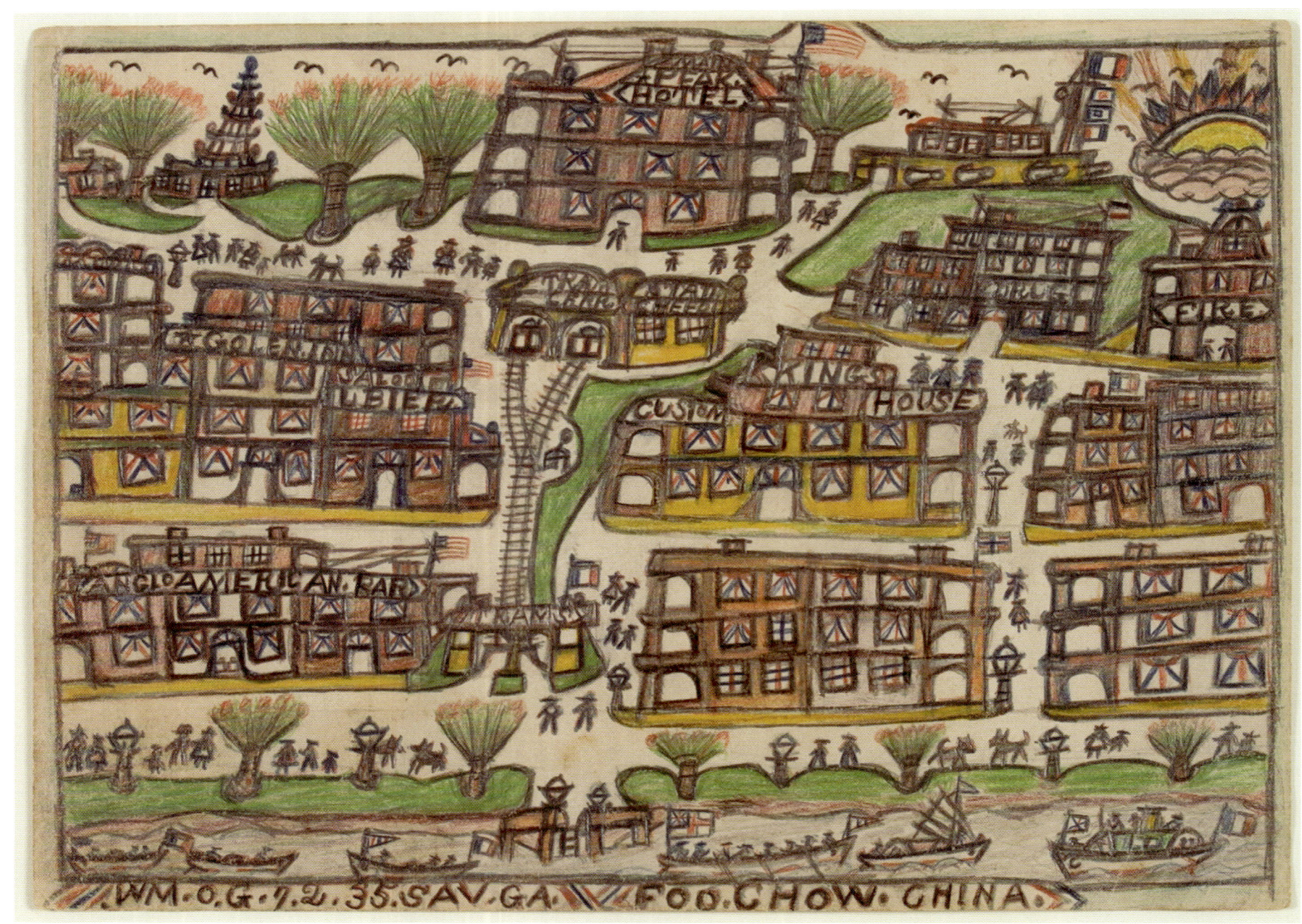

PLATE 52. *Foochow, China, 1935*

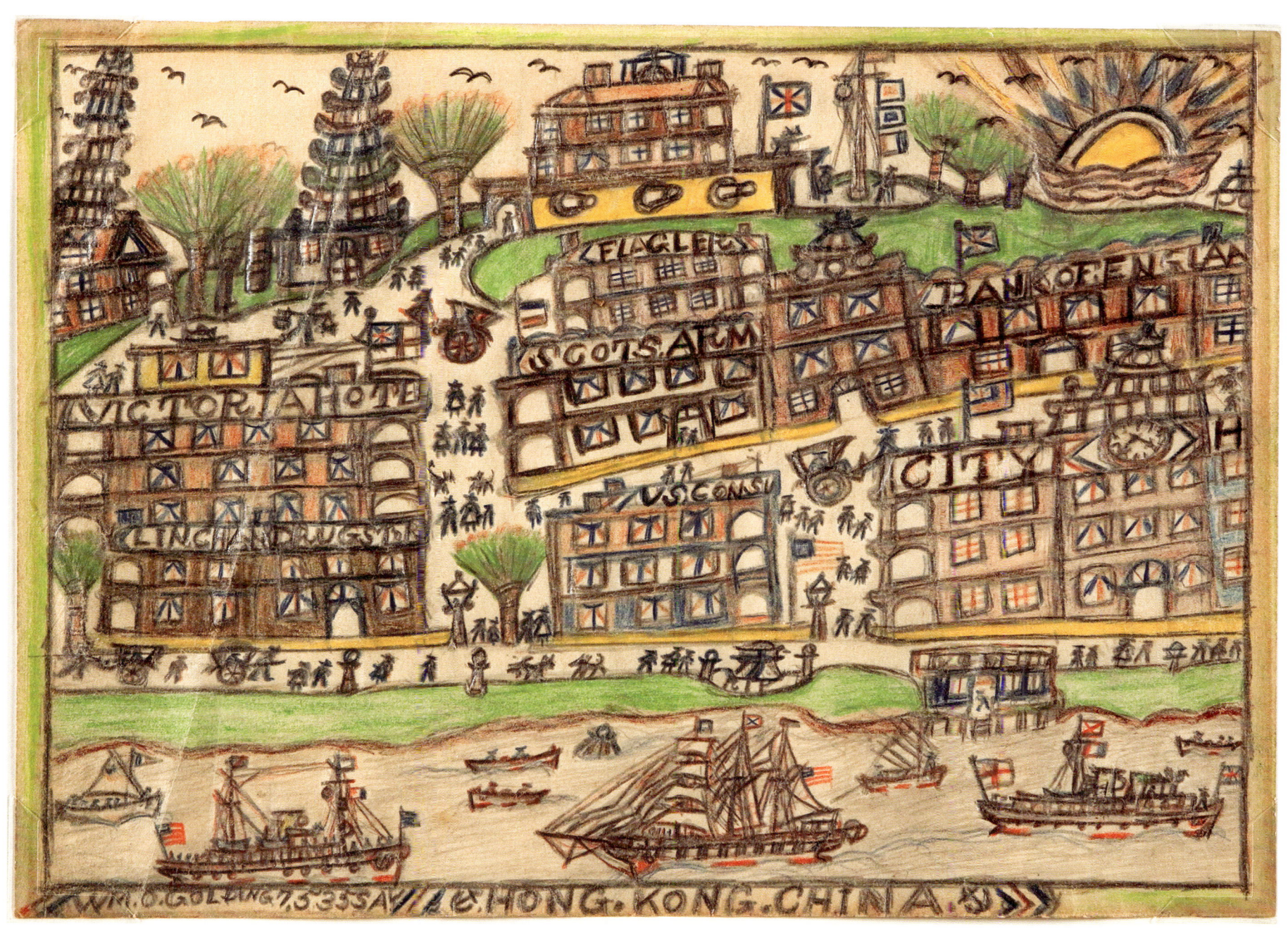

PLATE 53. *Hong Kong, China, 1935*

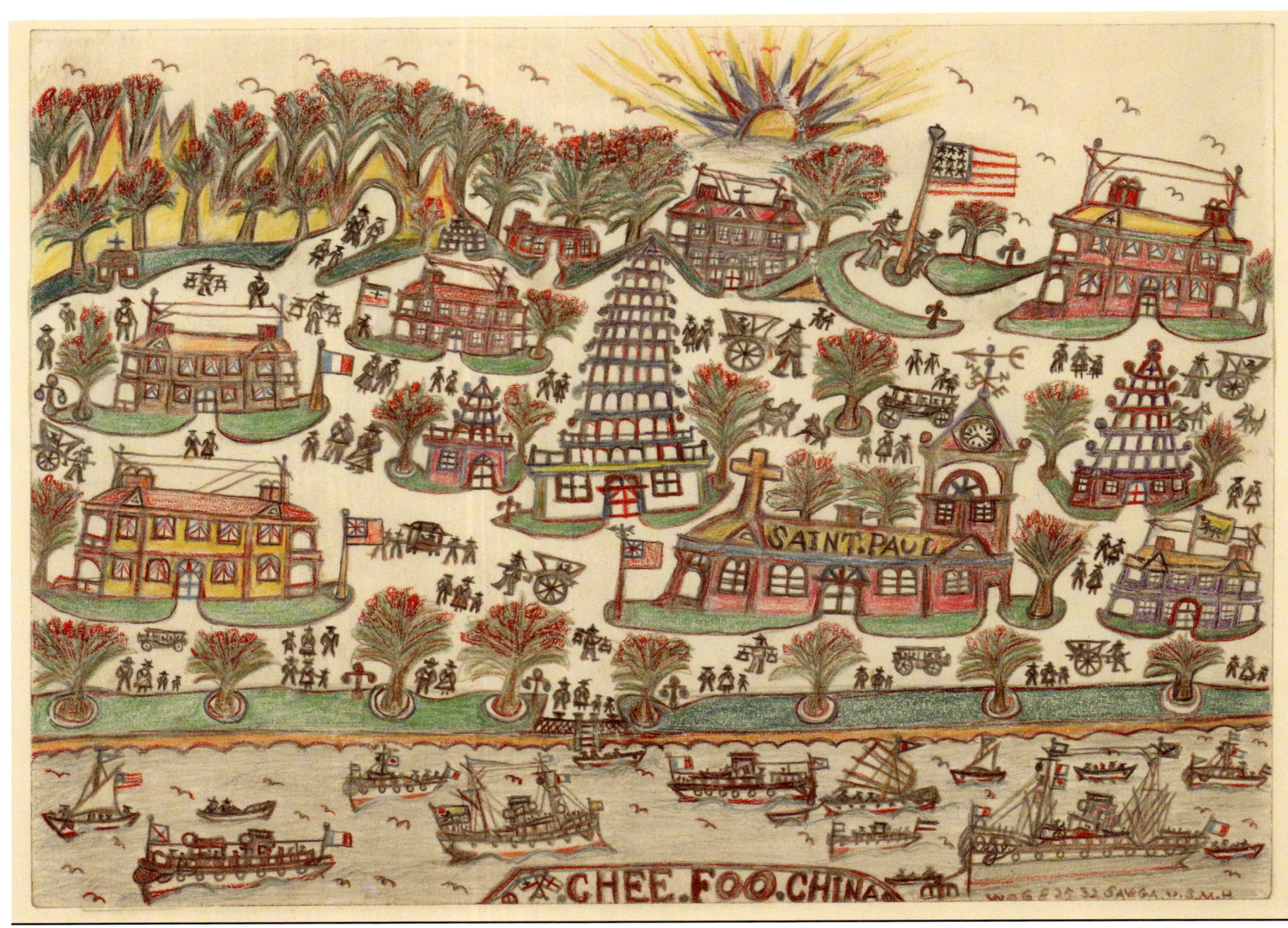

Chee Foo, China, 1932 (not included in the exhibition)

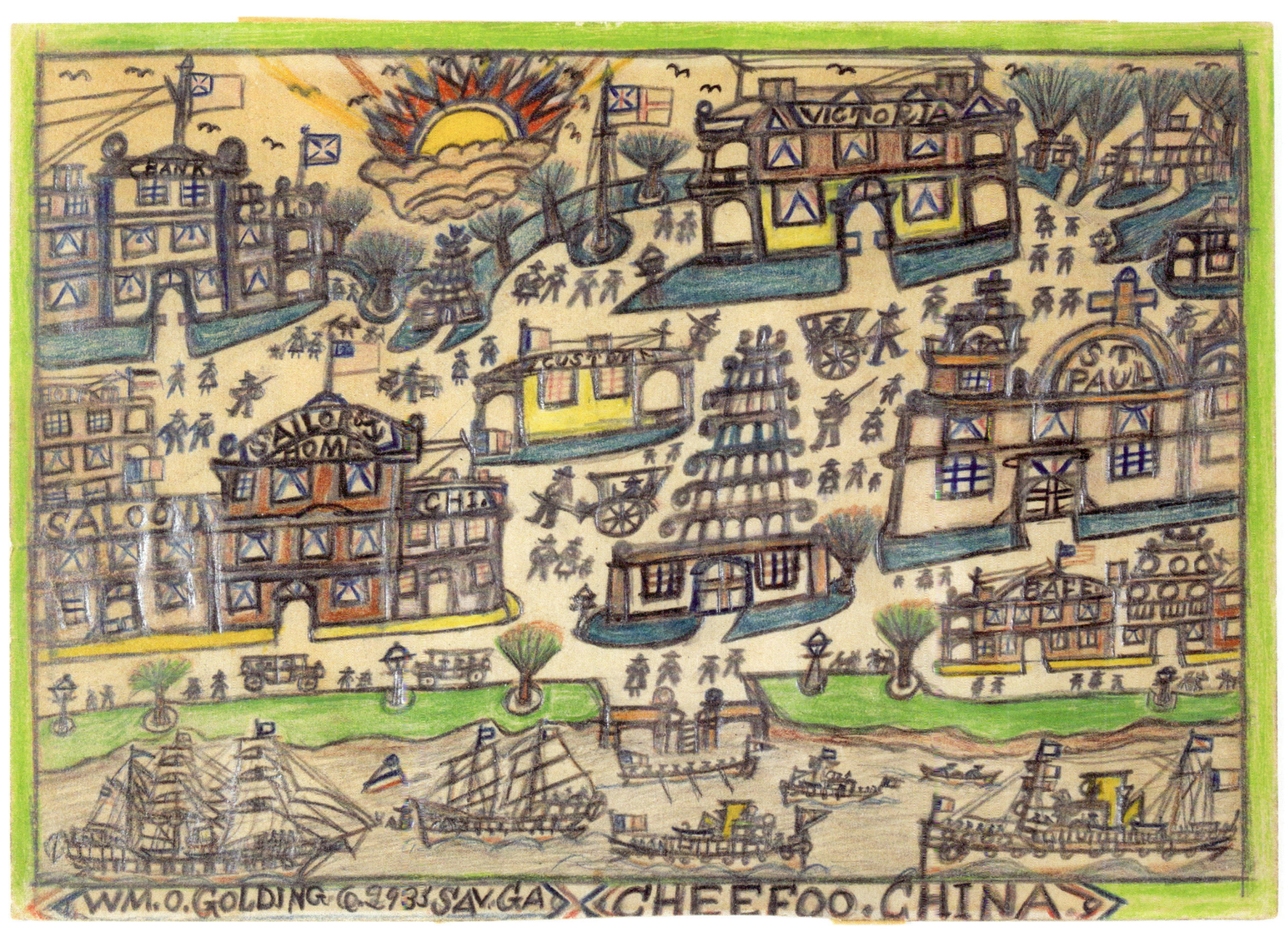

PLATE 54. *Cheefoo, China, 1935*

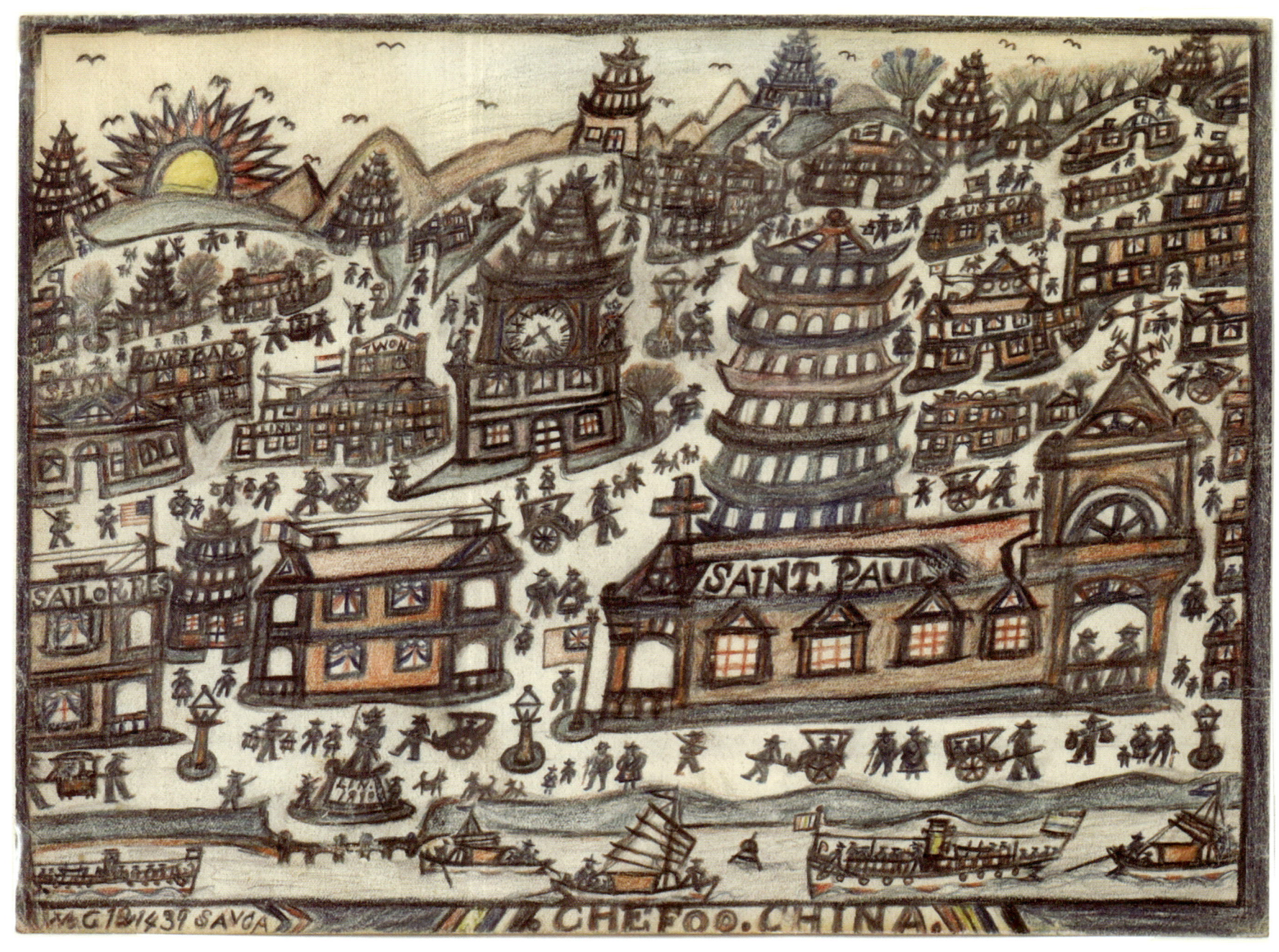

PLATE 55. *Chefoo, China, 1939*

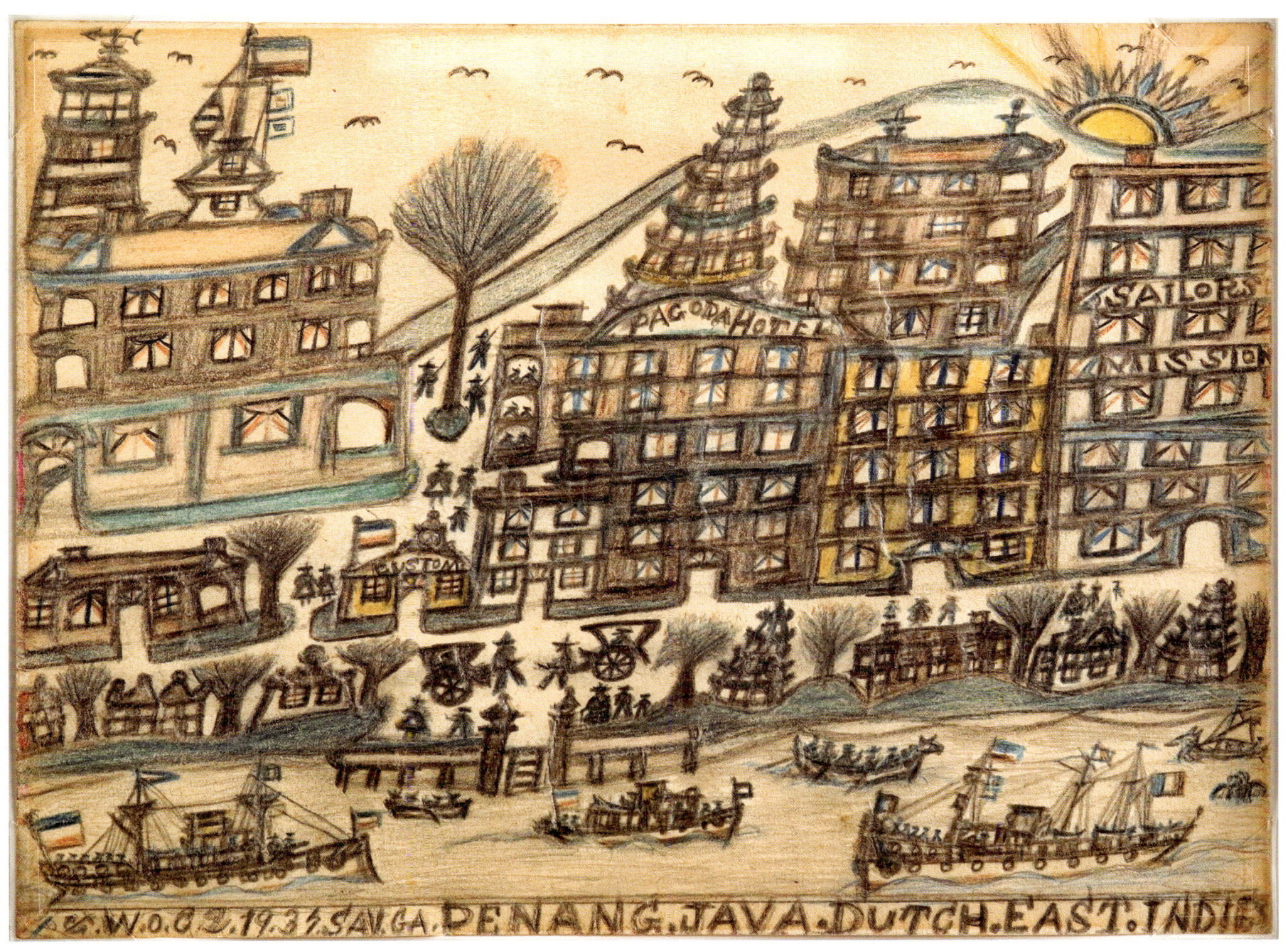

PLATE 56. *Penang, Java, Dutch East Indies, 1937*

THE SPANISH-AMERICAN WAR, THE PHILIPPINE WAR, AND WORLD WAR I

William O. Golden served in the US Navy for ten years between 1892 and 1902, a period encompassing the Spanish-American War in Cuba, defeat of Spain in the Philippines, and the war of resistance in the Philippine archipelago that followed. His drawings speak to the development of new armored cruisers and fortifications leading up to the Spanish-American War and even reference a war story closer to home in Savannah. He made two drawings of the Philippines potentially connected to his service there, and others that may reference an incident he experienced during World War I.

Golden's involvement in the Spanish-American War in Cuba is unknown, but he was clearly aware of vessels associated with the conflict, as evidenced by his portraits of the USS Texas and smaller depictions of US warships of the period in other drawings. The Texas was one of two new steel gunships ordered in the 1890s, along with the USS Maine, its principal claim to military fame coming during service in the battle of Santiago de Cuba in 1898 (Fig. 1). Golden's 1933 drawing of the Texas (Pl. 58) seems a composite of two different ships bearing that name. Although the ship's profile clearly resembles the 1892 cruiser, the large fore-and-aft guns are more reminiscent of the later dreadnought USS Texas

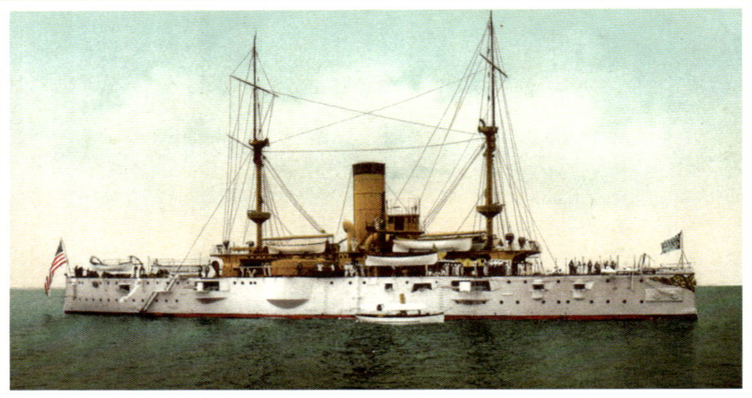

Fig. 1. *U. S. Protected Cruiser "Texas." 400 Officers and Men. Length 325 Feet. Main Battery 18 Guns. (Postcard), 1932. Edward H. Mitchell, Publisher, San Francisco.*

of World War I. His 1935 drawing of the Texas shows the casement-mounted guns of the earlier battleship. The question remains whether Golden merely knew of the Texas or saw the ship, perhaps when it was anchored near Savannah in Charleston, South Carolina, in 1908. [1]

A Spanish-American War story closer at hand to Savannah is represented in two drawings Golden made of the tugboat *Dauntless* in 1933 and 1934 (Pls. 59, 60). The *Dauntless* received national attention as one of several tugs based in Jacksonville, Florida, and coastal Georgia used for "filibustering" (unauthorized gun-running missions to Cuban independence fighters prior to the war). Built in 1893, the *Dauntless* was docked in Brunswick, south of Savannah, when purchased in 1895 by Jacksonville-based supporters of Cuban rebels, for the purpose of delivering guns, ammunition, and supplies to Cuba (Fig. 2). The *Dauntless*, a fast vessel, made numerous successful runs under Captain James W. Floyd, an African American mariner, notably identified by Golden in both drawings. Floyd's story was covered in the press and later commemorated in a 1929 article in W.E.B. Dubois' *The Crisis*. [2] In the earlier drawing Golden intriguingly locates the *Dauntless* "off Sapelo Island, GA, on 15 Jan. 1898." This detail may imply that

that Golden heard the story from someone close to the *Dauntless*, which was operating out of Savannah on that date. In both drawings, however, Golden draws the *Dauntless* flying the Cuban flag from its foremast, echoing a flag hoisted at a light station.

Two depictions of the Philippines speak to the artist's involvement there during the Philippine-American War. A currently unlocated drawing, pictured in a 1977 Sotheby Parke Bernet auction, is perhaps Golden's most direct depiction of this experience. This 1932 image of Cavite may be intended to show then-Commodore Dewey's Asiatic fleet in Manila Bay (Fig. 3). Eight or more warships or naval vessels and numerous smaller craft are pictured patrolling the bay. On the right, Golden depicts an armed fortification and lighthouse and a large building identified by the inscription "Dewey HQ." To the left of the bay, colonial structures are arrayed under an erupting volcano, possibly one of several dormant volcanoes near Manila or the active Mount Mayon located farther south.

Almost a year after drawing Cavite, Golding made a drawing entitled *Luson, P.I.*, perhaps picturing Manila's waterfront, again with an erupting volcano. As in many of Golden's port scenes, the waterfront bund is populated by figures as well as vehicles, including ice and coal trucks seemingly from a time after his Navy years. Waterfront establishments with swinging saloon doors offer the port's pleasures under a variety of names and flags: a British bar named "Chile Joes," an American bar called "Frisco Bill," a café flying a French flag ad-

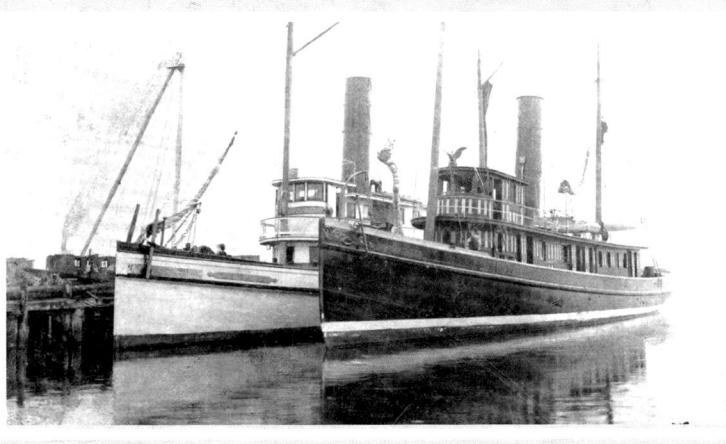

Fig. 2. *"The City's Famous Tugs: Three Friends and Dauntless,"* not dated. *Courtesy of the Jacksonville Historical Society, Family Album 12.*

vertising lunch and beds, and a sailor's mission. Unlike his view of Cavite, the waterfront here displays an American presence but little sign of military activity. Although Golden did not portray individual warships directly involved in the Philippines, he drew several vessels named *Petrel*, which was the name of a gunboat in Dewey's fleet. Vessels that Golden drew with the name *Petrel* include a whaler, a three-masted ship, and a steam yacht, although none match the ship from the Philippines conflict.

Aside from drawings referencing the war in Cuba and the Philippines, a military thread runs through Golden's work. He pictures coastal fortifications around the world, as well as naval training ships, historical battleships, and naval vessels in strategic ports. Coastal batteries with casements sporting anywhere from one to seven protruding cannons may be found in at least sixteen of Golden's drawings. Even his fanciful self-titled vessel (Pl. 22) includes a fortification in the background, indicating this type of installation was a familiar part of his experience. Fortifications dominate one of his two drawings of Fort Morgan, Alabama, a military base that saw multiple periods of use and was reopened during the Spanish-American War. In addition to the casements and guns of Fort Morgan's Endicott batteries, Golden depicts post buildings, such as an officers' club and a general's office labeled with a date of 1899.

Other drawings seemingly depict military confrontations or exercises of uncertain date. Golden made four drawings of the Rock

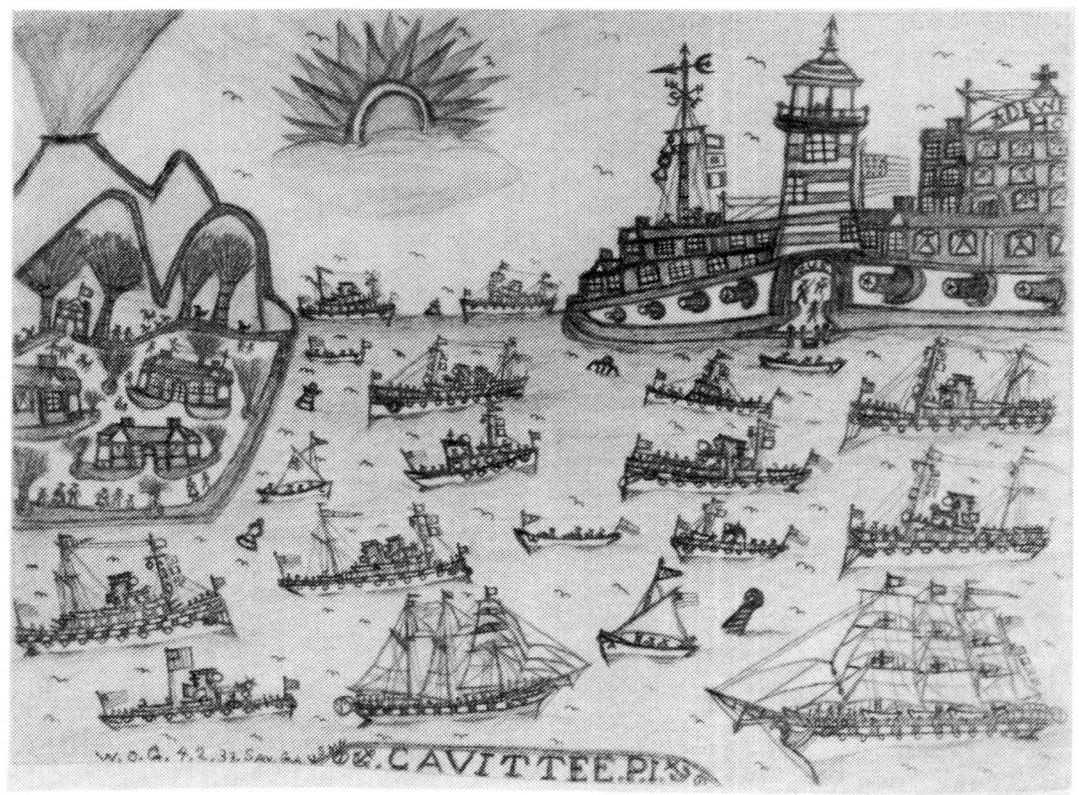

Fig. 3. William O. Golding, Cavitee, P.I., 1932
(unlocated), reproduced in Property from the Estate
of the Late Edith Kane Baker, Sale Number 4039,
Sotheby Parke Bernet Inc., New York, 1977.

of Gibraltar, a British territory and strategic outpost guarding the entrance to the Mediterranean. Golden references this military dimension of the famous monolith in two drawings from 1936 that both show a fleet of turn-of-the-century British warships steaming in from the left to greet a formation of American gunboats, led by a square-rigged American sailing ship. Golden may have been representing the international tour of the US Great White Fleet that stopped in Gibraltar in 1909 or the US Navy base established later at the fortified British outpost in 1917. [3]

Although he was discharged from the Navy in 1902, Golden's life as a mariner intersected dramatically with events of the First World War. A pair of his drawings depict strategic points on the English Channel: Eddystone Light, a key warning beacon south of Plymouth, and Ushant (Ouessant), a French island on the southwest side of the Channel. Neither drawing shows wartime events outright, but the Channel was the site of a dramatic episode in Golden's life. On June 27, 1917, The Brooklyn Daily Eagle reported the sinking of the American ship Galena two days prior in the English Channel by a German U-boat about 760 miles southwest of Ushant (Fig. 4). The Galena had just delivered seven thousand barrels of oil to Rouen and was returning to New York with a cargo of burlap. Aboard the Galena was a crew of eighteen, among them six African American seamen, including "W. O. Golding" of Savannah. [4] The Germans captured the Galena and sank it with bombs but allowed the crew to escape. Golden and the others were later rescued and taken to Brest, France. The same day, newspapers around the world announced the arrival in Brest of the first US troops in France, who had managed to elude the waiting German submarines. This episode highlights dangers faced by merchant seamen like Golden in the new era of globetrotting submarine warfare, with the English Channel a site of numerous sinkings of American merchant ships.

Golden's first drawing of the English Channel, his 1934 Eddystone

Light, features the beacon surrounded by steam and sailing ships but no obvious military activity. More telling is his drawing *Ushant, France,* from 1935 (Pl. 65). Golden depicts the island on the left, with a lighthouse and signal station flying the French flag. On the opposite side, by compressing distance, he may represent the French mainland. There, a French flag flies over armed fortifications from which an officer speaks through a bullhorn, accompanied by a rifle-carrying soldier. A trio of smaller American sailing vessels are shown on the left, one towing another, with French vessels appearing on the right. Although Golden's work sidesteps literal depictions of wartime conflicts, the military presence in this drawing affirms his experience.

Golden's drawings of steam yachts also figure into the years of the Spanish-American War and the Great War in that many private yachts were pressed into service by the US Navy. During World War I, private vessels were purchased by the US for use in different capacities: protecting merchant vessels and troop ships headed for France, hunting U-boats, and picking up the survivors of submarine attacks. Some steam yachts were operating in the English Channel, near the site of Golden's rescue, including the *Corsair,* which Golden depicted.

One of Golden's sailing-ship portraits references another World War I danger to merchant ships: German raiders. In 1939, Golden drew the *Seeadler,* notorious for destroying merchant vessels in the Atlantic and Pacific. Starting out as the British-built merchant ship *Pass of Balmaha,* the vessel was captured by a German submarine in 1915 and outfitted with weapons. [5] Renamed *Seeadler* ("Sea Eagle"), the ship captured and sank some sixteen vessels in 1916 and 1917. Golden depicts the *Seeadler* flying the German Imperial Navy jack from its mizzenmast. He names the ship's commander as "Capt. Von Luckner," meaning Felix von Luckner, noted for his cunning as well as his avoidance of loss of life in his raids. Golden, like other merchant mariners of the time would have been aware of the raider

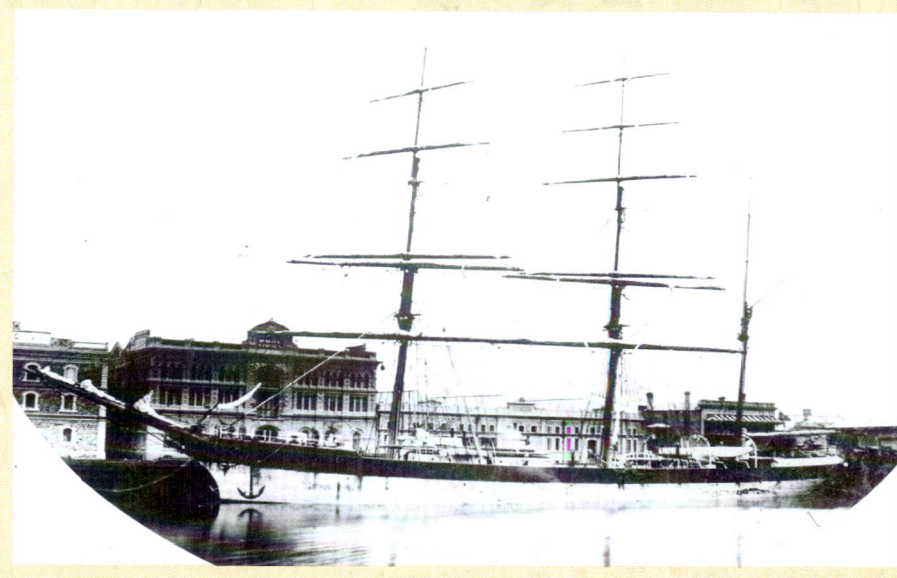

Fig. 4. Galena, *originally* Foomang Suey, *Honolulu. 1060 tons. Built at Glasgow. 1888. (Steel). gelatin silver photograph, 10.2 x 15.5 cm., Accession no: H99.220/2059, Brodie Collection, La Trobe Picture Collection, State Library of Victoria.*

from news accounts and could have heard about the *Seeadler's* demise four months after his survival of the *Galena* sinking. The romance of the *Seeadler,* the last sailing ship to be used in warfare, and its daring captain, likely appealed to Golden, who drew so many historic sailing vessels. —H.D.

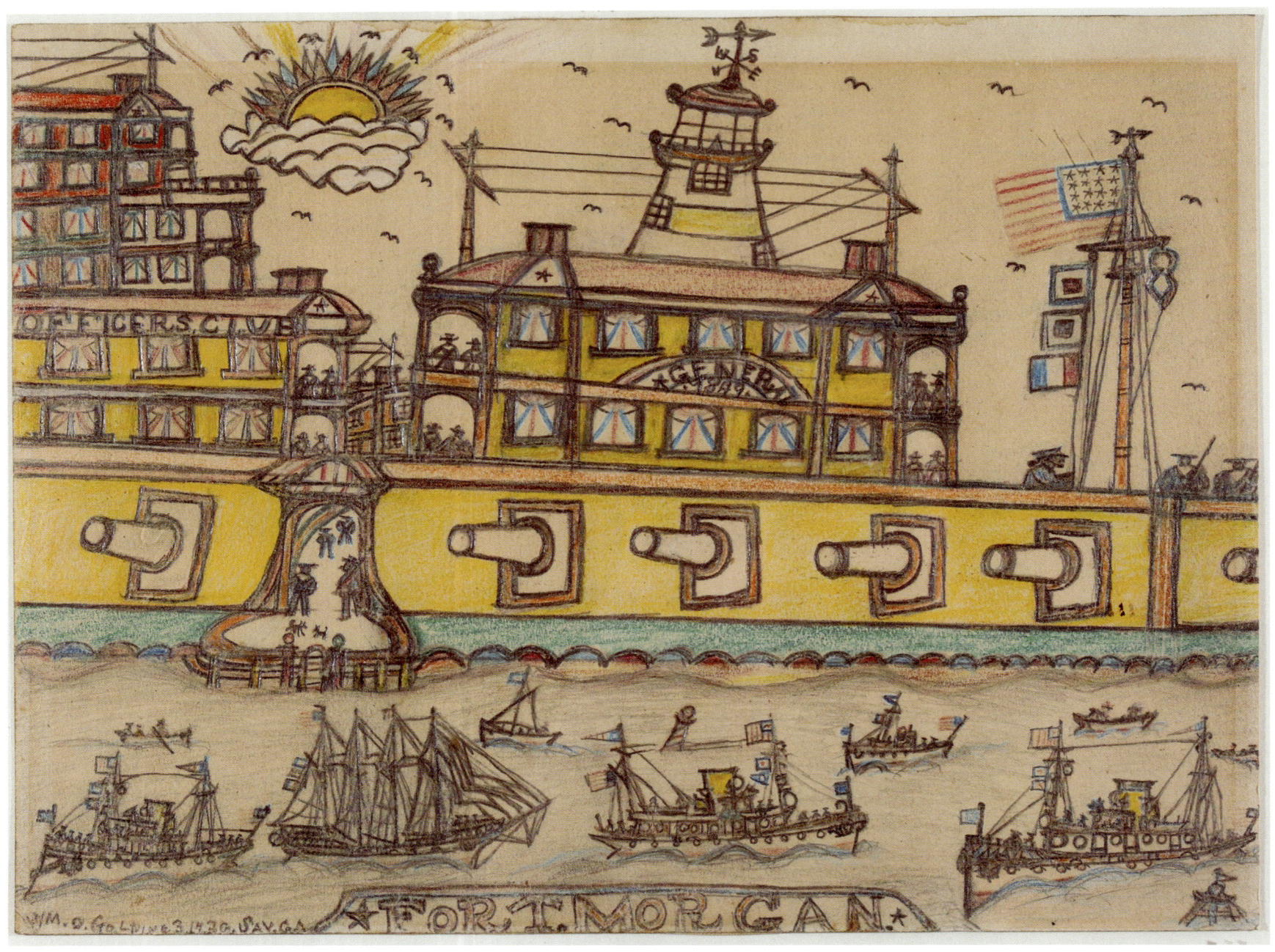

PLATE 57. *Fort Morgan, 1936*

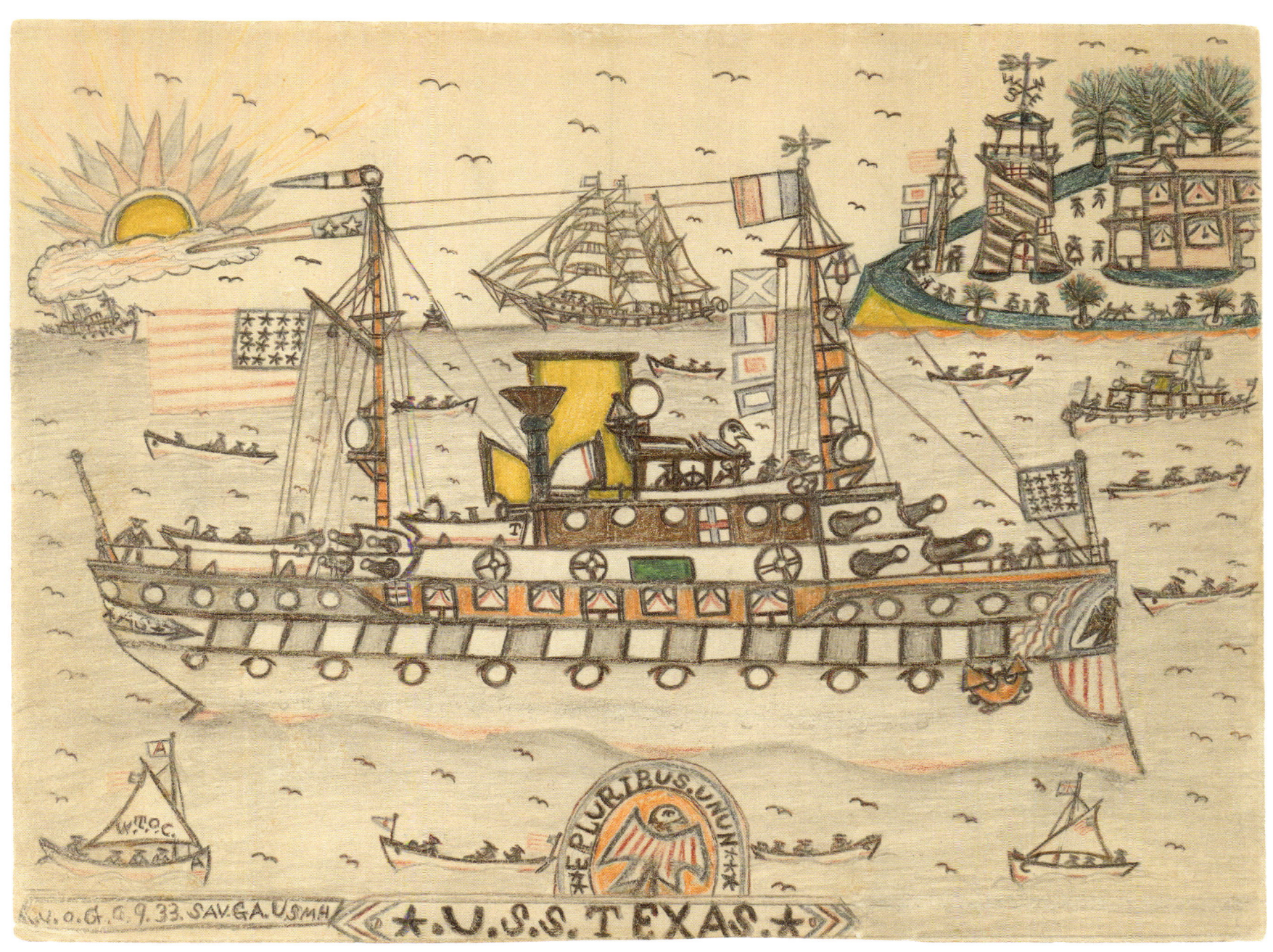

PLATE 58. *U.S.S. Texas*, 1933

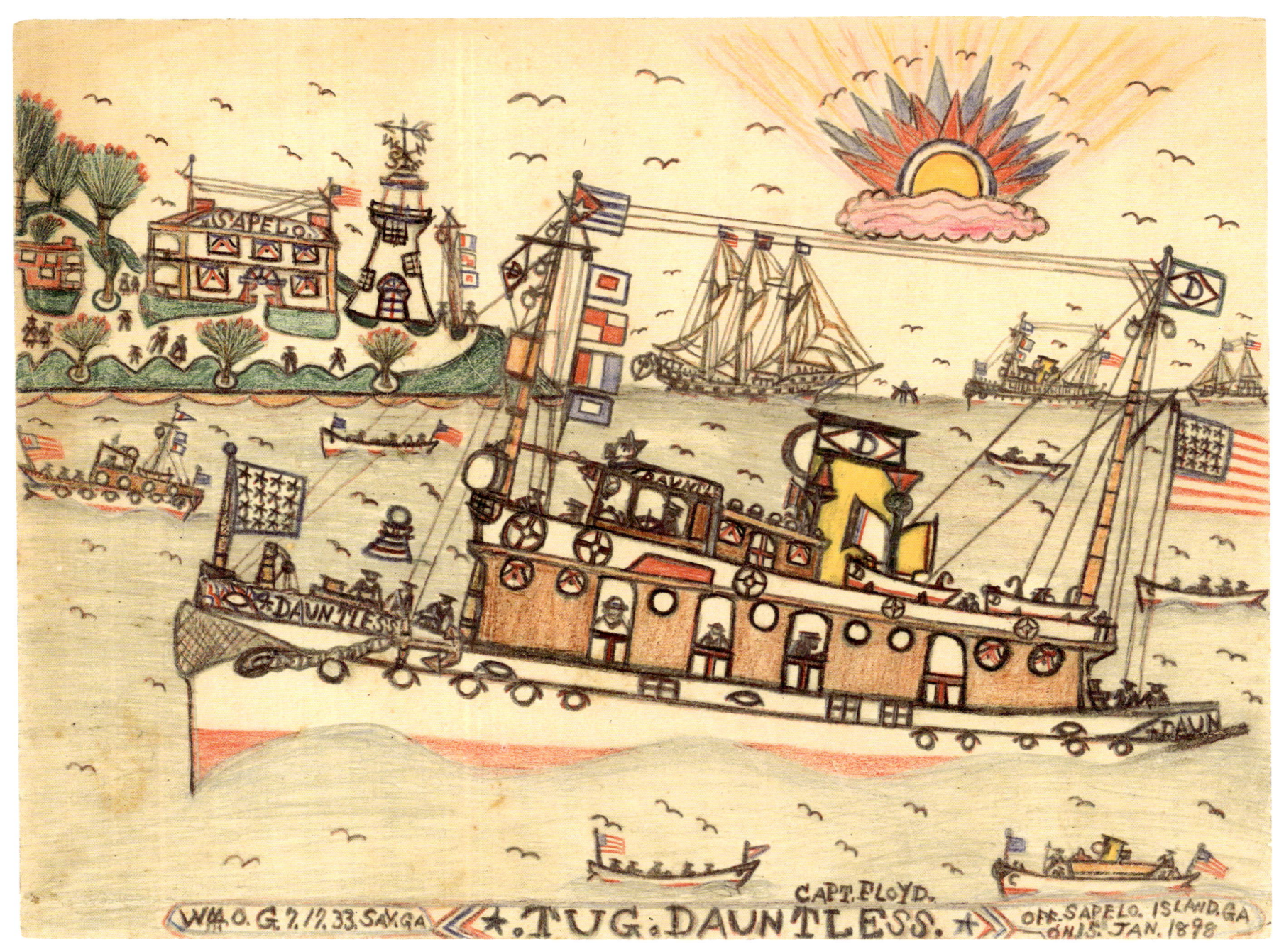

PLATE 59. *Tug Dauntless, Off Sapelo Island, GA on 15, Jan. 1898, 1933*

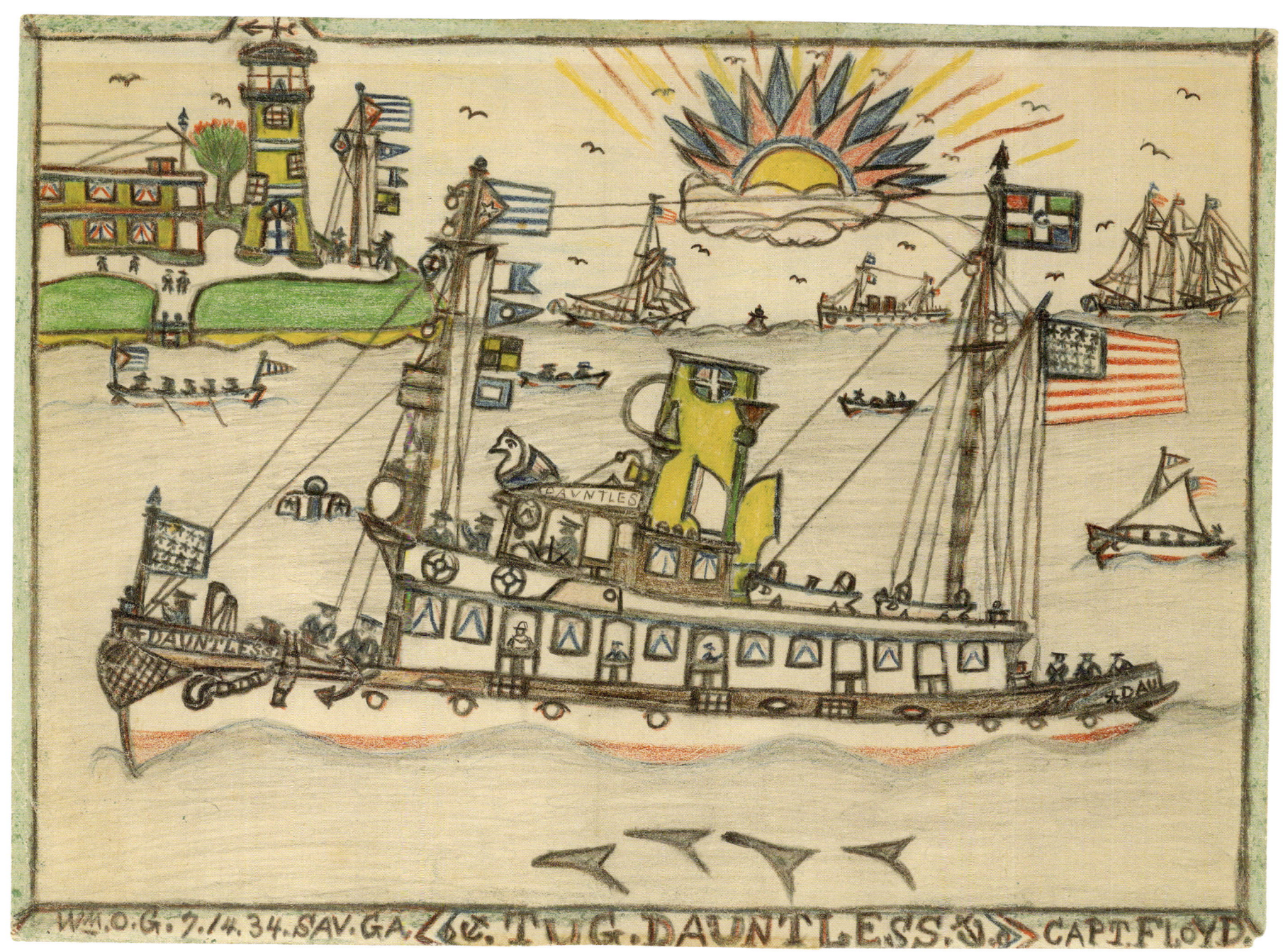

PLATE 60. *Tug Dauntless, Capt. Floyd,* 1934

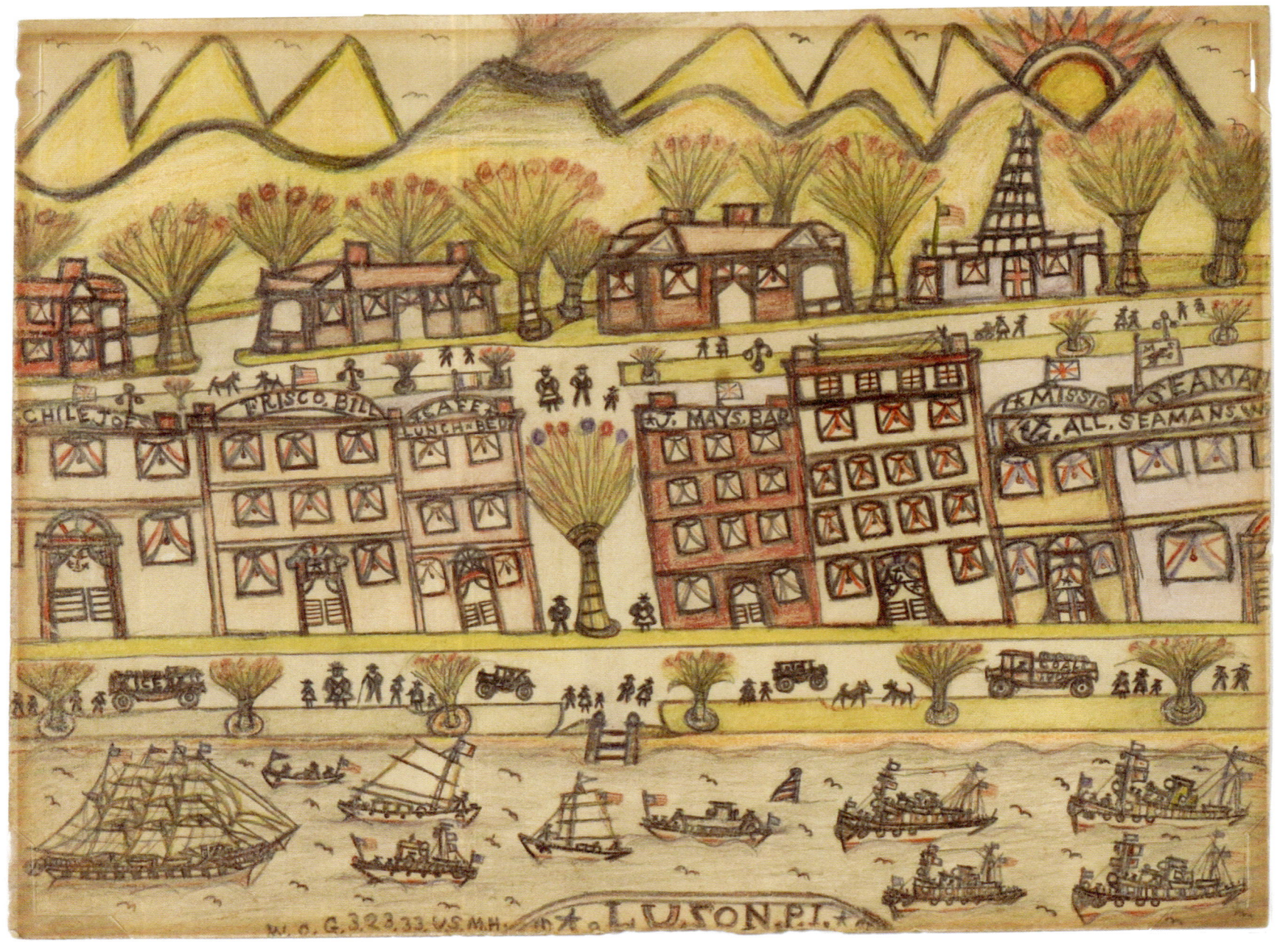

PLATE 61. *Luson, P.I.*, 1933

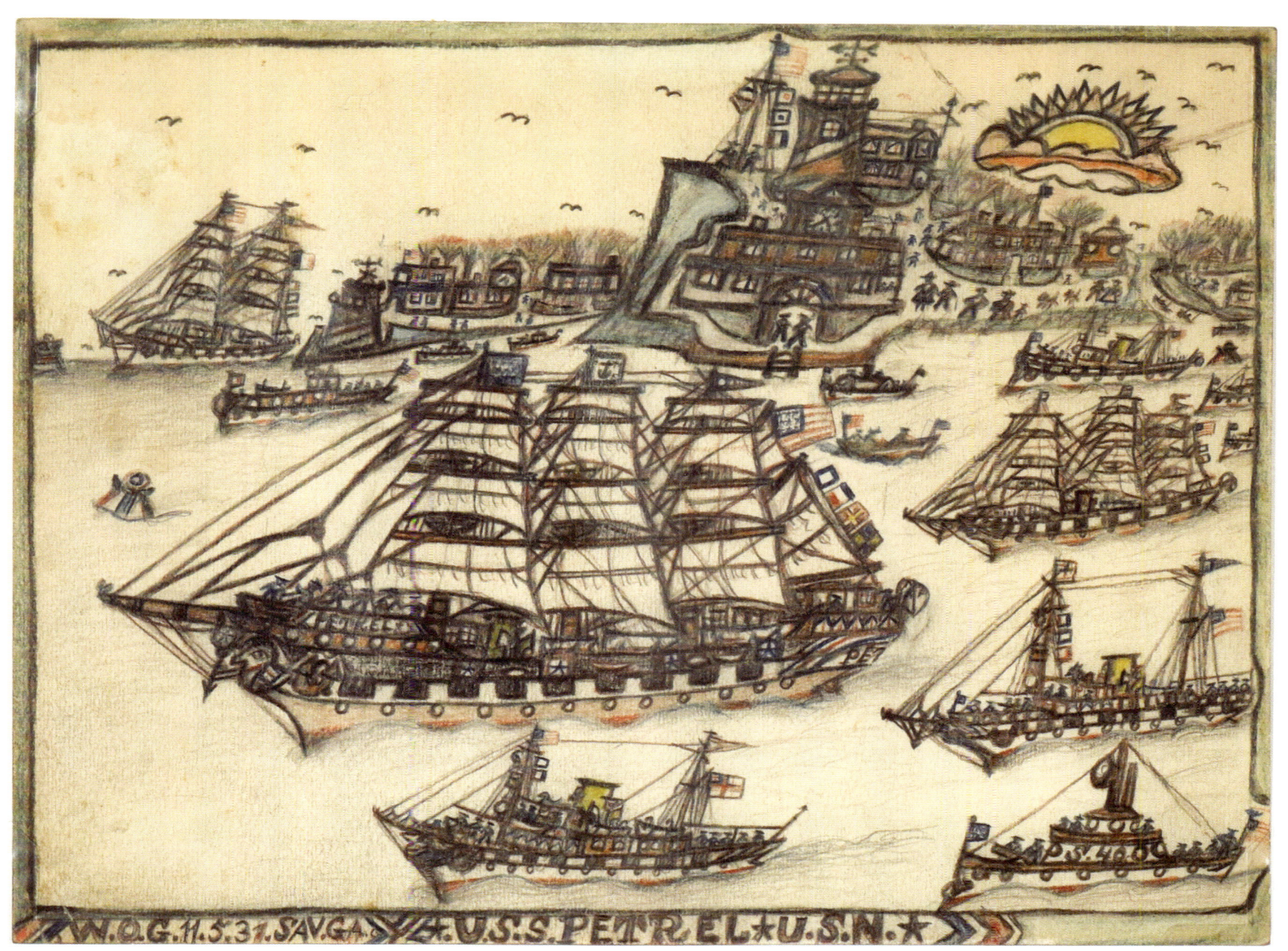

PLATE 62. *U.S.S. Petrel, U.S.N.,* 1937

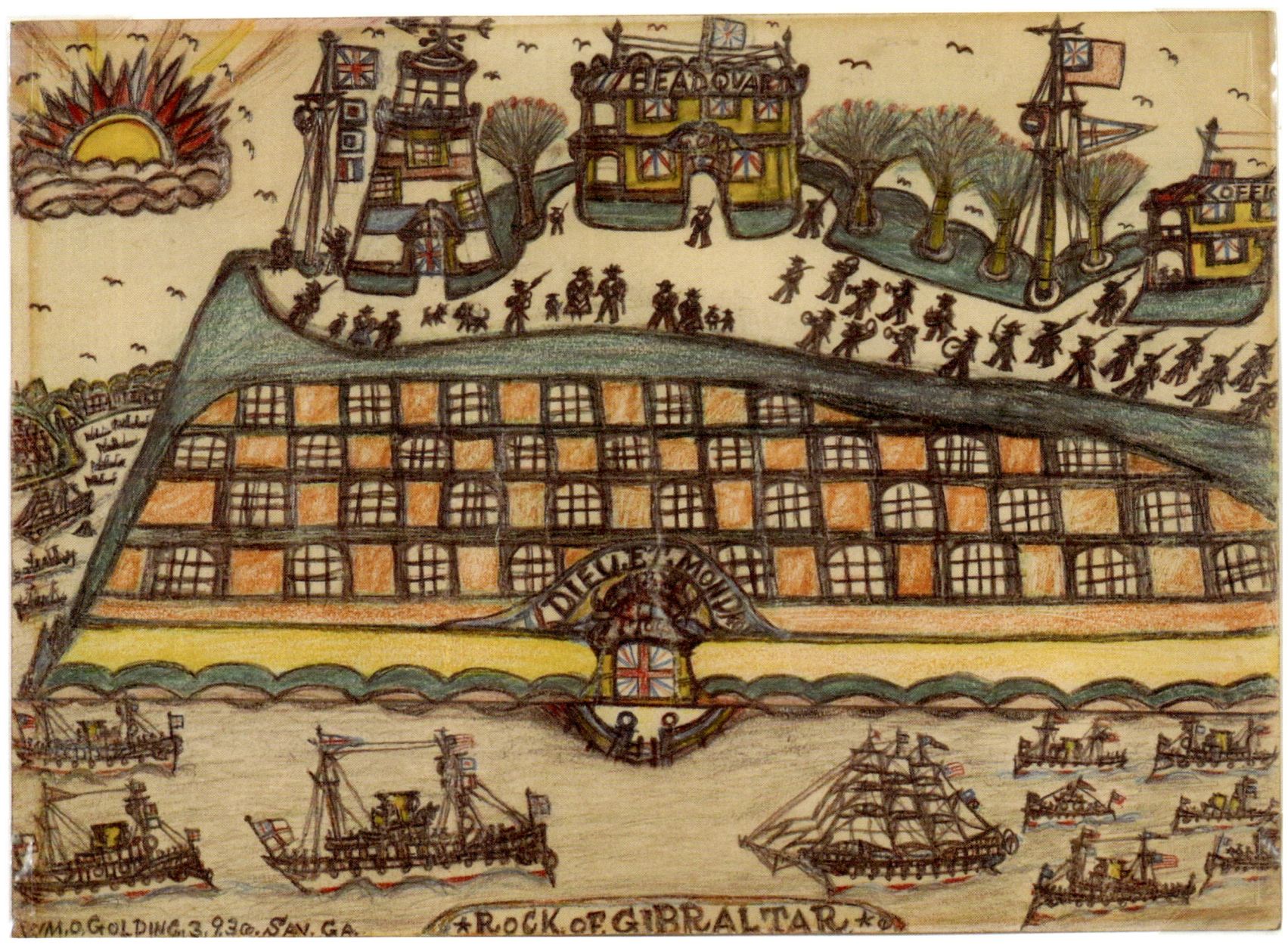

PLATE 63. *Rock of Gibraltar*, 1936

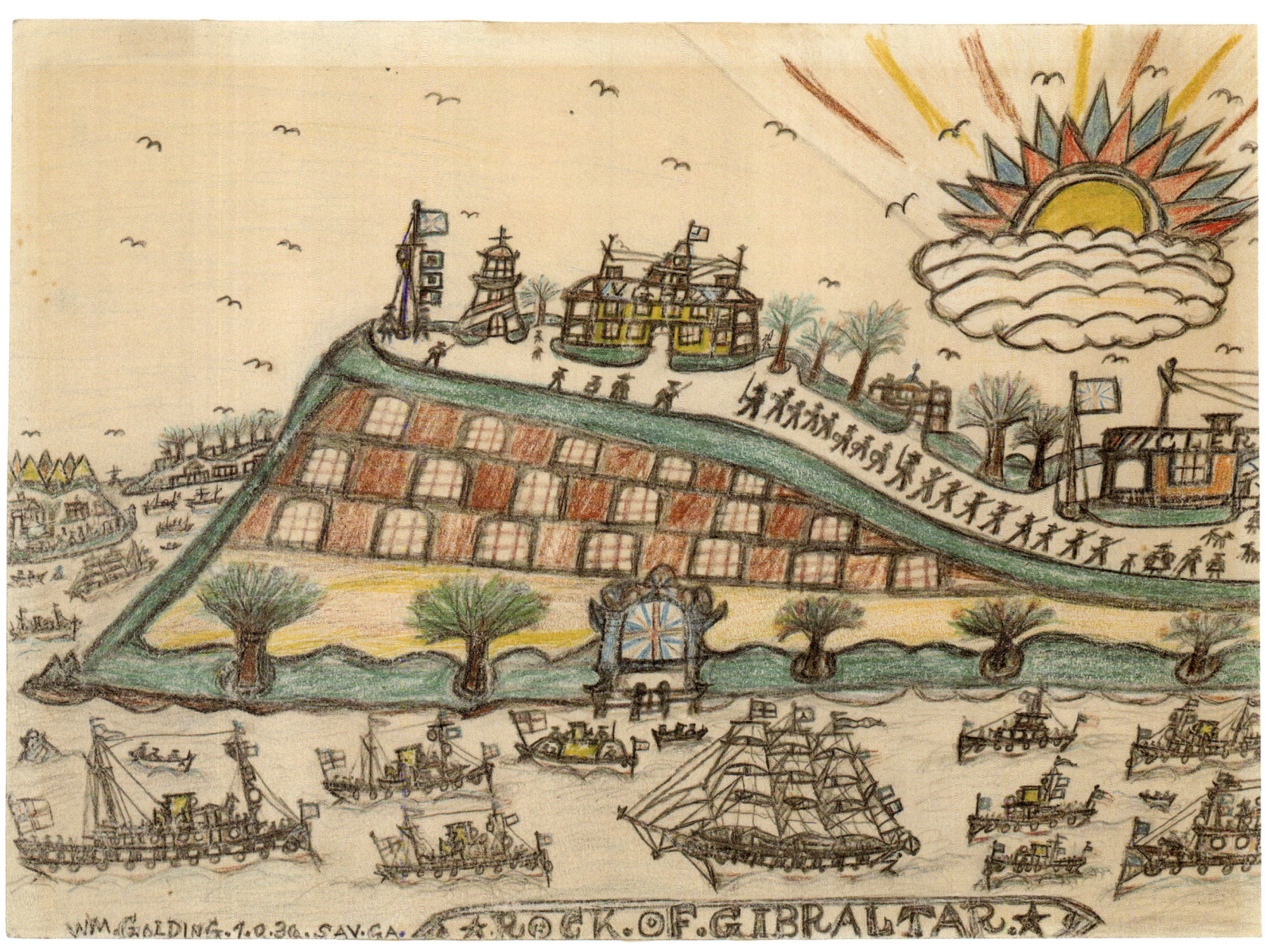

PLATE 64. *Rock of Gibraltar,* 1936

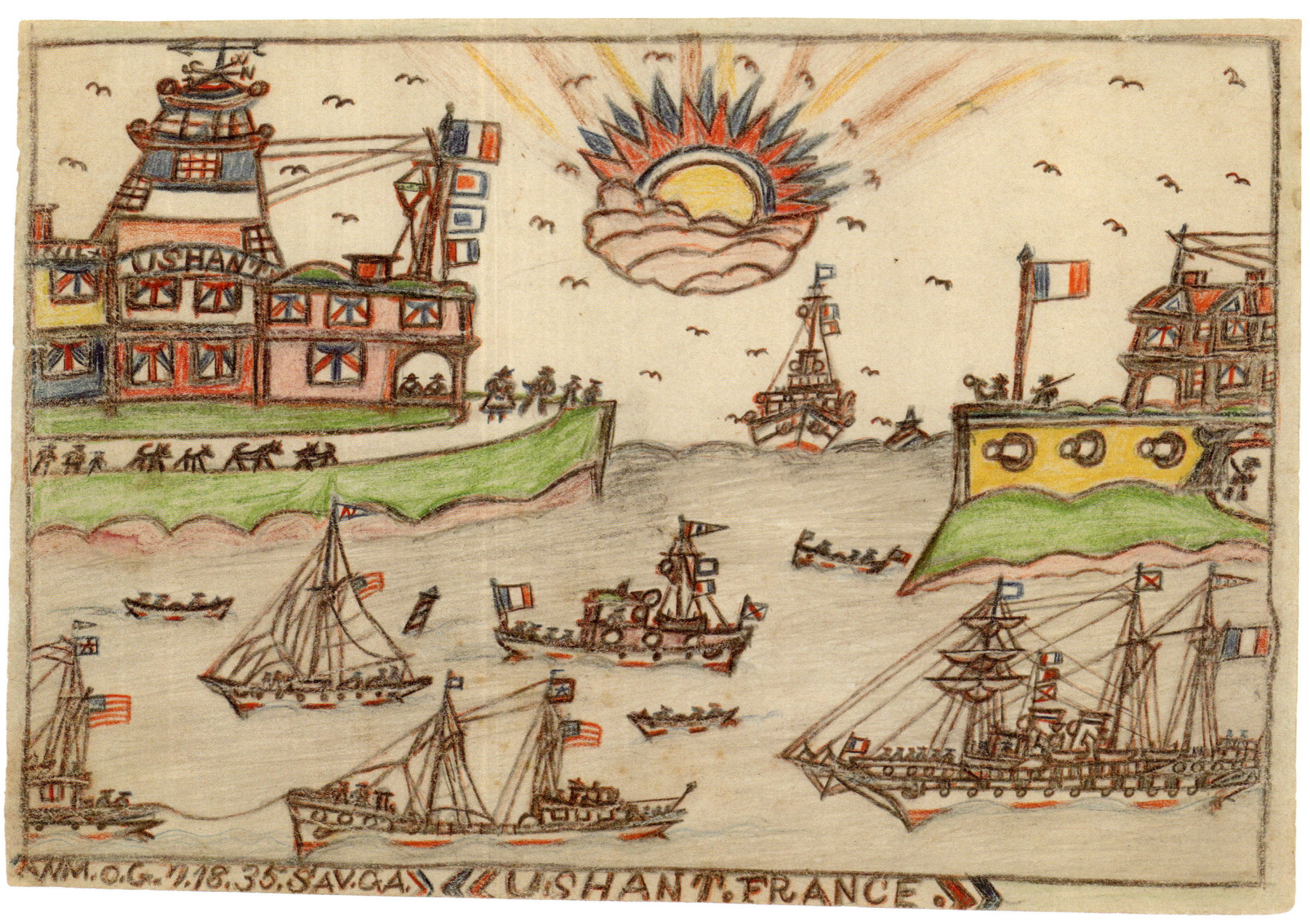

PLATE 65. *Ushant, France, 1935*

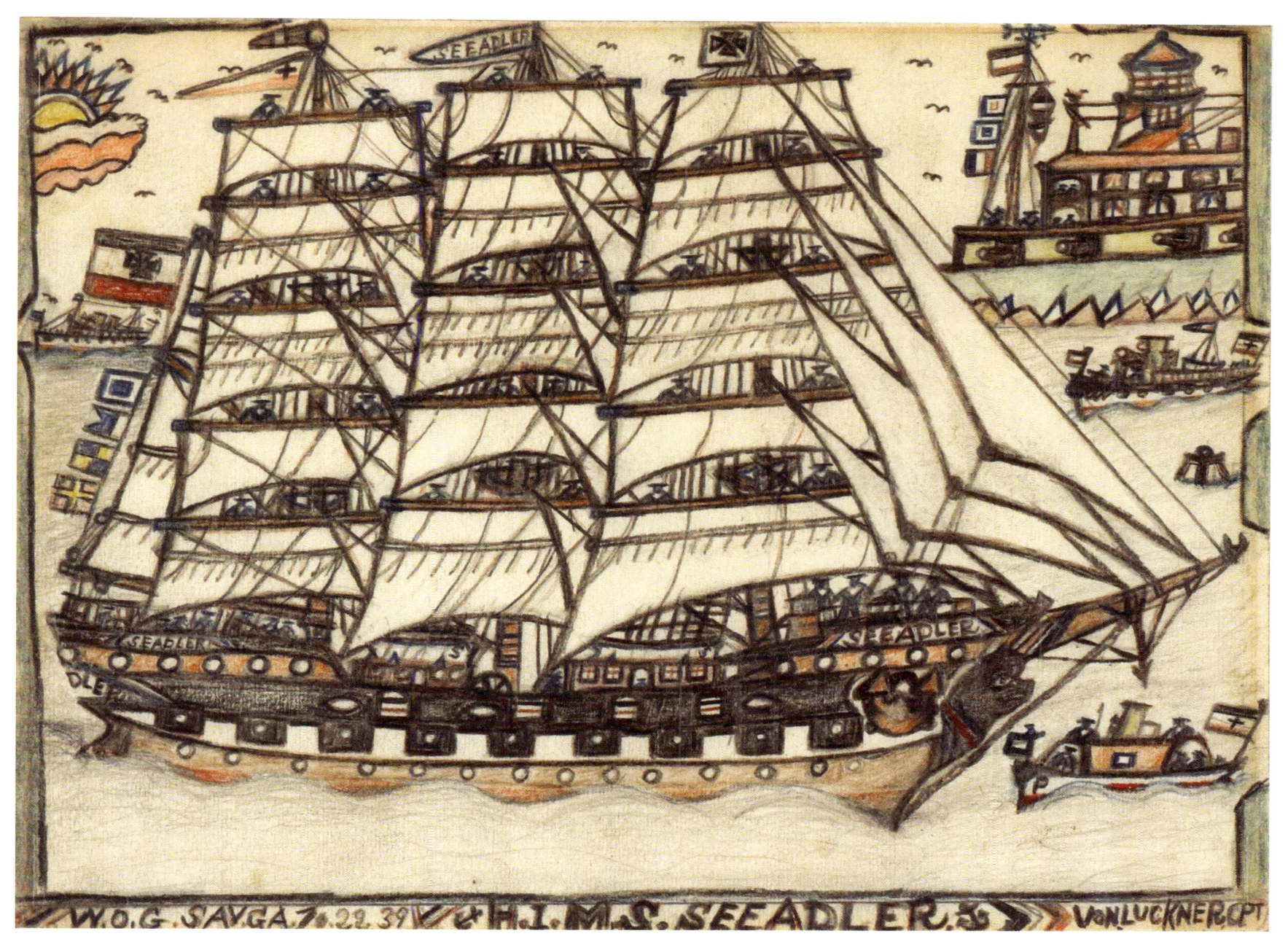

PLATE 66. *H.I.M.S. Seeadler, Von Luckner, Cpt., 1939*

THE HOME PORT: SAVANNAH

After decades working at sea, William O. Golden spent his later years in Savannah, most of that time apparently in the Marine Hospital. When Margaret Stiles first met him there, he only drew "sailing ships and the Savannah water front," suggesting that he began his artistic journey by drawing from his strongest memories, including the impressive sailing vessels of his early experience and the familiar local environment of his later years. [1] Although his earliest drawings of Savannah may be lost, seven known images by Golden include the city's waterfront, and a handful of others depict vessels he could easily have seen on visits home or during periods when he was not in the hospital.

A work illustrated in the *Savannah Morning News* and documented in folk art collector Herbert Hemphill's archives is Golden's only known drawing of Savannah's port without a featured vessel. On June 28, 1935, Golden drew this colorful depiction of Savannah as seen from the river, his lack of formal training in perspective resulting in a flattened image of the city in which buildings, watercraft, figures, and other details share equal importance (Fig. 1). A real-life ferry named the *Island Girl* is shown departing from the Seaboard Air Line Company's wharf. On River Street, Golden renders the Savannah Cotton Exchange with its distinctive underpass, Artley's contracting and constructing

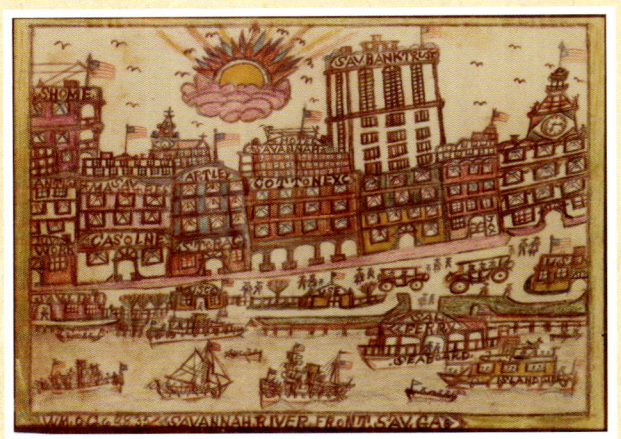

Fig. 1. *William O. Golding, Savannah River Front, 1935. Herbert Waide Hemphill papers, 1776-1998, AAA-hempherb_3222103.tif, Herbert Waide Hemphill papers, Archives of American Art, Smithsonian Institution.*

business, and "Jax," a saloon with swinging doors. On the far right Golden includes Savannah's City Hall, and beyond Bay Street and the bluff are the Savannah Bank and Trust building, the Hotel Savannah, and a sailors' home resembling the Marine Hospital.

Savannah's waterfront provides a backdrop for drawings of three other vessels, the tug *William F. McCauley*, the USS *Tybee*, and what Golden refers to as the US engineering vessel *Isendaga (Isondega)*. Golden's 1934 drawing *Tug Wm F. McAuley, Atlantic Towing Co.* (Pl. 67) depicts the titular vessel cruising downriver past the waterfront as if to meet a vessel entering the port. Built in 1894 for the Propeller Towboat Company of Savannah, the *McCauley* was named for the towing company's then-secretary–treasurer and, later, president of the Savannah Bank and Trust Company. That bank's fifteen-story building, then and now the tallest building in downtown Savannah, looms large at the center of this drawing. Other Savannah businesses featured include the Pulaski Hotel, the *Savannah Morning News*, Germania Bank, and Kress Department Store, all of which existed when this image was created. On the far left, however, Golden draws the old City Exchange building that overlooked the river from Bay Street when Golden left Savannah as a boy, but had been replaced by the current City Hall by 1905. By the time Golden completed this drawing, the *McCauley* had escorted yachts at local regattas, was commissioned by the US Navy in 1918, and sold in the 1920s to the Atlantic Towing Company (Fig. 2). [2]

Savannah's old City Exchange also appears in one of four drawings Golden made of the Corps of Engineers vessel *Isondega*, which is pictured in a published history of the Army Corps of Engineers Savannah District (Fig. 3). Built in South Boston, Massachusetts, the vessel was sold to the government in 1919 and renamed *Isondega*, which was believed to be a Native American name for the Savannah River. [3] The *Isondega* was active on in the Savannah harbor throughout the 1920s, appearing in annual reports of the Chief of Engineers for the US Army as a "steam inspection and survey boat." [4] Golden referred to the vessel with a slightly misspelled name and a variety of prefixes—*E.D.U.S.S., U.S.E.D.U.S.S.,* and *U.S.E.U.S.S.* to refer to the US Engineers (Pls. 71, 72). Though Golden's *Isondega* differs slightly from the real-life survey boat, he carefully renders the "castle" insignia of the Corps of Engineers on the yacht's funnel. Unidentified steam vessels bearing the Corps insignia appear in two other Golden drawings of local vessels, the passenger steamer *Pilot Boy* and the Coast Guard steamer *Tybee.*

The *Tybee*, a steam launch operated by the US Coast Guard Revenue Cutter Service, was built in 1895 in the Camden, New Jersey, shipyards that a year earlier had produced the tug *William F. McCauley.* The *Tybee* was taken over by the Navy during World War I, patrolled the Savannah harbor before returning to coast guard service, and was later sold by the government in 1930. [5] Golden drew the *Tybee* four times between 1932 and 1939, in two instances depicting the launch in the Savannah River. In two early portraits of the *Tybee* at Savannah, now in the collections of the Smithsonian American Art Museum and the Morris Museum of Art (Pl. 69), the vessel cruises past the Savannah Electric and Power Company's Plant Riverside. The *Tybee*, along with the *Isondega*, turns up in other Golden drawings, including one of the steam yacht *Nourmahal.*

Golden drew other vessels that frequented the Savannah River without including the city's waterfront, among them the paddle-wheel passenger steamer *Pilot Boy* (Pl. 68). Built in Charleston in 1885, the steamboat carried passengers on a regular basis between stops in coastal South Carolina. Sold to Savannah owners in the 1900s, the *Pilot Boy* carried passengers black and white between Savannah and its older cousin port city, Charleston (fig. 4). Golden's drawing presents the steamer dominating the composition, vastly out of scale with two nearby vessels, its paddle-wheel housing emblazoned with the words "Fast Service, Charleston. Savannah." Other vessels that worked out of Savannah depicted by Golden included the paddle-wheel steamer *Altamaha*, which operated between Savannah and Augusta, Georgia, in the 1920s and 30s. He also drew the tug *Dauntless*, which worked on occasion in Savannah.

Along with his drawings of Savannah, Golden may have commemorated his birthplace in rural Southeast Georgia. A list of images in Golden's 1932 letter includes a drawing intriguingly entitled *Liberty County*. Although it is unclear whether this work depicted a scene from Liberty County or a ship named for it, the title alone suggests a link to his personal story. This connection to coastal Georgia, along with drawings of the Savannah waterfront and of vessels that Golden knew on the local scene, anchor him to one particular spot, despite his worldwide travels. Tellingly, next to the signatures he left on his works, he always notes his location, the place where he made his mark as an artist, his home port of Savannah. —H.D.

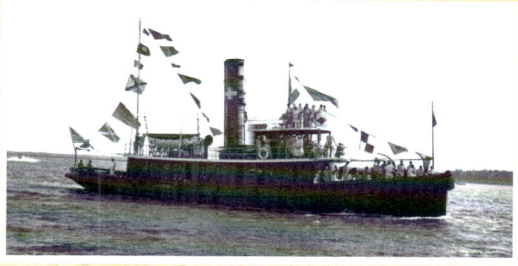

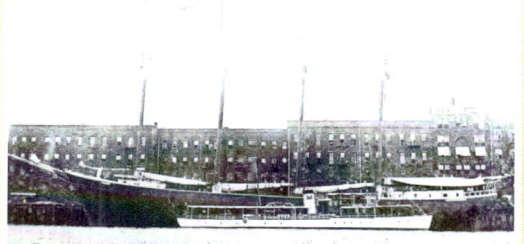

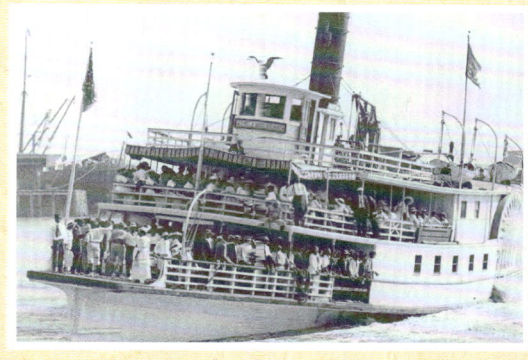

Top to bottom: Fig. 2. Yacht Racing, the William F. McCauley, 1934, MS 1360 Cordray-Foltz Photography Studio collection. Courtesy of the Georgia Historical Society, 1360-26-21-01.

Fig. 3. The Savannah District's inspection yacht Isondega, pictured in 1922 along the harbor front in Savannah, was used for inspection of the work done along the Intracoastal Waterway. Courtesy the Savannah District, Corps of Engineers.

Fig. 4. Pilot Boy steamboat, undated, MS 1361 Georgia Historical Society photograph collection. Courtesy of the Georgia Historical Society, 1361PH-29-18-5658.

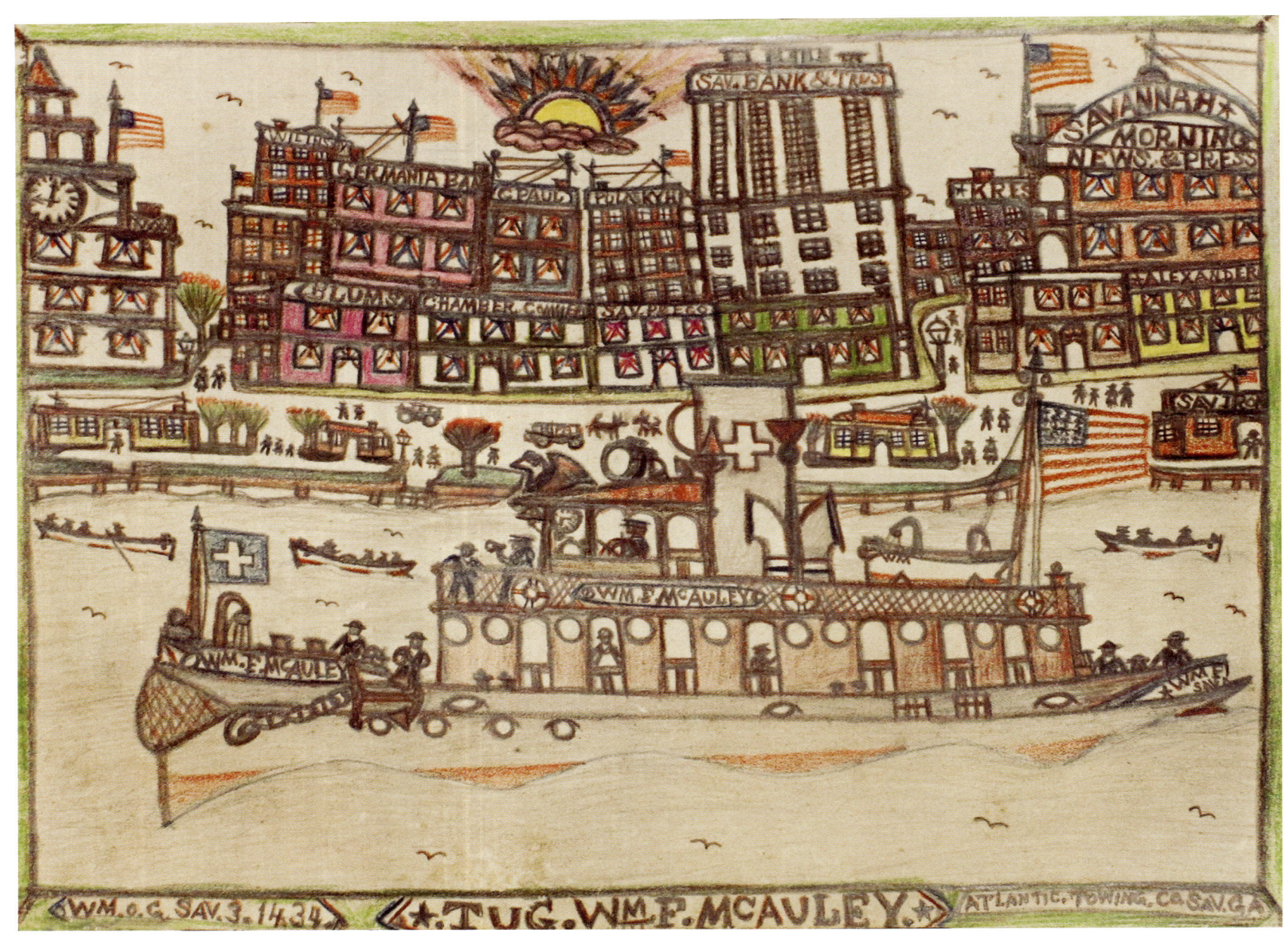

PLATE 67. *Tug Wm. F. McCauley, Atlantic Towing Co., Sav., Ga, 1934*

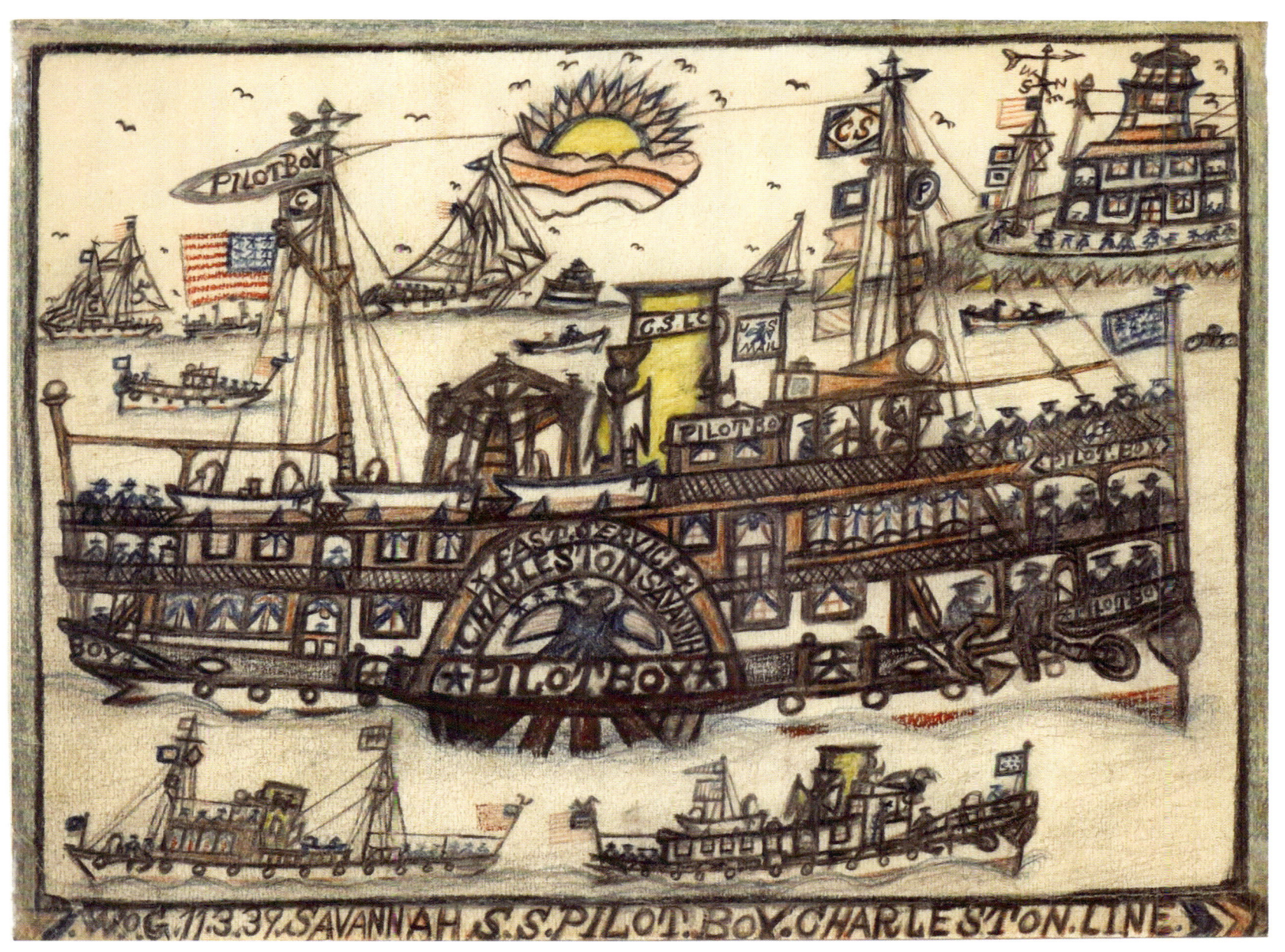

PLATE 68. *S.S. Pilot Boy, Charleston Line*, 1939

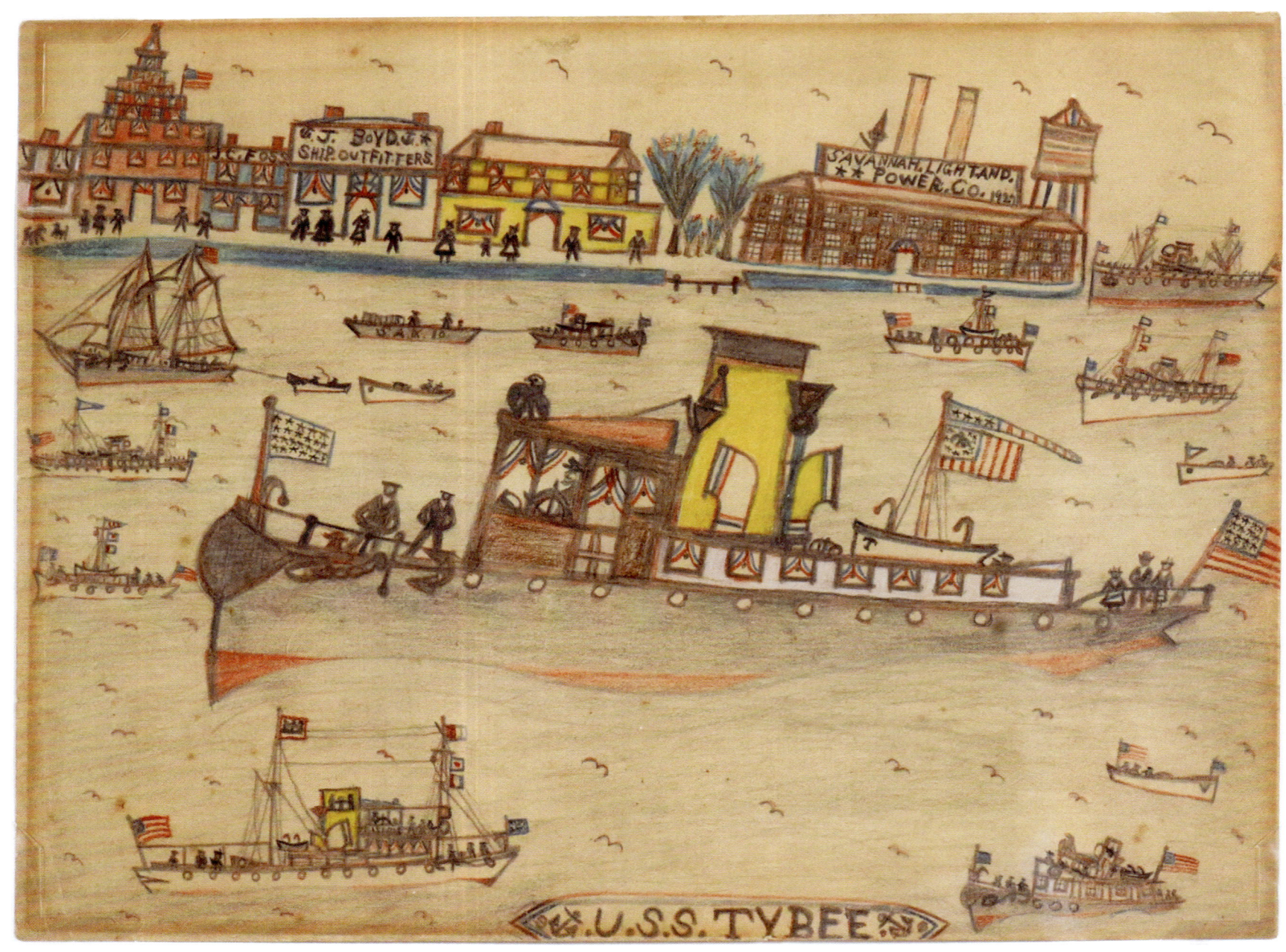

PLATE 69. *U.S.S. Tybee*, n.d.

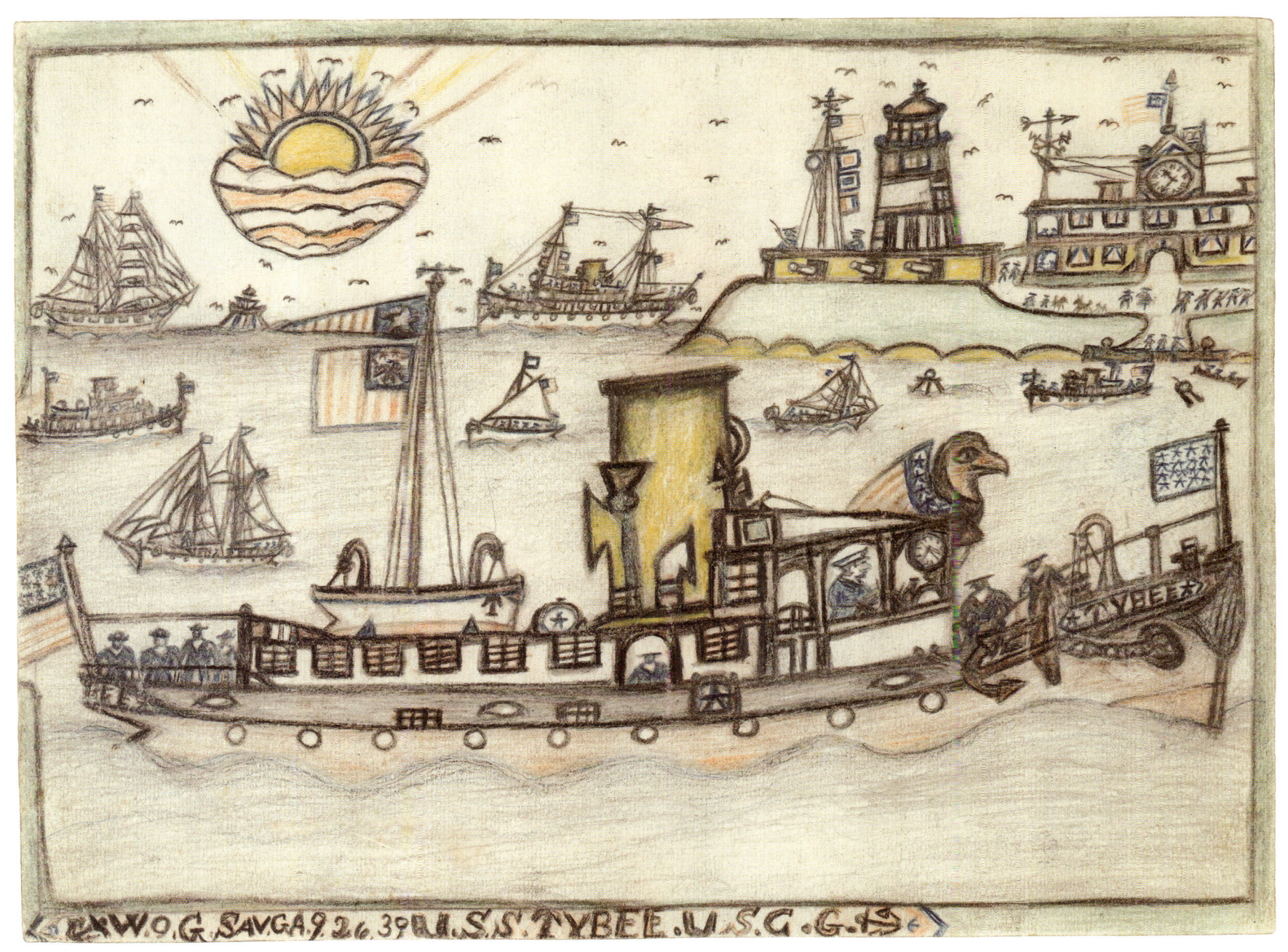

PLATE 70. *U.S.S. Tybee, U.S.C.G.,* 1939

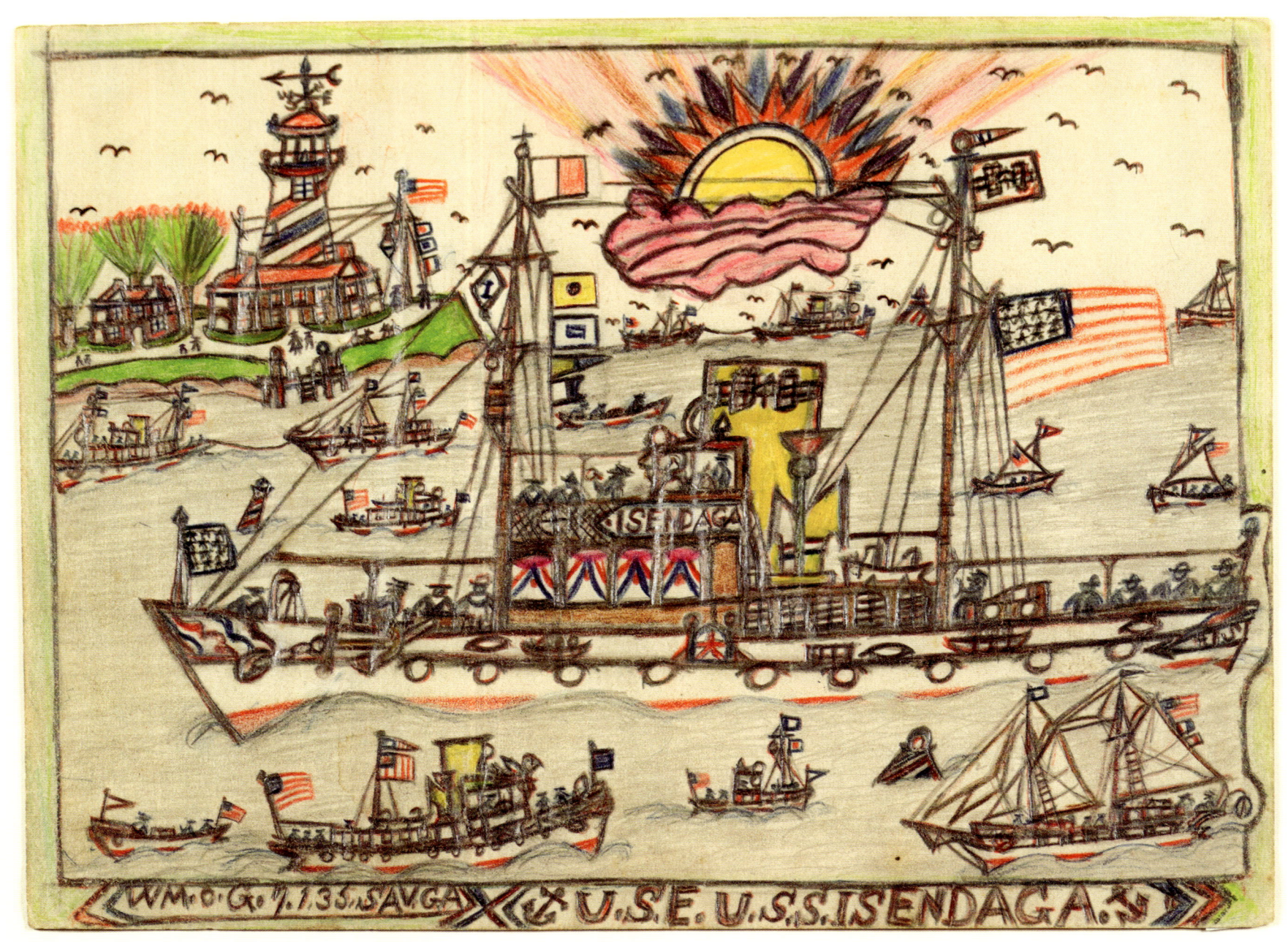

PLATE 71. *U.S.E.U.S.S. Isendaga*, 1935

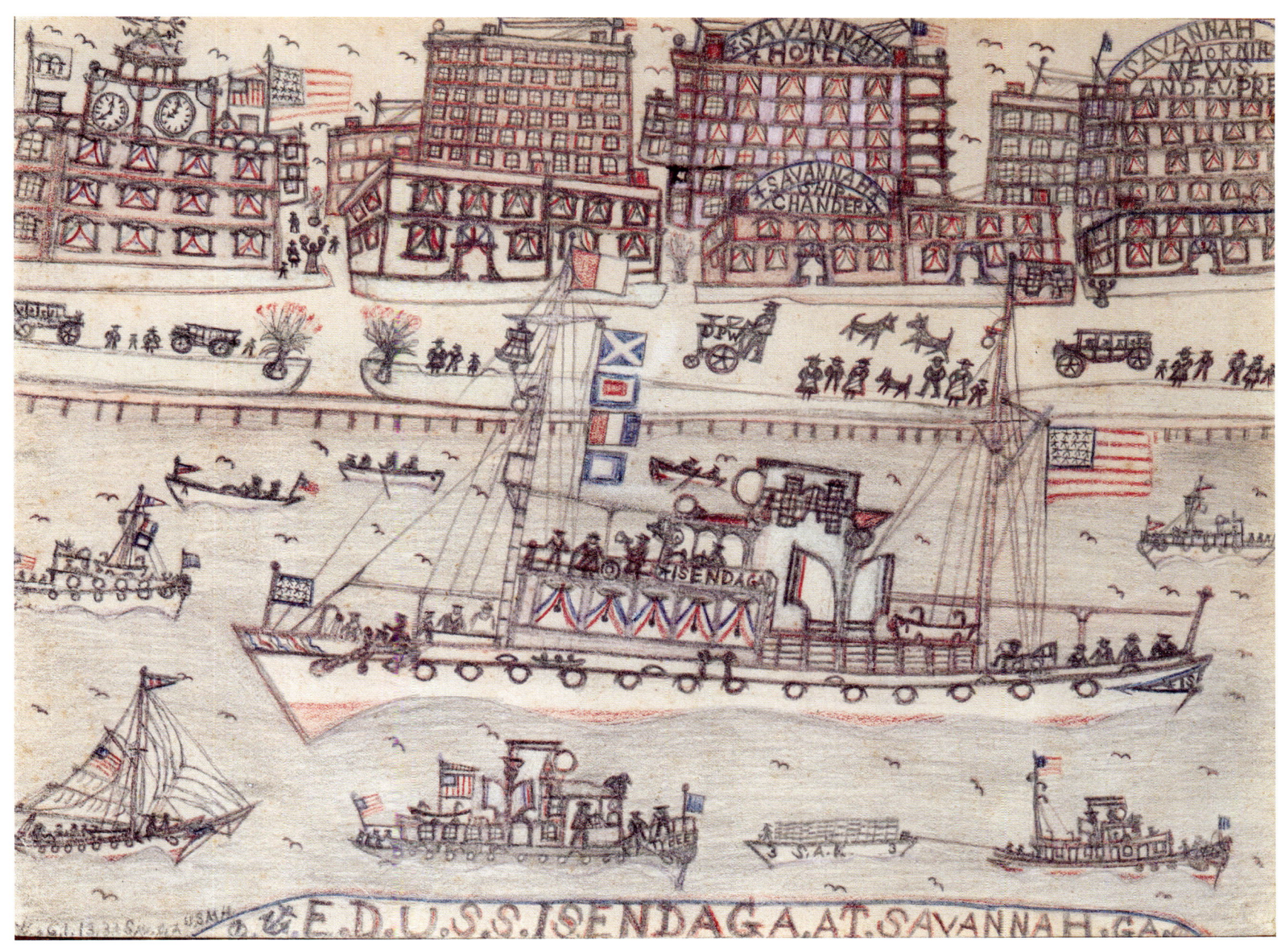

PLATE 72. *E.D.U.S.S. Isendaga at Savannah, GA*, 1932

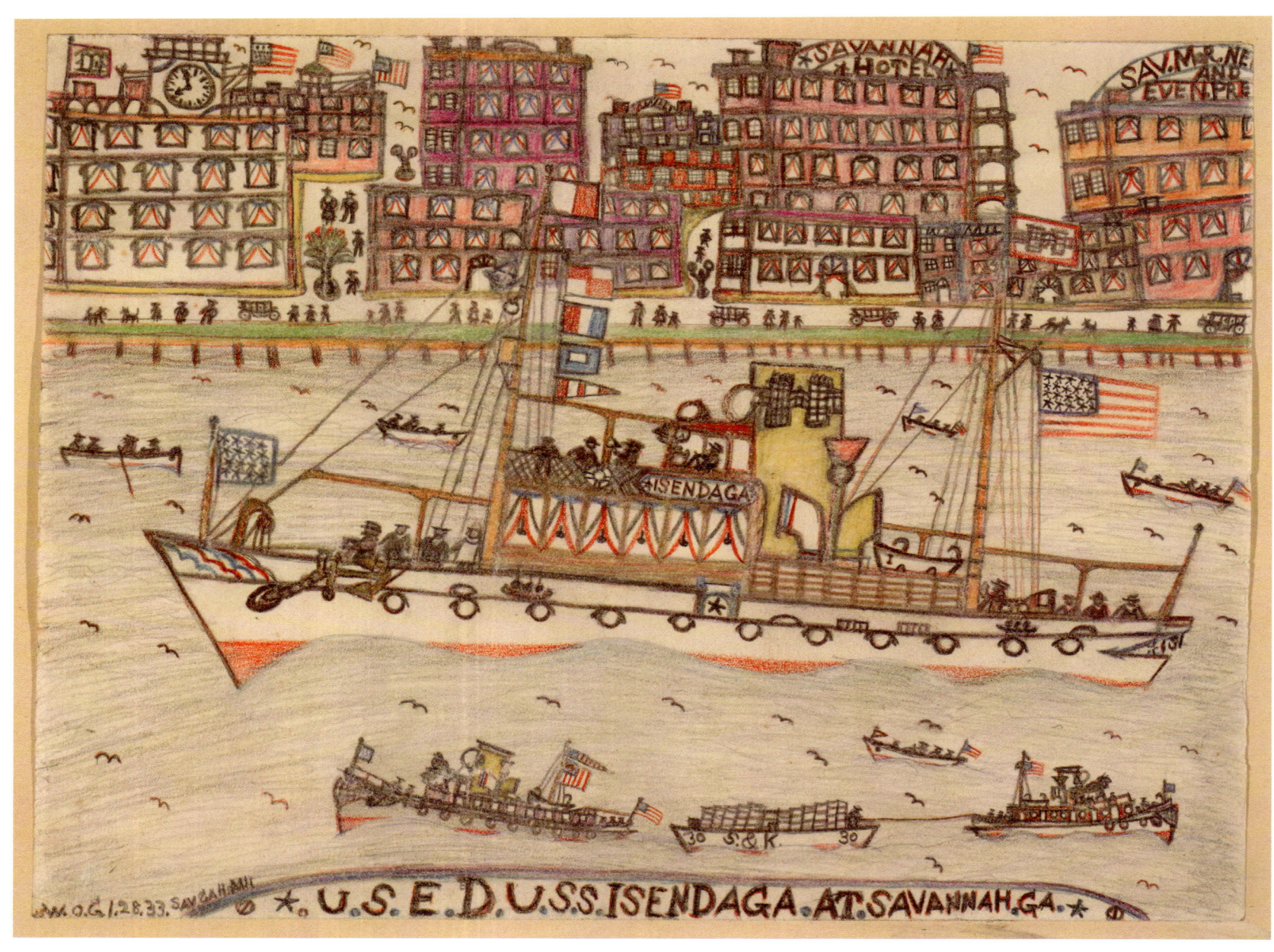

U.S.E.D. U.S.S. Isendaga at Savannah, GA, 1933 (not included in the exhibition)

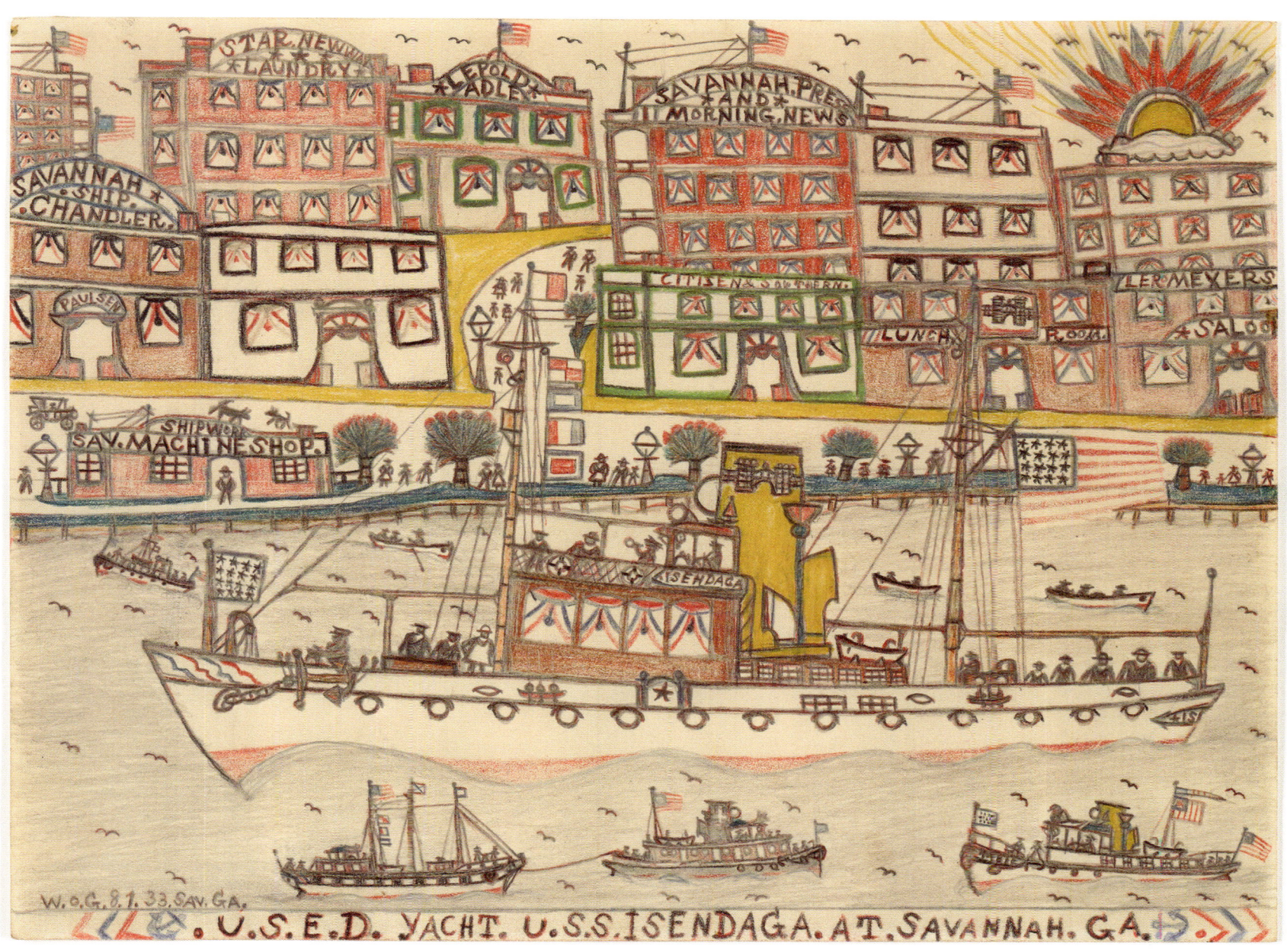

U.S.E.D. Yacht U.S.S. Isendaga at Savannah, GA, 1933 (not included in the exhibition)

ENDNOTES

William O. Golding: American Mariner and Artist (pp. 12–27)

[1] Jackie Cox-Crite, personal communication, December 12, 2019. Crite's father and grandmother knew him by the surname "Golden." See also "Crayon Sketch of 'Viking' by William Golden," typed biographical statement originally attached to his drawing *Steam Yacht Viking*, 1933, private collection, and Kai Olesen, "Black Savannah Seaman Captured Ports of Call in Pencil and Crayon," *Savannah Morning News—Evening Press*, August 24, 1975, 1-3F. Oleson, who interviewed former staff at the former Marine Hospital, reported the artist's actual surname as "Golden." The artist drew a ship named the "William O. Golden" (Telfair Museums, Savannah, Georgia) after himself, though he signed the drawing "Golding," perhaps signaling a preference for different private and public names. The surnames "Golden," "Golding" and other variations are found among African American residents in Liberty County at the time of William O. Golden's birth. He appears in various records with the surnames "Golding" and "Golden." See also Stacy Ashmore Cole, "Use of the Surname Golden/Golding/Gaulden/Gaulding Among African Americans in Liberty County, Georgia" (PDF), 2019, https://theyhadnames.net/golding-golden-surname-study/#

[2] "United States Census, 1880," database with images, FamilySearch (https://www.familysearch.org/ark:/61903/1:1:M8G8-V9W : 18 November 2021), Wm O Golding in household of Wm A Golding, District 15, Liberty, Georgia, United States; citing enumeration district , sheet , NARA microfilm publication T9 (Washington, D.C.: National Archives and Records Administration, n.d.), FHL microfilm.

[3] See Ahmauri Williams-Alford "Early Life: William A. Golden and the Dorchester Academy," in this catalogue.

[4] Olesen, "Black Savannah," 1-3F.

[5] Eric Foner, *Freedom's Lawmakers A Directory of Black Officeholders During Reconstruction*, (Baton Rouge: Louisiana State University Press), 1996, 88.

[6] William O. Golden to Margaret Stiles, July 10, 1932, photocopy of original letter, Telfair Museums, Savannah, Georgia, artist file. Copy provided by the Charleston Renaissance Gallery. Letter also quoted in Oleson, "Black Savannah". Original letter (partial) in collection of Fleisher/Ollman Gallery, Philadelphia.

[7] Atlantic Canada Shipping Project, and Memorial University of Newfoundland, *Ships and Seafarers of Atlantic Canada*. St. John's, Nfld: Maritime History Archive, Memorial University of Newfoundland, 1998. William Russell Potter listed as WR Potter in "Masters" table. For John Henry Potter see "John Henry Potter Master Mariner's Certificate of Competency," MS-2-469, SF Box 41, Folder 20, Dalhousie University Archives, Halifax, Nova Scotia, Canada.

[8] Ships of the Sea Maritime Museum Ships Registry, Savannah, Georgia (database), compiled 2002-2004. Registry includes ships in the port of Savannah up to 1890.

[9] Atlantic Canada Shipping Project, 1998. "Crews" tab, sorted by age shows a number of individuals ages 13 and younger aboard vessels.

[10] "United States, Veterans Administration Master Index, 1917-1940," database, *FamilySearch* (https://familysearch.org/ark:/61903/1:1:QPHJ-N9BR : 30 October 2019), William Golding, 23 May 1902; citing Military Service, NARA microfilm publication 76193916 (St. Louis: National Archives and Records Administration, 1985), various roll numbers.

[11] "United States Census, 1930," database with images, FamilySearch (https://familysearch.org/ark:/61903/1:1:3S2Z-D3Z : accessed 18 October 2021), William O Golding, Savannah, Chatham, Georgia, United States; citing enumeration district (ED) ED 25, sheet 1B, line 53, family, NARA microfilm publication T626 (Washington D.C.: National Archives and Records Administration, 2002), roll 344; FHL microfilm 2,340,079.

[12] James L. Mooney, ed., *Dictionary of American Naval Fighting Ships* (United States: Naval Historical Center, 1991), 173. The 1892-1893 cruise took the *Constellation* to Gibraltar, Naples and Le Havre to gather works of art for the 1893 World's Columbian Exposition.

[13] Frederick S. Harrod, *Manning the New Navy: The Development of a Modern Naval Enlisted Force, 1899-1940* (Westport: Greenwood Press, 1978), 10.

[14] "Crayon Sketch of 'Viking' by William Golden," typed biographical statement originally attached to the drawing *Steam Yacht Viking*, 1933, private collection. The statement is unsigned but due to a reference to "my aunt, Miss Stiles," the author is either Margaret Screven Tuck, or her husband at the time, A. J. M. Tuck.

[15] Olesen, "Black Savannah," 1F.

[16] Mike Walker, "The Locus of Hope: How Early Twentieth Century Clinical and Research Facilities in Savannah and New Orleans Embodied Progressive Allopathy and Governmental Involvement in Care" (Paper presented at the general meeting of the Southern Association for the History of Medicine and Science, New Orleans, 2020), 10-11.

[17] United States Census, 1930.

[18] "Society, People Coming and Going," *Savannah Morning News*, Thursday, October 2, 1902, 7.

[19] "Proceedings, Fifteenth Annual Meeting, Telfair Academy of Arts and Sciences," Savannah, Georgia, 1935, 3, 29-32. Margaret Stiles appears regularly in the annual reports of the Telfair Academy of Arts and Sciences beginning with her nomination to the board in 1931. She served on various committees into the 1940s. Her longest service was on the Mechlin Committee, on which she reported at Telfair's annual meetings. Stiles later served on the museum's Permanent Collection and Acquisitions Committee as noted in the museum's 1940 annual report.

[20] Edmund Berkeley, Jr., "Report on archives of William G. Haynes, Jr.," Ashantilly Center, Darien, Georgia, 1999.

[21] "Crayon Sketch of 'Viking' by William Golden."

[22] William O. Golden to Margaret Stiles, July 10, 1932

[23] William O. Golden to Margaret Stiles, August 10, 1933, typed transcript of original letter, Telfair Museums, Savannah, Georgia, artist file. Copy provided by the Charleston Renaissance Gallery. Letter also quoted in Oleson, "Black Savannah". Original letter (partial) in collection of Fleisher/Ollman Gallery, Philadelphia.

[24] William O. Golden to Margaret Stiles, August 10, 1933.

[25] William O. Golden to Margaret Stiles, August 10, 1933.

[26] A.J.M. Tuck to George F. Baker, Jr., August 15, 1933, private collection, Savannah, GA. Tuck. This letter, by Margaret Screven's husband, accompanied four drawings purchased by George F. Baker, Jr. in New York. The letter descended with a drawing of the steam yacht *Viking*, a vessel owned by Baker.

[27] *Pettus' Savannah 1940 Directory* (Luke P. Pettus, Savannah, Georgia, 1940), 779.

[28] United States Census Bureau, 1940; Census Place: Savannah, Chatham, Georgia; Roll: m-t0627-00650; Page: 1A; Enumeration District: 25-34. Source

ENDNOTES

Information: Ancestry.com. 1940 United States Federal Census [database on-line]. Provo, UT, USA: Ancestry.com Operations, Inc., 2012. Original data: United States of America, Bureau of the Census. Sixteenth Census of the United States, 1940. Washington, D.C.: National Archives and Records Administration, 1940. T627, 4,643 rolls.

[29] See Jackie Cox-Crite, "Searching for William Golding," this catalogue.

[30] Georgia Department of Public Health, "William O. Golding, Certificate of Death," August 28, 1943.

[31] Olesen, "Black Savannah," 1F.

[32] "Rediscovery: William O. Golding," *Art in America*, January-February, 1975, 84-85.

[33] Julia Weissman, Herbert Waide Hemphill, *Twentieth-Century American Folk Art and Artists.* (New York: E. P. Dutton & Co. Inc., 1974), 43.

[34] Anna Wadsworth et. al., *Missing Pieces: Georgia Folk Art 1770-1976* (Atlanta: Georgia Council for the Arts and Humanities, 1976), 44-47.

[35] Kai Olesen to Wallace M. Davis, Jr. Executive Editor *Savannah Morning News*, August 3, 1975, Letter and page of additional comments, Telfair Museums, Savannah, Georgia, artist file. Copy provided by the Charleston Renaissance Gallery, Charleston, SC.

[36] Stephen S. Lash, Daniel Finamore, Nicholas Whitman, Erik A. R. Ronnberg, *America and the Sea: Treasures from the Collections of Mystic Seaport* (New Haven: Yale University Press, 2005), 16.

[37] Whaleship logs are held by various institutions. For logbook drawings including drawings of whales and whaleships and whale stamps see the collections of the Nantucket Historical Society. Examples from Golden's lifetime include Log 108, Log of the ship *Horatio* (1880-1881), in the Ships' Logs Collection, Nantucket Historical Association https://nantuckethistory.org:443/permalink/?key=6000_m3868; Log 315, Log of the ship *Mermaid* (1876-1879), in the Ships' Logs Collection, Nantucket Historical Association https://nantuckethistory.org:443/permalink/?key=6000_m4072 ; Log 372; and others.

[38] Olesen to Wallace M. Davis, Jr.,1975.

[39] Silvanus Phillips Thompson, *The Rose of the Winds: The Origin and Development of the Compass-Card* (London: Oxford University Press, 1914) 3, 12-16. https://archive.org/details/roseofwindsorigi00thomrich/mode/2up

William O. Golden's Early Life: William A. Golden and the Dorchester Academy (pp. 28–29)

[1] Wm O Golding. Year: 1880; Census Place: District 15, Liberty, Georgia; Roll: 155; Page: 23B; Enumeration District: 067

[2] U.S., Southern Claims Commission Allowed Claims, 1871-1880.

[3] Georgia. General Assembly. Senate (1870). Journal of the Senate of the state of Georgia: at annual session of the General Assembly commenced at Atlanta, January 10, 1870.

[4] William A. Golding to AMA, November 22,1870, American Missionary Association Archives Amistad Research Center, New Orleans, Louisiana.

[5] Eliza A. Ward to Erastus M. Cravath, November 21,1871, AMAA.

Searching for William O. Golden (pp. 30–33)

[1] Now the Perez Museum of Art

[2] "Sarah Missouri Quarterman" may be listed as "Masouri Quarterman," the daughter of Sarah and Robert Quarterman of Liberty County in the 1920 US Census. "United States Census, 1920", database with images, *FamilySearch* (https://www.familysearch.org/ark:/61903/1:1:MJ6N-788 : 1 February 2021), Masouri L Quarterman in entry for Robert Quarterman, 1920. Sarah Quarterman is listed as William O. Golden's sister on his death certificate.

Golden's Age of Sail (pp. 36–37)

[1] Elliot Snow, Harpur Allen Gosnell, On the Decks of "Old Ironsides" (New York: Macmillan, 1932), 304.

[2] "NH 2391 USS *Ranger* Fires a Salute," image record, Naval History and Heritage Command, https://www.history.navy.mil/our-collections/photography/numerical-list-of-images/nhhc-series/nh-series/NH-02000/NH-2391.html, accessed 10/8/2021.

Steam Yachts and Steam Vessels (pp. 60–61)

[1] Erik Hofman, *Steam Yachts: An Era of Elegance* (Tuckahoe: John de Graff, Inc., 1970), 3-5.

[2] Kenneth Howard Goldman, *American Yachts in Naval Service: A History from the Colonial Era to World War II* (Jefferson, NC: McFarland, 2020), 66, 94. Noted here are private yachts drawn by Golden which saw military service including the steam yachts *Seneca* (built 1888) and *Corsair* (built 189).

[3] "Crayon Sketch of 'Viking' by William Golden," typed biographical statement originally attached to the drawing *Steam Yacht Viking*, 1933, private collection.

[4] A.J.M. Tuck to George F. Baker, Jr., August 15, 1933, private collection, Savannah, GA.

The Atlantic: Canada to Cape Horn (pp. 76–77)

[1] William O. Golden to Margaret Stiles, July 10, 1932, photocopy of original letter, Telfair Museums, Savannah, Georgia, artist file. Copy provided by the Charleston Renaissance Gallery. Letter also quoted in Kai Olesen, "Black Savannah Seaman Captured Ports of Call in Pencil and Crayon," *Savannah Morning News—Evening Press*, August 24, 1975. Original letter (partial) in collection of Fleisher/Ollman Gallery.

[2] Charles Henry Sewall, *Wireless Telegraphy; Its Origins, Development, Inventions, and Apparatus* (New York: D. Van Nostrand Company, 1903), 21-22.

[3] Rick Rennie, "Iron Ore Mines of Bell Island," Updated February, 2016, https://www.heritage.nf.ca/articles/economy/bell-island-mines.php

[4] William O. Golden to Margaret Stiles, July 10, 1932.

The Pacific: China and International Ports (pp. 72–93)

[1] William O. Golden to Margaret Stiles, August 10, 1933, typed transcript of original letter, Telfair Museums, Savannah, Georgia, artist file Copy provided by the Charleston Renaissance Gallery. Letter also quoted in Kai Olesen, "Black Savannah Seaman Captured Ports of Call in Pencil and Crayon," *Savannah*

ENDNOTES

Morning News—Evening Press, August 24, 1975. Original letter (partial) in collection of Fleisher/Ollman Gallery.

[2] *Hongkong, China* (United States Bureau of Navigation Under Authority of the Secretary of the Navy, 1920), 33.

The Spanish-American War, the Philippine War, and World War I (pp. 104–107)

[1] Navy Department, Naval History and Heritage Command, Dictionary of American Naval Fighting Ships, Published: Tue Sep 29 10:21:01 EDT 2015, https://www.history.navy.mil/research/histories/ship-histories/danfs/t/texas-i.html

[2] "Captain Floyd and Cuba Libre," *Crisis* (United States: Crisis Publishing Company, 1929), 230-31, 247.

[3] Christopher McMahon, "The Great White Fleet Sails Today? Twenty-First-Century Logistics Lessons from the 1907–1909 Voyage of the Great White Fleet," *Naval War College Review* 71, no. 4 (2018), https://digital-commons.usnwc.edu/nwc-review/vol71/iss4/6.

[4] "Four Brooklynites on Ship Sunk by a U-Boat, Galena a Famous Vessel," *Brooklyn Daily Eagle*, June 27, 1917, 1.

[5] United States Naval Institute Proceedings (US Naval Institute, 1917), 2716–2717.

Home Port: Savannah (pp. 118–119)

[1] "Crayon Sketch of 'Viking' by William Golden," typed biographical statement originally attached to the drawing *Steam Yacht Viking*, 1933, private collection.

[2] "William F. McCauley," Naval History and Heritage Command, Published: Mon Nov 02 13:10:48 EST 2015. https://www.history.navy.mil/research/histories/ship-histories/danfs/w/william-f-mccauley.html

[3] *Names in South Carolina* (Spartanburg, SC: Department of English, University of South Carolina, 1973), 22.

[4] Report of the Chief of Engineers U.S. Army, in 3 Parts, Part 3 (Washington, DC., 1920), 4526.

[5] "Tybee 1895," United States Coast Guard Historian's Office, United States Coast Guard, Department of Homeland Security, Published September 10, 2020, https://www.history.uscg.mil/Browse-by-Topic/Assets/Water/All/Article/2342261/tybee-1895/

EXHIBITION CHECKLIST

Golden's Age of Sail

1. *Wandering Jew, Liverpool, N.S.,* 1932
Pencil and crayon on paper
9 x 12 in.
Morris Museum of Art, Augusta, Georgia,
2004.066

2. *Ship Wandering Jew of Liverpool N.S.,* n.d.
Pencil and crayon on paper
9 x 12 in.
Telfair Museums,
Gift of Mrs. Frank Hollowbush and Mrs.
Julianna F. Waring, by exchange,
2021.14.1

3. *Yacht Muriel, Liverpool, N.S.,* 1939
Pencil and crayon on paper
9 x 12 in.
Morris Museum of Art, Augusta, Georgia,
2004.057

4. *Yacht Basuto,* 1934
Pencil and crayon on paper
8 ½ x 11 ⅞ in.
Morris Museum of Art, Augusta, Georgia,
2004.051

5. *U.S.S. Ranger, First Ship to Fly American
Flag,* 1935
Pencil and crayon on paper
9 x 12 in.
Morris Museum of Art, Augusta, Georgia,
2004.065

6. *U.S.S. Constitution, U.S.N.,* 1939
Pencil and crayon on paper
9 x 12 in.
Morris Museum of Art, Augusta, Georgia,
2004.068

7. *U.S.S. Constellation,* 1933
Pencil and crayon on paper
9 x 11 ¹⁵/₁₆ in.
Telfair Museums,
Museum purchase with funds provided by
the Gari Melchers Collectors' Society,
2013.3.2

8. *U.S.S. Constellation, U.S.N.,* 1939
Pencil and crayon on paper
9 x 12 in.
Morris Museum of Art, Augusta, Georgia,
2004.049

9. *H.M.S. Victory, Lord Horatio Nelson
Commanding,* 1933
Pencil and crayon on paper
9 x 12 in.
Private collection

10. *H.M.S. Hope,* 1939
Pencil and crayon on paper
8 ¹⁵/₁₆ x 12 in.
Telfair Museums,
Museum purchase funded by Linda Fisk Morris,
2020.8.7

11. *Confederate State Cruiser Alabama,* 1933
Pencil and crayon on paper
9 x 12 in.
Morris Museum of Art, Augusta, Georgia,
2004.052

12. *Confederate Cruiser Alabama,* 1934
Pencil and crayon on paper
9 x 12 in.
Private collection

13. *Sch. Alvena of Jacksonville, Fla.,* 1935
Pencil and crayon on paper
9 x 12 in.
Morris Museum of Art, Augusta, Georgia,
2004.071

14. *Sch. Thomas W. Lawson of Boston,
Mass,* 1939
Pencil and crayon on paper
9 x 12 in.
Morris Museum of Art, Augusta, Georgia,
2004.050

15. *Isobel,* 1932
Pencil and crayon on paper,
8 x 10 ½ in.
American Folk Art Museum, New York, Gift
of David L. Davies, 2004.22.1

16. *Bktn Josephine of Baltimore,* 1934
Pencil and crayon on paper
8 ¹⁵/₁₆ x 11 ¹³/₁₆ in.
Telfair Museums,
Museum purchase with Telfair Museum of
Art acquisitions endowment funds, 2020.8.1

17. *Whaler Petrel Chasing Whales in the
Artic Ocean,* 1933
Pencil and crayon on paper
8 ⅝ x 11 ¹³/₁₆ in.
Telfair Museums,
Museum purchase with Telfair Museum of
Art acquisitions endowment funds,
2020.8.15

18. *Whaler Neptune, Providence, R.I.,* 1939
Pencil and crayon on paper
9 x 12 in.
Morris Museum of Art, Augusta, Georgia,
2004.055

19. *Whaler Saluda Chasing Whales, in
Artic Ocean,* n.d.
Pencil and crayon on paper
8 ¹¹/₁₆ x 11 ¹³/₁₆ in.
Telfair Museums,
Museum purchase with Telfair Museum
of Art acquisitions endowment funds,
2020.8.16

20. *Saluda Chasing Whales, North Cape, Artic,* 1939
Pencil and crayon on paper
9 x 12 in.
Morris Museum of Art, Augusta, Georgia, 2004.053

21. *Whaler Saluda Chasing Whales in the Artic Ocean,* 1934
Pencil and crayon on paper
9 x 12 in.
Private collection

Steam Yachts and Steam Vessels

22. *Wm. O. Golden,* 1936
Pencil and crayon on paper
8 15/16 x 11 13/16 in.
Telfair Museums,
Museum purchase with Telfair Museum of Art acquisitions endowment funds, 2020.8.17

23. *Steam Yacht Viking, George Bakers, owner,* 1933
Pencil and crayon on paper
9 x 12 in.
Private collection

24. *S.S. Nourmahal, Owner J. J. Astor,* 1933
Pencil and crayon on paper
9 x 11 7/8 in.
Telfair Museums, Gift of Ervin and Diane Houston, 2014.1.3

25. *Steam Yacht Nourmahal, John Jacob Astor Owners,* 1934
Pencil and crayon on paper
9 x 12 in.
Morris Museum of Art, Augusta, Georgia, 2004.073

26. *Rosa Lee,* 1932
Pencil and crayon on paper
9 x 12 in.
The Miller Collection

27. *St. Yacht Rosalie, N.Y.,* 1935
Pencil and crayon on paper
9 x 12 in.
The Miller Collection

28. *St. Yacht Ramona,* 1935
Pencil and crayon on paper
8 3/4 x 11 3/4 in.
Morris Museum of Art, Augusta, GA, 1989.01.063

29. *St. Yacht Thelma of Bangor, ME,* 1935
Pencil and crayon on paper
9 x 12 in.
Morris Museum of Art, Augusta, Georgia, 1993.C0302

30. *St. Yacht Petrel,* 1935
Pencil and crayon on paper
9 x 12 in.
The Miller Collection

31. *St. Yacht Wydabiity (sic),* 1935
Pencil and crayon on paper
9 x 12 in.
Private collection

32. *S.S. Vina Del Mar,* 1932
Pencil and crayon on paper
8 3/8 x 11 7/8 in.
Telfair Museums,
Museum purchase with Telfair Museum of Art acquisitions endowment funds, 2020.8.9

33. *Scarlet,* 1934
Pencil and crayon on paper
9 1/4 x 12 3/8 in.
Morris Museum of Art, Augusta, Georgia, Gift of the Robert Powell Coggin Art Trust 1993. C0336

34. *Steamer Swan,* 1939
Pencil and crayon on paper
8 15/16 x 11 15/16 in.
Telfair Museums,
Museum purchase with Telfair Museum of Art acquisitions endowment funds, 2020.8.10

The Atlantic: Canada to Cape Horn

35. *Table Island, N.S.,* 1934
Pencil and crayon on paper
9 x 12 in.
Morris Museum of Art, Augusta, Georgia, 2004.054

36. *Belle Island, Newfoundland,* 1934
Pencil and crayon on paper
9 x 12 in.
Morris Museum of Art, Augusta, Georgia, 2004.058

37. *Cape Breton, Newfoundland,* 1935
Pencil and crayon on paper
9 x 12 in.
Morris Museum of Art, Augusta, Georgia, 2004.062

38. *Cape Brenton NF,* 1939
Pencil and crayon on paper
8 15/16 x 11 7/8 in.
Telfair Museums,
Museum purchase with Telfair Museum of Art acquisitions endowment funds, 2020.8.3

39. *Gay Head*, 1935
Pencil and crayon on paper
9 x 12 in.
Morris Museum of Art, Augusta, Georgia,
2004.064

40. *Gay Head*, n.d.
Pencil and crayon on paper
8 $^{15}/_{16}$ x 12 in.
Telfair Museums,
Museum purchase with Telfair Museum of Art
acquisitions endowment funds, 2020.8.5

41. *Gay Head*, 1936
Pencil and crayon on paper
8 $^{15}/_{16}$ x 12 in.
Telfair Museums,
Museum purchase with Telfair Museum of Art
acquisitions endowment funds
2020.8.6

42. *Off Barnegat*, 1935
Pencil and crayon on paper
8 $^7/_8$ x 11 $^{11}/_{16}$ in.
Georgia Museum of Art, University of
Georgia; University purchase. GMOA
1977.3619

43. *Cape Henlopen*, 1933
Pencil and crayon on paper
9 x 12 in.
Ashantilly Center, Inc., Darien, Georgia

44. *Trinidad, Port of Spain, W. I.*, 1937
Pencil and crayon on paper
9 x 12 in.
Morris Museum of Art, Augusta, Georgia,
2004.059

45. *Santa Helena with Tomb of Napoleon*,
1936
Pencil and crayon on paper
9 x 12 in.
Private collection

46. *Cape Horn*, 1933
Pencil and crayon on paper
9 x 12 in.
Telfair Museums,
Gift of Mrs. Frank Hollowbush and Mrs.
Julianna F. Waring by exchange, 2021.14.2

47. *Cape Horn*, 1935
Pencil and crayon on paper
8 $^{11}/_{16}$ x 11 $^{13}/_{16}$ in.
Telfair Museums,
Museum purchase with Telfair Museum of Art
acquisitions endowment funds, 2020.8.4

The Pacific: China and International Ports

48. *Tahiti*, 1935
Pencil and crayon on paper
8 $^7/_8$ x 11 $^7/_8$ in.
Telfair Museums,
Museum purchase with Telfair Museum of Art
acquisitions endowment funds, 2020.8.11

49. *Saigon, China, Under French Protection*, 1934
Pencil and crayon on paper
8 $^1/_2$ x 12 in.
Telfair Museums,
Museum purchase with funds provided by the
Gari Melchers Collectors' Society, 2013.3.1

50. *Macaco* (sic), *China*, 1933
Pencil and crayon on paper
9 x 12 in.
Collection of Mr. and Mrs. E. Brian Culver,
Savannah, Georgia

51. *Canton, China*, 1935
Pencil and crayon on paper
8 $^5/_8$ x 11 $^{13}/_{16}$ in.
Telfair Museums,
Museum purchase with Telfair Museum of Art
acquisitions endowment funds, 2020.8.2

52. *Foochow, China*, 1935
Pencil and crayon on paper
9 x 12 in.
Private collection

53. *Hong Kong, China*, 1935
Pencil and crayon on paper
8 $^3/_4$ x 11 $^7/_8$ in.
Morris Museum of Art, Augusta, Georgia,
2004.048

54. *Cheefoo, China*, 1935
Pencil and crayon on paper
9 x 12 in.
The Miller Collection

55. *Chefoo, China*, 1939
Pencil and crayon on paper
9 x 12 in.
Morris Museum of Art, Augusta, Georgia,
2004.069

56. *Penang, Java, Dutch East Indies*, 1937
Pencil and crayon on paper
9 x 12 in.
Morris Museum of Art, Augusta, Georgia,
2004.060

The Spanish American War, Philippine War, and World War I

57. *Fort Morgan*, 1936
Pencil and crayon on paper
9 x 12 in.
The Miller Collection

58. *U.S.S. Texas*, 1933
Pencil and crayon on paper
9 x 11 $^7/_8$ in.
Telfair Museums,
Museum purchase funded by Linda Fisk
Morris, 2020.8.13

59. *Tug Dauntless, off Sapelo Island, GA on 15, Jan. 1898*, 1933
Pencil and crayon on paper,
9 x 12 in.
Ashantilly Center, Inc., Darien, Georgia

60. *Tug Dauntless. Capt. Floyd*, 1934
Pencil and crayon on paper
8 15/16 x 12 in.
Telfair Museums,
Museum purchase with Telfair Museum of Art acquisitions endowment funds, 2020.8.12

61. *Luson, P.I.*, 1933
Pencil and crayon on paper
9 x 12 in.
Morris Museum of Art, Augusta, Georgia, 2004.067

62. *U.S.S. Petrel, U.S.N.*, 1937
Pencil and crayon on paper
9 x 12 in.
Morris Museum of Art, Augusta, Georgia, 2004.063

63. *Rock of Gibraltar*, 1936
Pencil and crayon on paper
9 x 12 in.
Morris Museum of Art, Augusta, GA, 2004.072

64. *Rock of Gibraltar*, 1936
Pencil and crayon on paper
8 7/8 x 11 7/8 in.
Telfair Museums,
Museum purchase with Telfair Museum of Art acquisitions endowment funds, 2020.8.8

65. *Ushant, France*, 1935
Pencil and crayon on paper
8 1/16 x 12 in.
Telfair Museums,

Museum purchase with Telfair Museum of Art acquisitions endowment funds, 2020.8.14

66. *H.I.M.S. Seeadler, Von Luckner, Cpt.*, 1939
Pencil and crayon on paper
9 x 12 in.
Morris Museum of Art, Augusta, Georgia, 2004.070

"The Home Port"

67. *Tug William F. McAuley, Atlantic Towing Co., Sav, GA*, 1934
Pencil and crayon on paper
9 x 12 in.
Telfair Museums,
Museum purchase, 2009.23

68. *S.S. Pilot Boy, Charleston Line*, 1939
Pencil and crayon on paper
9 x 12 in.
Morris Museum of Art, Augusta, Georgia, 2004.061

69. *U.S.S. Tybee*, n.d.
Pencil and crayon on paper
9 x 12 in.
Morris Museum of Art, Augusta, Georgia, 2004.056

70. *U.S.S. Tybee, U.S.C.G.*, 1939
Pencil and crayon on paper
9 x 12 in.
Collection of Mr. and Mrs. Edwin H. Culver, Savannah, Georgia

71. *U.S.E.U.S.S. Isendaga*, 1935
Pencil and crayon on paper
8 3/4 x 11 7/8 in.
Georgia Museum of Art, University of Georgia; University purchase. GMOA 1977.3620

72. *E.D.U.S.S. Isendaga at Savannah, GA*, 1933
Pencil and crayon on paper
9 x 12 in.
Collection of Joey and Amy Trotz, Atlanta, GA

Not Included in the Exhibition

Page 59. *Whaler Saluda Chasing Whales in Artic Ocean*, 1933
Crayon and pencil on paper mounted on board
Overall: 9 x 11 15/16 in.
Williams College Museum of Art, Williamstown, MA: Gift of Anne Waring Lane (Mrs. Mills Bee Lane), 54.21.2

Page 100. *Chee Foo, China*. 1932
Crayon and pencil on paper mounted on board
Overall: 8 7/8 x 12 3/16 in.
Williams College Museum of Art, Williamstown, MA: Gift of Anne Waring Lane (Mrs. Mills Bee Lane), 54.21.1

Page 126. *U.S.E.D.U.S.S. Isendaga, at Savannah, GA*, 1933
Pencil and crayon on paper
9 1/16 x 11 7/8 in.
Williams College Museum of Art, Williamstown, MA
Gift of Anne Waring Lane (Mrs. Mills Bee Lane), 54.21.3

Page 127. *U.S.E.D. Yacht U.S.S. Isendaga at Savannah, GA*, 1933
Pencil and crayon on paper
9 x 11 15/16 in.
Collection of Anne d'Harnoncourt and Joseph Rishel, Courtesy the Philadelphia Museum of Art.

CONTRIBUTING WRITERS

Benjamin T. Simons is Executive Director and CEO of Telfair Museums in Savannah, Georgia. He served previously as Director of the Academy Art Museum in Maryland, and as the Robyn & John Davis Chief Curator at the Nantucket Historical Association. He received an AB in Philosophy from Harvard College, an MA/MPhil in English Literature from Yale University, and an MA in the History of Art from the Courtauld Institute of Art, London, England. He is a graduate of the Getty Museum Leadership Institute. Simons has written several catalogues including, *Island Treasures: Gifts of the Friends of the Nantucket Historical Association, 1986–2011*, and *The Nantucket Art Colony, 1920–45*; and co-authored the books, *Maritime Maverick: The Maritime Collection of William I. Koch*, and *A Yachtsman's Eye: The Glen S. Foster Collection of Marine Paintings*. He was the Editor of the award-winning quarterly *Historic Nantucket*.

Kevin Grogan, Director of Augusta, Georgia's Morris Museum of Art since 2002, has worked in museums since 1971, first at The Phillips Collection in Washington, DC, and later at museums in Tennessee and Virginia. Over the length of his career, he has participated in the organization of hundreds of exhibitions and authored, edited, or contributed to dozens of publications. He has lectured widely and served on the boards of numerous organizations. A native of Washington, DC, he was educated at Franklin & Marshall College, American University, and Vanderbilt University.

Harry DeLorme, Jr., is Director of Education and Senior Curator at Telfair Museums, Savannah, Georgia. He holds BFA and MFA degrees in Drawing and Painting from the University of Georgia, Athens, with training in museum education and curatorial work. Since 1990, DeLorme has curated thirty-four exhibitions at Telfair, including an experiential learning gallery, Telfair's PULSE Art and Technology Festival, and related exhibitions exploring artificial intelligence, virtual and augmented reality, and video games. DeLorme's many exhibitions on Southern artists include the first museum survey of William O. Golding's art (2000), and *Bonaventure: A Historic Cemetery in Art* (2018). He has written entries and essays for books including *Looking Back: Art in Savannah 1900-1960* (Telfair Museums, 1996), *The New Encyclopedia of Southern Culture: Folk Art* (University of North Carolina Press, 2013), *The Morris at 25* (Morris Museum of Art, 2019), and *Curators' Choice: Telfair Museums* (2021).

Ahmauri Williams-Alford is the Assistant Curator of Historical Interpretation and Programs at Telfair Museums. Williams-Alford holds a master's degree in Social Sciences and a bachelor's degree in Anthropology from Georgia Southern University. Her research interests include archaeological curation, sociocultural anthropology, and public education. Much of her research includes African American and Native American history and culture. She has recently been working with the Willow Hill Heritage and Renaissance Center in Portal, Georgia, on a large-scale curatorial project.

Jackie Cleveland Cox-Crite is co-founder, along with her late husband Allan Rohan Crite, of the of the Allan Rohan Crite Research Institute & Library, established in 1998. Her prior work experience was in corporate finance, however, her true avocation and personal love for over 45 years has been supporting the arts—Theater, Music, Dance, Visual Arts—and befriending artists. She has curated and installed exhibitions and lectured extensively on her late husband's wide body of artwork. She has also represented Boston artists, including photographers, ceramicists, sculptors, public artists, and painters.

ACKNOWLEDGMENTS

When I first saw a pair of unusual drawings of ships in a private collection in the mid-1990s, I had little idea that those works and their maker would take me on an intermittent voyage of more than two decades. I was intrigued by the limited information I could find about the artist, William O. Golding (a.k.a. Golden), who had made these works in Savannah's Marine Hospital in the 1930s. Although my involvement with the artist's work dates to 1996, the idea for a larger exhibition was sparked by an essay I was invited to write on Golding in 2018. Returning to his work by deeply analyzing a single image, I realized that I had only scratched the surface in the small exhibition I curated at Telfair in 2000—then the first solo museum exhibition of the artist's work. I realized that there were worlds contained within his drawings, with many facets yet to be explored. Exhibition plans solidified following Telfair's acquisition of seventeen Golding drawings in 2020, making the museum one of the two largest repositories of his work. The acquisition and subsequent funding from the National Endowment for the Arts underscored the necessity of a catalog, despite a short time frame. There have been many mysteries to solve and many which remain from this attempt to bring Golden into focus, although recent research has revealed important information about his family and years at sea. The global pandemic provided opportunity in the form of research time, but also significant obstacles, in particular the closure of key archives. Large parts of Golden's life remain opaque, but my hope is that this first publication devoted to his art will bring him greater recognition and open the door to further exploration of his work and world.

Telfair Museums thanks the funders who have made the exhibition and catalogue possible, in particular the National Endowment for the Arts. A donation to the Telfair Museums' Labelle and Meyer Tenenbaum endowment by Davida Deutsch in memory of Arnold and Lorlee Tenenbaum has underwritten interpretive components of the exhibition. Additional investment and funding have been provided by the City of Savannah, the Georgia Council for the Arts, and by Inge Brasseler.

This project could not have taken place without the time and assistance of many individuals, among them former Director of Curatorial Affairs Courtney McNeil, who supported Telfair's acquisition of Golding works, and former Director of Collections and Exhibitions Jessica Estes, for her coordination of loans and conservation. Telfair's Executive Director and CEO Benjamin Simons has provided enthusiastic support for this project, bringing his maritime collections knowledge and connections to bear, reading essays, and writing a foreword to this catalogue. David Kaminsky expertly photographed and prepared images of works in Telfair's collection. Many talented Telfair Curatorial and Education staff members have played a part in the catalogue, exhibition design, and related programming. Beth Moore and Margaret Von Spreecken assisted with coordination of photography and cataloging, respectively. Heath Ritch, Andrew Gatti, and Melissa Hill have contributed to the design of the exhibition. Education team members Kip Bradley, Rachel Stayer, Carey Daughtry and Deja Chappell have developed related public programs and interpretation. I am indebted to Janice Shay of Pinafore Press for her indefatigable work on the design and packaging of this book, and to copy editor John Harris.

My colleague Ahmauri Williams-Alford has been an essential fellow researcher and important contributor to the catalog, and I have valued her advice and assistance in the process of uncovering Golden's life. Telfair Director of Curatorial Affairs Alex Mann brought his sharp eye and editorial skills to the proofing of the catalogue. Dr. Elyse Gerstenecker read the lead essay and provided feedback, along with Dr. Kurt Knoerl, maritime historian and Assistant Professor of History at Georgia Southern University. My son, Caleb DeLorme, and mother, Rita DeLorme, both far better writers than I, and my wife Rachel Green, were important sounding boards.

Telfair Museums thanks all who graciously loaned works, including the Miller Collection, Brian and Edward Culver, and the Trotz family. Many thanks are due to Wilson Morris for his support, as well as Ervin Houston and the late Diane Houston who made the first donation of a Golding drawing to Telfair. Many colleagues at other museums have assisted with loans, photography or research including Kevin Grogan, Director and Curator, Stacey Thompson, Registrar and Cary Wilkins, Librarian and Archivist at the Morris Museum of Art; Valérie Rousseau, Senior Curator & Curator of Self-Taught Art and Art Brut, and Director of Collections Ann-Marie Reilly of the American Folk Art Museum, New York; Lisa Dorin, Deputy Director for Curatorial Affairs/Curator of Contemporary Art at the Williams College Museum of Art; Jun P. Nakamura, Suzanne Andrée Curatorial Fellow, and colleagues at the Philadelphia Museum of Art: and William U. Eiland, Director, and Registrars Christy Sinksen, and Sarina Rousso, at the Georgia Museum of Art; Harriet Langford, Board President of the Ashantilly Center; and Amy Folk, Manager of Collections at Oysterponds Historical Society.

Several nationally-noted maritime scholars graciously considered Golden's work at my request or answered questions. Local colleagues Luciana Spracher, City of Savannah Archives Director, and Wendy Melton, Director of the Ships of the Sea Maritime Museum, pointed me toward a fantastic historical registry of ships visiting the port of Savannah. Historian Vaughnette Goode-Walker helped make the connection between William O. Golden and his stepfather William Anthony Golden, and Mayor Bill Austin welcomed us to Dorchester Academy, founded by the elder Golden. Hugh Golson shared important information and photographs regarding Margaret Stiles and family. Longtime gallerists Stuart Feld of Hirschl and Adler Gallery, and Robert Hicklin provided invaluable documentation. John Ollman of Fleisher/Ollman Gallery shared vital information about his long association with Golden's art and coordinated several loans, including drawings and the remnants of Golden's letters. I greatly am obliged to Kevin Grogan at the Morris Museum of Art, who has shared my enthusiasm for Golden's art throughout the years, partnered with Telfair Museums to make this exhibition possible, and provided an introduction to this catalogue. Most of all I am grateful to William O. Golden's great grand-niece Jackie Cox-Crite, who shared her personal journey and family story with Telfair Museums. Hers was a crucial voice in this project and a reminder of a personal legacy beyond works of art through which William O. Golden left his mark on the world.

Harry DeLorme

© 2022 Telfair Books

The Art of William O. Golding
Hard Knocks, Hardships, and Lots of Experience

By Harry DeLorme

Published in conjunction with the exhibition of the same name, organized by Telfair Museums, Savannah, Georgia.

Exhibition itinerary:
Telfair Museums, Savannah, Georgia, April 1–August 28, 2022
Morris Museum of Art, Augusta, Georgia, September 10–December 30, 2022

Photography by:
David J. Kaminsky: Front cover, back cover, pp. 39, 44, 47, 49, 53. 56, 62, 64, 71, 72, 74, 75, 83, 84, 90, 91, 94, 95, 96, 97, 109, 11, 115, 116, 120, 123
Mark Albertin: pp. 45, 48, 50, 51, 57, 65, 68, 69, 73, 78, 79, 80, 82, 112, 113, 117, 121, 122,
John Harpring: pp. 38, 40, 41, 42, 43, 55, 88, 98, 102, 103, 114
Andrew Gatti: p. 58
Gavin Ashworth: p. 52
Christopher Michael Wong: pp. 66, 67, 70, 101, 108
Courtesy Fleisher/Ollman Gallery: pp. 46, 63, 89, 98
Courtesy Ashantilly Center, Inc.: pp. 86, 87, 110
Courtesy the Williams College Museum of Art: pp. 59, 100, 126
Courtesy the Georgia Museum of Art: pp. 85, 124
Courtesy the Philadelphia Museum of Art: p. 127

Images:
Cover (front): *Saigon, China, Under French Protection*, 1934 (Pl. 49)
Cover (back): Detail, *U.S.S. Constellation*, 1933 (Pl. 7)
P. 1: From *Rock of Gibraltar*, 1936 (Pl. 64)
P. 2: *St. Yacht Ramona*, 1935 (Pl. 28)
P. 11: Detail, *Chefoo, China*, 1939 (Pl. 55)

Library of Congress Catalogue Control Number: 2021923996
ISBN: 9780933075221

Printed and bound in Canada by Friesens

Design by Pinafore Press

www.telfair.org